Second Language Use Online and its Integration in Formal Language Learning

SECOND LANGUAGE ACQUISITION

Series Editors: Professor David Singleton, *University of Pannonia, Hungary* and **Fellow Emeritus,** *Trinity College, Dublin, Ireland* and **Associate Professor Simone E. Pfenninger,** *University of Salzburg, Austria*

This series brings together titles dealing with a variety of aspects of language acquisition and processing in situations where a language or languages other than the native language is involved. Second language is thus interpreted in its broadest possible sense. The volumes included in the series all offer in their different ways, on the one hand, exposition and discussion of empirical findings and, on the other, some degree of theoretical reflection. In this latter connection, no particular theoretical stance is privileged in the series; nor is any relevant perspective – sociolinguistic, psycholinguistic, neurolinguistic, etc. – deemed out of place. The intended readership of the series includes final-year undergraduates working on second language acquisition projects, postgraduate students involved in second language acquisition research, and researchers, teachers and policymakers in general whose interests include a second language acquisition component.

All books in this series are externally peer-reviewed.

Full details of all the books in this series and of all our other publications can be found on http://www.multilingual-matters.com, or by writing to Multilingual Matters, St Nicholas House, 31-34 High Street, Bristol, BS1 2AW, UK.

SECOND LANGUAGE ACQUISITION: 153

Second Language Use Online and its Integration in Formal Language Learning

From Chatroom to Classroom

Andrew D. Moffat

MULTILINGUAL MATTERS
Bristol • Jackson

DOI https://doi.org/10.21832/MOFFAT3627
Library of Congress Cataloging in Publication Data
A catalog record for this book is available from the Library of Congress.
Names: Moffat, Andrew D., author.
Title: Second Language Use Online and its Integration in Formal Language Learning: From Chatroom to Classroom/Andrew D. Moffat.
Description: Bristol, UK; Jackson, TN: Multilingual Matters, [2022] | Series: Second Language Acquisition: 153 | Includes bibliographical references and index. | Summary: "This book addresses questions surrounding online second language (L2) communicative activities and formal language learning. It provides empirical evidence and analysis of the scale and nature of L2 English communicative activities online and explores the possibilities for language teaching practices that engage with learners' L2 online activities"—Provided by publisher.
Identifiers: LCCN 2022001042 (print) | LCCN 2022001043 (ebook) | ISBN 9781800413627 (hardback) | ISBN 9781800413641 (epub) | ISBN 9781800413634 (pdf)
Subjects: LCSH: Second language acquisition. | English language—Web-based instruction. | English language—Computer-assisted instruction for foreign speakers. | English language—Study and teaching—Foreign speakers. | Internet in education.
Classification: LCC P118.2 .M64 2022 (print) | LCC P118.2 (ebook) | DDC 401/.93—dc23/eng/20220316
LC record available at https://lccn.loc.gov/2022001042
LC ebook record available at https://lccn.loc.gov/2022001043

British Library Cataloguing in Publication Data
A catalogue entry for this book is available from the British Library.

ISBN-13: 978-1-80041-362-7 (hbk)

Multilingual Matters
UK: St Nicholas House, 31-34 High Street, Bristol, BS1 2AW, UK.
USA: Ingram, Jackson, TN, USA.

Website: www.multilingual-matters.com
Twitter: Multi_Ling_Mat
Facebook: https://www.facebook.com/multilingualmatters
Blog: www.channelviewpublications.wordpress.com

Typeset by Deanta Global Publishing Services, Chennai, India.

Contents

Figures

Tables

Acknowledgements

Huge thanks are due to everybody whose influence and support made this book possible. I am especially grateful to Svenja Adolphs and Alex Lang at the University of Nottingham, who both showed me great kindness, patience and faith: Svenja guided me through the complexities of the research process and provided me with great optimism; Alex provided invaluable feedback even at time-sensitive moments, speed-reading drafts on long-haul flights. Both have had occasion to act as crisis counsellors when the need arose! I am also extremely grateful to everyone at Cambridge University Press who went out of their way to help with my project. In particular: Laura Grimes, who worked with me to get the questionnaire up and running, and helped me arrange and settle in to my internship; and to Claire Dembry, who made me answer difficult (but very necessary) questions.

Thanks are also due to others who have been kind enough to give up their time to offer their thoughts, particularly Zoltán Dörnyei, for his thoughts on the questionnaire analysis, and Christine Muir, for advice on dealing with 10,000 questionnaire responses.

I'm grateful to my colleagues in the School of English and in the Horizon Centre for Doctoral Training. I'm very lucky to have had such fantastic peers, even if I have been notably absent from Nottingham for a large part of the last four years. My Brunch WhatsApp group have been a great source of support and banter, not to mention inspiration for the research itself (lol).

Many thanks to Laura Longworth and Rosie McEwan at Multilingual Matters for all their help with the publishing process.

And finally, and in the chief place, I am forever grateful for the love and support of my family. On to the next adventure!

Abbreviations

AT	Activity theory
CA	Communication apprehension
CALL	Computer-Assisted Language Learning
CANELC	Cambridge and Nottingham E-Language Corpus
CEFR	Common European Framework of Reference (for languages)
CIC	Cambridge International Corpus
CMC	Computer-mediated communication
CMD	Computer-mediated discourse
CUP	Cambridge University Press
EE	Extramural English
EFL	English as a foreign language
EL2	English as a second/foreign language
ESL	English as a second language
FASIL	Fully autonomous self-instructed learner
ICT	Information and communications technology
IDLE	Informal digital learning of English
IM	Instant messaging
ISLL	Informal second language learning
L2	Second/foreign language
LA	Language awareness/language anxiety (check context)
MALU	Mobile-assisted language use
MIM	Mobile instant messaging
OILE	Online informal learning of English
SFL	Systemic functional linguistics
SLA	Second language acquisition
SMS	Short messaging service
STC	Socio-technical configuration (of CMC)

1 A Thoroughly Modern Medium

Internet-based communication continues to become 'ever-increasingly embedded into our daily lives' (Knight, 2015: 20), and as it permeates our everyday communicative activities its significance as a site, or multitude of sites, of language use for second language (L2) learners to engage with grows accordingly. Internet-enabled modes of communication which 20 years ago were limited to a minority of technology enthusiasts have become so ubiquitous as to be 'squarely mundane in the business of daily life' (Squires, 2016: 1). Furthermore, the explosive growth of smartphone usage over the last decade has marked a shift from static information terminals that required users to move to a certain physical location in order to access online communication media, to portable communication terminals carried, or even worn, by users. This has led to a situation in which we are *permanently online* and *permanently connected* (Vorderer *et al.*, 2016), inseparable from our channels of telecommunication. Social interaction online is no longer a specialist hobby, but an integral part of a 21st-century identity.

For people learning an L2, today's hyper-connectivity has the potential to present new domains of engagement with and exposure to their target language. Exposure to the target language, defined as both the reception of linguistic *input* and the opportunity for authentic, meaning-driven *interaction* with other speakers, is accepted as a necessary condition for language learning (Spolsky, 1989), and computer-mediated communication (CMC) has the potential to connect learners with expert and non-expert speakers of the target language, regardless of geographical location. Such exposure is not an automatic consequence of access to internet-enabled devices however: the internet is not a monolithic entity (Pasfield-Neofitou, 2012: 7) and learners may continue to be immersed in online networks of speakers of their mother tongue.

For L2 learners who do engage with the language online, the learning benefits are increasingly documented. Incidental learning can take place even where communicative activities are initiated for their own sake, with no explicit intention to practice the language (Sockett, 2014). This can aid language learning directly, through the acquisition of words or phrases, or indirectly, by helping learners find their voices as independent language users, entitled to participate in a global anglophone community (Lam, 2000).

The level of target language engagement made possible by the internet has the potential to significantly increase the complexity of the language learning process, providing new avenues of exposure and communicative interaction. Language teaching practices must evolve to anticipate the needs of hyper-connected learners, both to support them in their online activities, and to maximize the potential learning benefits that such activities may provide.

1.1 Aims of the Book

In response to these developments in the nature of language learning in a hyper-connected world, this book will do the following:

- provide empirical evidence of the scale and nature of L2 English communicative activities online among a broad range of English learners;
- investigate the nature of the language that L2 English users may encounter in online interactions;
- explore the possibilities for language teaching practices that support and integrate learners' L2 English online activities.

These processes will be based on analysis of empirical data, supported and contextualized through a synthesis of existing research in a number of relevant fields.

1.2 Focus on Computer-Mediated Communication

This book is concerned with text-based communicative activity mediated by internet-based technologies, under the umbrella term *computer-mediated communication*. This term includes an array of forms of communication, including email, discussion boards, blogs, instant messaging, social media and chat rooms. Short messaging service (SMS) messaging is also included under the umbrella, in spite of the technical difference that SMS data are not transmitted via the internet, but via cellular networks. SMS is nevertheless included due to its functional similarity to, and increasing indistinguishability from, mobile instant messaging. This is discussed in detail in Chapter 6.

There is a great deal of research and scholarship examining CMC from a variety of disciplinary perspectives, including communications research, information systems, organizational research, human–computer interaction, sociology and applied linguistics. Terminological debate has been an inevitable by-product: the term CMC arose from work in the field of communication studies, such as Walther (1996), while linguistic approaches to the phenomenon give rise to language-oriented terms, such as *e-language* (Knight, 2015) and *Netspeak* (Crystal, 2001). The study of discourse in online environments has been labelled *computer-mediated discourse* (Herring & Androutsopoulos, 2015). The older term, CMC, is adopted here, reflecting the focus on a broad set of communicative contexts and practices, rather than a language variety or set of discourse characteristics. Baron (2008: 12) highlights the fact that much CMC now takes place using devices such as smartphones and tablets that may not be thought of as being *computers* in the lay sense of the word, and proposes *electronically mediated communication* instead. However, for present purposes, the term CMC is retained, with the *computer* element to be understood as referring more broadly to the information technologies that underlie the forms of hardware on which such communication takes place.

The book is further concerned with the use of English as an L2 in interactions facilitated by CMC technologies. There is a growing body of research looking at L2 communicative and literacy practices online, and the effect of such activities on language learning. Efforts to define and label the phenomenon have produced a number of different terms: online informal learning of English (OILE; Sockett, 2014), extramural English (EE; Sundqvist & Sylvén, 2016), informal digital learning of English (IDLE; Lee, 2017), fully autonomous self-instructed learner (FASIL; Cole & Vanderplank, 2016) and mobile-assisted language use (MALU; Jarvis & Achilleos, 2013). Some approaches have focused on languages other than English (Inaba, 2019; Pasfield-Neofitou, 2012). Many of the findings of the above studies regarding the effects of L2 exposure facilitated by internet connectivity are applicable to any language. However, the global lingua franca status of English gives its learners greater potential for exposure, and a wider range of possible situations in which its use might be required.

1.3 Defining the Object of Study

A number of parameters further restrict the scope of the book and delineate the object of attention. These are discussed in greater detail in Chapter 2, but they are stated here for conceptual clarity, as they are fundamental theoretical positions.

1.3.1 Online language activities motivated by an authentic communicative need

Whether it be emailing a colleague, discussing a hobby or interest on a discussion board, exchanging WhatsApp messages with friends or merely playing around in a chat room, the book is concerned with activities initiated by a desire to communicate with other people, or to achieve some practical purpose such as making a purchase on eBay. The book does not concern itself with activities undertaken for the express purpose of language learning. There is a large body of literature looking at the use of CMC for language learning, in the field of computer-assisted language learning (CALL). More recently, however, an awareness has emerged that regarding CMC as a tool for language learning does not adequately describe a range of L2 activities, enabled and facilitated by the internet, in which L2 users don't necessarily regard themselves as primarily engaged in learning (Inaba, 2019; Pasfield-Neofitou, 2012; Sockett, 2014; Sundqvist & Sylvén, 2016). These are the interactions with which this book concerns itself, as they represent a 'back door' to language exposure which formal language teaching may overlook.

This characteristic of the object of study rests on a distinction between language learning and language use, and concomitant subject positions of learner and user. This is noted by Sockett (2014: 14) and Sundqvist and Sylvén (2016: 29), and by others whose work is not directly concerned with informal language learning, such as Cook (2011). However, Van Lier (2004), who shares with Sockett a theoretical stance that emphasizes complexity and ecology in language learning, contests this. He insists that '[f]rom an ecological perspective, the distinction must be rejected forcefully' (Van Lier, 2004: 223). While it is true that learning and use do not represent entirely distinct cognitive processes, it is not unreasonable to separate them on grounds of context and identity. To class someone as a language learner when they are, say, in the bank applying for a mortgage, or emailing a supplier about a delayed shipment, is to obscure the nature of the activity. Indeed, in the terms of activity theory used throughout this book (and to which Van Lier [2004: 211] also refers), the difference between learning and use can be encoded in the motives of the activity. This book therefore follows Sockett and Sundqvist and Sylvén in continuing to use the distinction. It is acknowledged that learning occurs in situations of use, and vice versa – indeed, this is crucial to the conclusions of the book – but activities are said to be primarily learning-oriented or use-oriented, and it is on the latter that the book focuses.

1.3.2 Online language activities which are interactive and dialogic in nature

The book does not concern itself with 'passive' language activities such as watching target-language films, television programs or videos or listening to music. Sundqvist and Sylvén (2016) take a broader approach, surveying all forms of non-class-related (what they term 'extramural') English language activities among classes of primary school pupils in Sweden. The resulting web of activities is conceptualized by the authors as a two-storey house, with monologic, receptive activities on the ground floor and dialogic, interactive activities, whose higher level of cognitive demand is metaphorically represented by the effort of 'climbing the stairs', on the upper floor (Sundqvist & Sylvén, 2016: 139). It is on the upper floor that this book focuses. This focus on the interactive component of these activities reflects the assertion in second language acquisition (SLA) theory that the use of language in conversational interaction 'forms the basis for the development of language' (Gass, 2003: 234).

Of the studies cited in Section 1.2, only Pasfield-Neofitou (2012) focuses on CMC activities. The L2 in this case is Japanese, and as discussed above, while many of Pasfield-Neofitou's findings are transferrable to English, the global status of English has implications that are not addressed in a study of Japanese learners.

1.3.3 Online language activities which are primarily conducted textually

Despite the continuing development of more 'information-rich' (Daft & Lengel, 1984) online media such as video conferencing, and indeed the explosive growth in the use of these technologies in response to the Covid-19 pandemic, text-based forms of communication remain perennially popular. Text-based CMC is generally regarded as a 'lean medium' (Rice, 1992), unable to transmit a wide array of extra-linguistic channels of information which shape face-to-face interaction in subtle but fundamental ways, such as gesture, timbre and intonation of voice, social cues such as physical appearance and dress, and the location and relative positions of interlocutors (lying on the sofa in a dressing gown versus standing in front of the manager's desk). Nevertheless, many people often choose to send a message when they could make a phone call, suggesting that efficient transmission of information is not the sole determiner of medium choice. Recent research into the pragmatics of online communication has suggested communicative and social functions unique to text-based online communication, that therefore cannot be achieved by other means (Yus, 2011). This suggests that text remains as salient an object of study as ever, showing no signs of obsolescence, and a major site of potential L2 use. The book therefore focuses on text, and does not concern itself with 'richer' online media such as video conferencing.

1.4 Research Gap and Contributions to Knowledge

The discussion in the preceding sections established the object of study as L2 English dialogic interactions in text-based CMC, undertaken for primarily non-learning purposes. It also demonstrated a gap in the literature with regard to this combination of characteristics. A number of studies have investigated L2 English activities online, but not focused on CMC activities in detail (Sockett, 2014; Sundqvist & Sylvén, 2016); others have investigated L2 CMC activities, but in a language other than English (Pasfield-Neofitou, 2012). Furthermore, while the studies discussed in previous sections include a range of methodological approaches, they all use relatively small participant sample sizes, and participants are limited to certain contexts. This book investigates activities defined by the characteristics stated above, on a large scale, recruiting participants from a wide range of language learning contexts.

This approach contributes the following to the body of knowledge regarding L2 CMC and informal language learning:

- A broad and detailed picture of L2 English communicative activities online by L2 English users in a wide variety of contexts and locations.
- An understanding of the needs of L2 English users as they engage in these activities.
- An approach to English teaching that supports these activities and maximizes their positive effects on language learning.

1.5 Partnership with Cambridge University Press

The research on which this book is based was undertaken in collaboration with Cambridge University Press (CUP). As one of the world's leading providers of English language teaching and learning materials, CUP are keen to understand the impact of online communication on tomorrow's language users and learners. CUP has an increasing emphasis on digital products and online or blended on/offline learning materials, and an ongoing research interest in 'how we use, teach and learn written and spoken language, particularly English'.[1]

CUP were instrumental in the questionnaire that provided the data for the analysis presented in Chapter 4, collaborating in its development and allowing it to be promoted on the Cambridge Online Dictionary. Furthermore, the study made direct and indirect use of a number of valuable resources made available by CUP. The analysis presented in Chapter 5 utilizes one of CUP's proprietary corpora, the Cambridge International Corpus (CIC), of which a component is the Cambridge and Nottingham E-Language Corpus (CANELC), and I am grateful for their kind permission to republish this analysis in this book. The Cambridge Online Dictionary was itself utilized at times during the writing of the book, when it was necessary to refer to conventional word meaning and usage.

1.6 Research Questions and Research Design

This book is based on research that addressed the following questions:

- RQ1: How widespread are L2 English CMC activities?
- RQ2: What challenges do L2 English users face in online interactions?
- RQ3: How does the English language used in CMC differ from the language more generally? What kinds of language knowledge are important for learners in this regard?

- RQ4: How can L2 English CMC activities be supported and integrated in formal language learning?

The first three of these research questions were investigated in two main phases of empirical research, followed by a synthesis of the findings that addressed the potential implications for language teaching (RQ4). The first empirical phase investigated RQ1 and RQ2 by means of a questionnaire-based survey, eliciting data from respondents regarding activities, contexts and difficulties of L2 English CMC use. The questionnaire also probed respondents' attitudes to the inclusion of L2 English CMC activities in formal learning. The second empirical phase, which investigated RQ3, used corpus analysis to explore the English language as it is used in online spaces.

Further methodological discussion is presented in Chapter 3.

1.7 Structure of the Book

The book is divided into nine chapters. Following this introduction, Chapter 2 explores the positions outlined in Sections 1.2 and 1.3, along with other related concepts, in more detail. Relevant literature is critically discussed both to situate the subsequent research in its proper context, and to build a conceptual and theoretical foundation for the empirical research. Chapter 3 presents a methodological account of the research process, from ideation to design, data collection and analysis. The following three chapters each focus on a particular element of the primary data gathered through a large-scale survey. Chapter 4 explores the notion of language activities defined functionally, and presents the findings of the questionnaire component probing respondents' feelings of comfort or discomfort when engaged in these activities. Chapter 5 turns to the socially and technically described contexts of CMC interactions, drawing on questionnaire data to show which forms of L2 CMC are most commonly engaged with. Chapter 5 concludes with a study of questionnaire respondents' attitudes to their English language CMC and its relationship with their language learning. Chapter 6 exchanges the quantitative lens for a qualitative lens, using a thematic analysis of text comments in the questionnaire data to inductively explore the kinds of difficulties and challenges encountered by L2 English users in their online interactions.

Chapter 7 explores the language of digital discourse, presenting a corpus analysis of two corpora of language used in online communication to better understand how learners might be better prepared to encounter and use language online, and provide examples of the linguistic manifestations of the phenomena described by questionnaire respondents.

Chapter 8 builds on the findings from the previous chapters bringing L2 English CMC and classroom learning together to propose an approach to English teaching that supports learners' online activities while maximizing their learning benefits. Finally, Chapter 9 brings the book to a conclusion by revisiting the research questions and discussing how they were addressed in the book, before acknowledging the limitations of the book and its implications for future research directions.

Note

(1) https://languageresearch.cambridge.org.

2 Situating the Research

This chapter presents overviews of some key concepts and their associated research, in order to position this book within the relevant fields and provide contextual knowledge in support of the analyses and discussions in subsequent chapters. First, in Section 2.1 the research is positioned within the field of informal second language learning (ISLL), including a critical discussion of some of the fundamental characteristics of that field and the seminal works that have led to its emergence. Then, in Section 2.2 the focus returns to computer-mediated communication (CMC): its relation to informal learning, its implications for the notion of language learning context and the implications of 'extramural' second language (L2) CMC for formal language learning. Drawing on aspects of second language acquisition (SLA) theory, I demonstrate the progression from language exposure to language acquisition, identify key cognitive processes that are required and show how these are facilitated by L2 CMC. The latter part of the chapter, Sections 2.3 and 2.4, turns to the identification and elaboration of a suitable theoretical foundation that enables the simultaneous consideration of both formal and informal aspects of learning. I outline the growth of complexity-oriented approaches to L2 learning and development, before entering into a deeper exploration of cultural historical activity theory (AT) as one such approach that provides a suitable perspective.

2.1 Informal Second Language Learning

This book complements and develops an expanding body of literature in a subfield which has emerged over the past two decades, and that has to a large extent coalesced around the term *informal second language learning*. Such research begins with the observation that the communicative affordances enabled by ubiquitous internet connectivity provide an unprecedented array of contexts of target language interaction, and that for many individuals, this exposure has the potential to change the nature of their relationship with the language and the learning process. In some cases, the individuals in question are not engaged in formal language learning of any kind, instead owing their language proficiency entirely to such naturalistic exposure. That this is a novel phenomenon worth particular study is due to its emergence from and through the explosive growth, since the turn of the millennium, of internet connectivity, Web 2.0 technologies and ubiquitous smartphone ownership. Together, these have greatly expanded the range of potential contexts of language use, and locations of interlocutors, with which the 21st-century individual comes into contact on a daily basis.

A substantial amount of research can be said to fall within the purview of the ISLL community (see Dressman & Sadler, 2020, for an overview). Research exploring online, out-of-class L2 English language activities has been carried out in a wide range of geosocial contexts: in Asia (Lai *et al.*, 2015; Lamb & Arisandy, 2019; Lee, 2017, 2019b, 2019a), Scandinavia (Henry, 2013; Sundqvist & Sylvén, 2014, 2016; Sylvén & Sundqvist, 2012), Europe (Jarvis & Achilleos, 2013; Kusyk, 2017; Sockett, 2014; Toffoli & Sockett, 2015; Trinder, 2017) and South America (Cole & Vanderplank, 2016). There are commonalities among these approaches, but also some fundamental ontological and epistemological differences.

A key differentiating factor within the field is the conception and usage of the term 'informal'. A distinction has long been drawn between *naturalistic* or *informal* learning or learning environments on the one hand and *formal* learning or learning environments on the other. Spolsky's (1989) discussion of the typical characteristics of the two categories is summarized in Table 2.1.

In informal learning contexts, then, the individual is concerned with co-constructing meaning with other target language speakers in 'the real world' using 'normal' language, while in formal contexts the individual exchanges stretches of 'controlled' language with other non-expert L2 learners, with a focus on form for the primary purpose of learning the language. This is admittedly a rather reductive analysis of classroom learning, particularly in light of the development of meaning-focused language teaching methodologies such as communicative language teaching and task-based language teaching (Brandl, 2020). In addition,

Table 2.1 Contrasting conditions of informal and formal learning environments

	Informal	**Formal**
Goal of language use	Communication	Learning
Interlocutors	Expert L2 speakers	Non-expert L2 learners
Context	The real world; L2 community	Classroom only
Language	'Free and normal'	Controlled, simplified
Focus	Meaning	Form

Source: Adapted from Spolsky (1989: 171).

the assumption of 'expert L2 speakers' in informal learning contexts implies that they exist primarily or solely as immersion situations in native-speaking L2 locations. This is one of the most significant disruptions caused by internet connectivity: individuals physically located in strongly monolingual first language (L1) communities may nevertheless find themselves interacting online with L2 speakers with a wide variety of backgrounds, L1s and degrees of L2 proficiency. Despite these shortcomings, Spolsky's (1989) analysis demonstrates the fundamental difference between what might be more simply labelled in-class and out-of-class learning.

This latter term was taken up by Benson (2011), who proposed a set of four dimensions to provide a consistent framework in which to locate a range of terminology arising in previous research into different forms of learning inside and outside the classroom. *Location* was proposed to cover such terms as 'out-of-class', 'out-of-school', 'after-school', 'extracurricular' and 'extramural'; it is apparent that this range necessitates conceiving 'location' on different levels of abstraction: physical location ('out-of-school'), temporal location ('after-school') and location within institutional structures ('extracurricular'). *Formality* refers to 'the degree to which learning is independent of organized courses leading to formal qualifications' (Benson, 2011: 10) and covers such terms as 'formal', 'informal' and 'non-formal'. *Pedagogy* refers to the degree and source of instruction taking place in the activity, as well as, to some extent, the intention behind the activity. 'Instructed', 'self-instructed' and 'non-instructed' clearly reference the former, while Benson states that in the 'naturalistic' position on the pedagogy dimension, 'there is no instruction … and, in principle, no intention to learn'. *Locus of control* concerns whether the driving force behind the activity stems from within the individual, or from an external source such as a teacher.

The term 'informal' appears in Benson's (2011: 10) analysis as a value in his 'formality' dimension, which as a whole refers to 'the degree to which learning is independent of organized courses leading to formal qualifications'. Informal learning is distinguished from formal learning (institutionalized schooling leading to high-stakes examinations and societally recognized qualifications) and non-formal learning (similar in structure but undertaken on an elective basis and without the imperative provided by the need to obtain certain scores). In defining informal learning, Benson (2011) borrows a definition from Livingstone: 'anything people do to gain knowledge, skill, or understanding from learning about their health or hobbies, unpaid or paid work, or anything else that interests them outside of organized courses'. A substantial proportion of the ISLL literature uses the term 'informal' in this way: activities motivated by a desire to learn, undertaken voluntarily, independently of any formal learning also being undertaken, and organized and structured entirely by the individual.

Elsewhere, however, an additional characteristic is assumed in the use of the term 'informal', relating to the intentionality or motivation behind the activity. This can be seen in the adoption of the term by the Council of Europe in its recommendations on the validation of non-formal and informal learning: 'informal learning means learning resulting from daily activities related to work, family or leisure and is not organised in terms of objectives, time or learning support; it may be unintentional from the learners' perspective' (Council of the European Union, 2012: 5). This defines informal learning as an outcome of an activity, not as an activity in itself, and makes it clear that the learning outcomes may be quite unrelated to the primary purpose of the activity. To an extent, this characteristic is present in Benson's (2011: 11) 'pedagogy' dimension as 'naturalistic learning', in which there is, 'in principle, no intention to learn'. However, Benson clearly finds this difficult to reconcile with his overall framework, noting that naturalistic learning 'may be a hypothetical state'. This difficulty arises because the four dimensions categorize learning activities; this second form of informal learning, as an outcome or, indeed, 'state', does not sit comfortable anywhere within them. It may be that a fifth dimension, that of *intentionality*, might help to expand Benson's framework and rectify this.

This distinction between activity and outcome is a crucial aspect of the term informal learning as it is used in some, but not all, of the literature. It is a differentiation that has been made for some time in the field of continuing adult education. Marsick and Watkins (1990: 12) distinguished formal and informal learning, but then noted, as a sub-category of informal learning, *incidental learning*, defined as 'a byproduct of some other activity, such as task accomplishment, interpersonal interaction, sensing the organizational culture, trial-and-error experimentation, or even formal learning'. This 'byproduct' characteristic is particularly salient in defining this second variant of informal learning, and is notably used by Sockett (2014) in his formulation of the online informal learning of English (OILE), discussed further below.

There are, then, two distinct 'flavors' of informal learning, and two main manifestations of the difference. The first manifestation is the distinction between informal learning as an activity and as an outcome. The latter still assumes the existence of an activity of some sort, however, and the second manifestation is in the fundamental difference in the purpose or motivation behind the activity: in one, the activity is undertaken primarily for the purpose of learning; in the other, it is not. This is summarized in Table 2.2.

It may ultimately be preferable to use the term *incidental* in place of *informal* for the second variant of informal learning, in order to recognize the ontological difference and prevent confusion and conflation. However, as is often the case, the need for conceptual clarity is tempered by the need for parsimony and communal identity. Either way, it is

Table 2.2 Two flavours of 'informal'

	Informal 1	Informal 2 (incidental)
'Learning' is...	An activity	An outcome (a byproduct)
The activity is...	Motivated by learning	Motivated by something else

important to clarify which form is intended. This book, then, is concerned with the second sense of the term informal learning – Marsick and Watkins' (1990) incidental learning – and more specifically the English language, communicative, online activities through which informal (incidental) learning may take place.

2.1.1 Learners and users

To characterize an individual as a 'learner' when they are engaged in an activity whose primary purpose or motivation is not learning related would seem to be unsatisfactory, or indeed counterproductive. It is difficult therefore to regard the study of informal language learning (in the second sense of the term) as the study of language learners. An alternative may be found in the notion of L2 users, individuals who are 'exploiting whatever linguistic resources they have for real-life purposes' (Cook, 2002: 2). The terms *user* and *learner* are not mutually exclusive in an individual, referring instead to situational roles. While students in a language classroom could certainly be characterized as *learners*, '[s]ome of these L2 learners become L2 users as soon as they step outside the classroom' (Cook, 2002: 3). *Learning* refers to activities undertaken with the explicit goal of developing knowledge and abilities in the language, while *use* refers to situations in which an individual is carrying out tasks or engaging in a communicative activity involving the co-creation of meaning with other speakers of the language, in response to an authentic communicative need.

Concern with an unhelpful preoccupation with *learners* in SLA research was voiced by Firth and Wagner (1997) in a much-cited article that marked the beginning of a move toward sociocultural approaches in the field of SLA. They argued that such a focus comes 'at the expense of other potentially relevant social identities' (Firth & Wagner, 1997: 288). Chen (2013: 162–163) notes a shift from learner to user in the self-perceived identities of Chinese immigrants to the US, manifest in their social media activity and enabling them to 'assume a more central role as a local participant'. Hanna and de Nooy (2003) observe that students who approached L2 interactions in a French discussion forum explicitly indexing their *learner* identities (by stating a desire to practice their French) were less successful in participation than students who, after briefly excusing their French, joined or initiated meaningful debates.

This is not to say that there is anything inherently objectionable about the term *learner*. Someone actively in the process of learning a language might very well regard himself or herself as a learner without any sense of disempowerment. However, where an individual is engaging in interactions or undertaking tasks that require the use of the L2 only coincidentally, to characterize them as a learner risks misrepresenting the situation and portraying them as a subordinate participant.

2.1.2 Strands of prior research in ISLL

Parallel research strands exploring aspects of language learning beyond the classroom have given rise to several terms to characterize the phenomena, with both senses of the term 'informal' being represented. Most influential in the literature have been extramural English (EE), OILE and informal digital learning of English (IDLE). These are used in the following to group related studies.

The term 'extramural English' was coined by Pia Sundqvist (2009) in her doctoral thesis to characterize the naturalistic exposure to English occurring in the day-to-day activities of Swedish schoolchildren. Sundqvist makes clear that EE is a characteristic of the individual and the context: the degree to which English appears in their life. Any learning or acquisition of the language that may result from this contact is considered separately from the basic concept itself. As such, this is clearly an example of the second form of informal learning, incidental learning, and the notion of EE refers to the activities through which informal learning outcomes may emerge.

Sundqvist and Sylvén (2016: 10) expand Benson's (1989) framework by explicitly relating location with locus of control and demonstrating where EE-induced learning sits in the resulting two-dimensional matrix. However, they also highlight that, contrary to Benson, they prefer to avoid the term *learning* altogether, due, among other things, to its connotations of intentionality. As such, EE sits uneasily within Benson's taxonomy, precisely because the activities constituting EE are not language learning activities in the first instance.

Sundqvist and Sylvén conceptualize the array of EE activities as an 'EE house', with monologic, receptive activities, such as watching English language movies and listening to English language music, on the ground floor, and dialogic, interactive activities, whose higher level of cognitive demand is metaphorically represented by the effort of 'climbing the stairs', on the upper floor (Sundqvist & Sylvén, 2016: 139). Upstairs are located the library, representing English language reading, and the office, representing online language use including multiplayer gaming. In several collaborations (Sundqvist & Sylvén, 2014, 2016; Sylvén & Sundqvist, 2012), the authors demonstrate a substantial amount of EE activity among Swedish primary schoolchildren, along with evidence of improved English language proficiency. They do not differentiate the kinds of interactive language activities which are the focus of this book, however, with 'internet use' covering a broad range of such activities. They do place particular emphasis on the apparent benefits of gaming, however, demonstrating the power of meaning-driven interaction.

Sockett (2014: 7) introduces the concept of the OILE to refer to a wide range of English language activities online which may lead to learning outcomes, but which are not primarily motivated by them. Sockett makes it clear that his use of the term 'informal learning' is intended to reference learning outcomes that emerge as a 'byproduct' of language activities whose primary motivation is not assumed to be learning related. This characteristic falls more naturally within Benson's 'pedagogy' dimension, rather than his 'formality' dimension, and as with EE, OILE ultimately rests uneasily in a framework for categorizing forms of language learning.

Sockett's seminal monograph presents evidence from questionnaires and interviews with students at a French university, showing frequent engagement with English in online activities, and evidence of language learning benefits, both subjectively in the form of participant perceptions, and objectively in the form of vocabulary test scores associated with higher frequency of OILE activities.

Kusyk (2017) expands on the notion of OILE, surveying students in both French and German universities. The nature and frequency of OILE activities are again probed using questionnaires, and Kusyk tracks the development of the complexity, accuracy and fluency of participants' English over a period of five months. Kusyk's data emphasize the fact that engagement with English online is a dynamic phenomenon, with shifting patterns of use over time. To the French and German data, Jurkovič (2019) adds a study of undergraduate students in Slovenia, and Lyrigkou (2018) moves beyond the higher education (HE) context to explore the relationship between OILE activities and learner agency in adolescent learners in Greece. Trinder (2017) conducts a similar survey among students at an Austrian university, again finding widespread engagement with English in leisure-time activities.

A separate strand of research leading to similar ideas proposed the notion of IDLE, the 'informal digital learning of English' (Lee & Dressman, 2018). This formulation is a development of research into computer-assisted language learning (CALL), a field which has typically regarded technology as a potential instrument in formal language learning, but which began to consider the role of technology in the wider learning ecosystem after observations such as that by Young *et al.* (2014: 265), who argued, in relation to studies of pragmatic competence development through CMC, that it is 'questionable how much learner's [sic] experiences in using pragmatic features in these "inauthentic" media can tell us about learning of the target items and use of these features in "real world" CMC contexts'. IDLE encompasses activities which are intentionally learning-oriented (regarded as 'extracurricular' IDLE), and those which are undertaken for leisure-, social- or information-seeking purposes. A number of IDLE studies have focused on the twin dimensions of quantity and quality (or diversity) of online language activities (Lai *et al.*, 2015). The latter refers to a balance between focus on meaning and focus on form (while maintaining differentiation from activities whose primary goal is learning related) and data suggest that this is a key variable in enhanced learning outcomes (Lee, 2019b).

Lee and Dressman (2018) do not analyze their use of the term 'informal' as rigorously as Sockett (2014) does, and it is apparent that they use it in a more generic sense to mean self-directed learning outside institutional education structures – the first definition of informal in the analysis above. They demonstrate an awareness of the need to differentiate between activities along the lines discussed above, but their analysis is hampered by a failure to consider the motive of the activity, and to move beyond activities motivated primarily by learning. Instead, they utilize Benson's (2011) terminology to make a somewhat forced distinction between 'L2 learning in the extramural digital context' and 'L2 learning in the extracurricular digital context'. They explain the difference as follows:

> The latter notion [extra-curricular] indicates students' autonomous English learning on their own initiative in out-of-class, digital contexts, which is still assessed by a teacher. For instance, EFL learners take the initiative in completing school assignments or projects, either alone or in groups, outside the institutional context, with the help of digital materials.... Later, the teacher evaluates their performance. In contrast, the former situation [extramural] signifies that students are involved in autonomous English learning in digital, unstructured, out-of-class environments that are not linked with a formal program. That is, EFL learners perform *English learning activities* on their own initiative, but these activities are not structured or assessed by the teacher.
>
> (Lee, 2019a: 694, my emphasis)

Elsewhere (Lee, 2019b: 115), both extracurricular and extramural variants are presented as flavors of IDLE. However, the definition given above of the extracurricular variant seems merely to be students doing their homework. It is difficult to see how 'completing school assignments or projects' falls into the category of informal learning, or indeed how students display autonomy and initiative in so doing. The extramural variant certainly seems to fit the nature of informality, but the use of the phrase 'English learning activities' clearly shows it to correspond to the first definition of informality in the current analysis.

Lee (2019b) introduces a further level of differentiation between form-focused and meaning-focused extramural IDLE activities, building on previous work that explores the notion of diversity in out-of-class learning activities (Lai *et al.*, 2015). This begins to acknowledge the possibility of non-learning-oriented activities, but without relinquishing the fundamental perspective of intentional learning the result is contradictory and awkward, not least in the fact that form-focused IDLE seems to be drifting back toward the extracurricular position. Acknowledging the difficulty of clearly separating meaning-focused from form-focused activities, the two are ultimately distinguished 'based on individuals' perceptions and *intentions* identified during the interviews' (Lee, 2019b: 118, my emphasis).

The paradoxical outcomes of maintaining a focus on learning activities are evident in the work on which Lee's discussion of diversity is based (Lai *et al.*, 2015, 2018). Lai *et al.* (2018) conducted interviews with undergraduate university students in Hong Kong, yielding three types of out-of-class, technology-mediated language learning experiences: instruction-oriented, entertainment- and information-oriented, and social-oriented. The latter was engaged with by 'a much smaller proportion of interview participants' (Lai *et al.*, 2018: 9) than the other two. Participants reported feelings of anxiety, discomfort and awkwardness in these interpersonal encounters, and some reported finding them inauthentic and boring (Lai *et al.*, 2018: 10). These were interactions initiated from a desire to practice the language, but beyond that they had little communicative purpose, and so there was little to say. That this was surprising to participants and researchers alike demonstrates the fundamental fixation on learning-oriented activities. One participant demonstrated an awareness of this, however: 'Interaction for the sake of interaction did not entice me. I spoke with others when I really had things to share or to discuss. I didn't like engaging someone in Spanish conversation for the sake of practicing the language, which basically led to fake, boring conversations' (Lai *et al.*, 2018: 11). This, again, illustrates the focus of this book: interactions driven by having something to share or to discuss, not simply to practice the language.

A different response to the need for evolution in the principles of CALL research is outlined in Jarvis and Achilleos (2013). Presenting data demonstrating substantial engagement with English using mobile devices among international undergraduate students at a UK university, Jarvis and Achilleos argue that both the 'computer' and 'learning' elements of CALL should be reconsidered. They propose 'mobile-assisted language use' as an alternative, a terminological choice that cleaves to our second definition of informality.

Largely independently of the research strands described above, Cole and Vanderplank (2016) present evidence of successful language acquisition by what they term 'fully autonomous self-instructed learners' (FASILs) in Brazil. These FASILs had 'acquired the majority of their English through informal contact with the language', rather than through dedicated self-study, and the authors conclude that 'adult learners can and do achieve high levels of English language proficiency without formal training'.

2.2 L2 English Computer-Mediated Communication

This book diverges from the literature discussed above by focusing solely on interactive, dialogic, CMC interactions. CMC activities are found in almost all the aforementioned studies to constitute a small minority of overall L2 English use online and, as a consequence, CMC is somewhat neglected by the field. However, there are firm theoretical grounds, outlined in the following discussions, for proposing that this form of activity has the greater potential for language development. L2 CMC, as distinct from language activities more generally, has been studied at length in the CALL literature as a tool for enhancing formal learning (see Lin, 2015, for a comprehensive meta-analysis). As with the ISLL literature, however, there has been an acknowledgement, since the turn of the century, of the importance of leisure-time L2 CMC interactions.

Studies in this area tend to take an ethnographic approach, longitudinally exploring the nature of engagement with others using an L2 online, and the effects of this contact on language and identity development. A seminal case study in this area is Lam (2000), who presents the case of an adolescent Chinese immigrant to the US, overcoming the stigma of being a remedial English as a second language (ESL) learner at school through online engagement with an international English-speaking community of pop music fans. Widening the perspective, Pasfield-Neofitou (2012) and Inaba (2019) use interviews, diaries and conversation analysis to explore language and identity development through the L2 CMC activities of Australian learners of Japanese. Pasfield-Neofitou (2012: 162) finds numerous aspects of CMC that provide unique language learning benefits, such as the durable, visual trace characteristic of most forms of CMC that can help learners notice non-standard forms of language that are common in colloquial speech, and the blurring of private and public boundaries in CMC that can allow learners to observe naturally occurring language use between others. Inaba (2019: 110) notes the importance of considering L2 identity development as a part of language development.

While the work of both Pasfield-Neofitou and Inaba contains a wealth of valuable insights into the workings of L2 development via CMC, studies of Japanese as an L2 leave unexplored the implications of the lingua franca status of English. In adopting this focus on L2 English CMC (henceforth EL2 CMC), this book brings together this strand of research with the more psycholinguistic-oriented informal language learning literature. Furthermore, I address two hitherto overlooked methodological aspects of these research areas. Firstly, all the studies discussed above involve relatively small sample sizes, Trinder's 179 participants being the largest by some margin. These populations are usually accessed in educational environments: schools, universities and private language academies, and are often engaged in the formal study of the L2 in question. There is very little exploration of how working life presents opportunities and obligations for L2 use online.

This book presents the results of a study that was able to access a large sample of L2 English users with a broad age range, outside of formal learning institutions, in locations all over the world, in order to provide valuable baseline data for the field to build upon.

2.2.1 EL2 CMC and language acquisition

This section invokes a number of key concepts from the field of SLA to demonstrate how EL2 CMC can lead to improved language proficiency, and to build a theoretical framework which will be used later to consider how best to address/exploit/integrate EL2 CMC in formal learning. It begins with an observation that online interactions can provide exposure to the target language in a similar way to being immersed in a physical target language community, before introducing a chain of concepts that model how language encountered in the environment comes to be used for the derivation of new language knowledge, and the cognitive conditions and processes that are required.

Extramural L2 CMC can provide 'opportunities for authentic social interaction' (Pasfield-Neofitou, 2012: 12), contexts in which the L2-speaking individual can interact as an autonomous language user. Such contact with the target language in a naturalistic setting is examined using the concept of *exposure*, a common-sense term that is given more technical depth in the literature on SLA. Exposure is regarded as necessary for language learning, and the potential of CMC for providing it makes online communication a great asset to the learner. In order to clearly illustrate the value of CMC in this regard, the concept of exposure is explored in some detail in the following sections.

SLA theorists tend to agree that being exposed to the target language in some form is 'a necessary condition for learning' (Spolsky, 1989: 166). As Susan Gass (1997: 1) observes: 'It is trivial to point out that no individual can learn a second language without input of some sort'. The term 'exposure' in a lay sense has connotations of contact with environmental phenomena, to light, sun or 'the elements', and as discussed further in a moment in relation to language learning context, it is often regarded as an environmental variable.

Influential work by Krashen (1981: 1; 1982) distinguished the processes of language *acquisition*, the 'picking-up' of language from environmental exposure, and language *learning*, undertaken formally and consciously. Krashen (1982: 15) argued that acquisition was the superordinate process, with formal linguistic *learned* knowledge serving to monitor output between ideation and verbalization. Exposure to language in naturalistic environments is therefore a critical process in the formation of a competent language user, as it provides input for acquisition. Krashen's (1982: 20–22) input hypothesis postulates that acquisition will take place when comprehensible input – that is, language of a degree of complexity a little higher than the learner's existing knowledge (presented as the formula $i + 1$) – is received. The comprehensibility condition recognizes that not all input will become 'utilized primary linguistic data' (Krashen, 1981: 46), which Krashen terms *intake*, following Friedlander *et al.* (1972).

Later developments of Krashen's model address what was perceived as a problem of the absence of negative evidence in an input-only scenario. White (1987) argues that there are scenarios in which input can draw attention to the inadequacy of the learner's current state of knowledge (Krashen's *i*), but not allow for the inference of new rules in order to progress to $i + 1$. The interaction hypothesis addresses this oversight, stating that language encountered at the input stage must be used for the negotiation of meaning in communicative interaction for learning to take place (Gass, 2003: 234). CMC has the potential to provide both exposure to language-in-use and opportunities for interaction.

The distinction between input and intake is explored by Schmidt (1990), in an article which also challenges Krashen's assumption of the non-conscious nature of acquisition. Schmidt finds a lack of clarity in the use of the concept of *consciousness* in the SLA literature. He identifies three main meanings: consciousness as awareness, consciousness as intention and consciousness as knowledge (Schmidt, 1990: 131). Furthermore, he differentiates three levels of awareness: *perception*, *noticing* and *understanding*. Perception is a minimal state of awareness, noticing is a state of 'focal awareness', in which the noticed phenomena are distinguished from the perceived background, and understanding is a state in which noticed phenomena are subject to cognitive processes such as analysis. Schmidt (1990: 139) therefore defines intake as 'that part of the input that the learner notices', and goes on to declare that learning without any awareness of stimulus is impossible (Schmidt, 1990: 149). This is all neatly summed up by Ellis (1995: 89) as 'no noticing, no acquisition'.

Figure 2.1 visualizes the relationships between the processes discussed in this section. Exposure provides linguistic input, salient parts of which are converted to intake when they are noticed. Language intake that is used in meaning-driven interaction is then acquired.

With regard to consciousness as intention, Schmidt (1990) relates this to the concept of incidental learning. Incidental learning is unconscious in the specific sense that it takes place without the intention to learn on the part of the learner. It is in this sense that it is a 'byproduct' of some other activity. This definition does not require incidental learning to take place without awareness on the part of the learner: in fact, awareness-as-noticing is crucial for it to occur. The capacity for noticing salient features of the

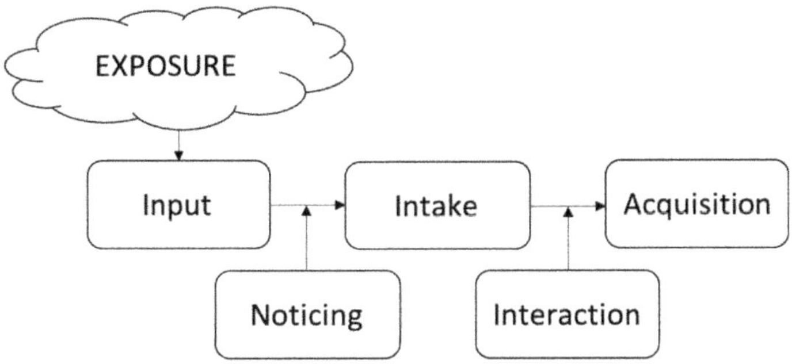

Figure 2.1 From exposure to acquisition

input and thus converting them to intake, triggering the mechanisms of acquisition, is independent from the intentionality to engage in learning in the interaction. Schmidt (1990: 149) concludes that incidental learning is possible 'when task demands focus attention on relevant features of the input'. Adopting the theoretical perspective of AT (see Section 2.4), McCafferty *et al.* (2001) provide empirical evidence that, within activity systems, actions which have as their goal a linguistic item will be more likely to result in the acquisition of that item than activities in which the same item is only tangentially involved. Noticing, then, involves the emergence of a secondary activity, with language as its object.

Pasfield-Neofitou (2012: 163) notes that the permanent textual trace characteristic of most forms of CMC can help learners notice non-standard forms of language that are common in colloquial speech, and that this textual record combined with the blurring of private and public boundaries in CMC can allow learners to observe naturally occurring language use between others (Pasfield-Neofitou, 2012: 162).

The importance of noticing, and the underlying awareness it implies, has resulted in the emergence of the concept of *language awareness*, and an attendant approach to language teaching (Svalberg, 2007). This approach views language awareness as a learner characteristic that can be learned and taught, and which functions as a predisposition to notice aspects of language. Svalberg (2007: 288) quotes the Association for Language Awareness as defining the concept in the following way: 'Explicit knowledge about language, and conscious perception and sensitivity in language learning, language teaching, and language use'. She further outlines five principles of a language awareness approach to language teaching as follows:

1. It involves an ongoing investigation of language as a dynamic phenomenon rather than awareness of a fixed body of established facts.
2. It involves learners in talking analytically about language, often to each other.

3. It considers essential the involvement of learners in exploration and discovery.
4. It aims to develop not only the learners' knowledge about and understanding of language but also their learning skills, thus promoting learner independence.
5. The aim is to involve learners on both a cognitive and an affective level.

(Svalberg, 2007: 290–291)

Language awareness can provide a link between informal and formal learning. This will be explored at length in Chapter 6.

2.2.2 EL2 CMC and attitudes to language learning

EL2 CMC has the potential to benefit language learning by changing the nature of the relationship between the individual and the language. Attitudes toward languages, language communities and language learning have received considerable attention throughout several decades of research into language learning motivation. Influential early work in this area, based on studies of immigrants to Canada learning ESL, identified an *integrative orientation* as a key factor behind the motivation to learn a language, defined as 'a sincere and personal interest in the people and culture represented by the other group' (Gardner & Lambert, 1972: 132). Krashen (1981: 22–23; see further discussion in Section 2.2.1) incorporates integrative motivation, in conjunction with instrumental motivation, into the *affective filter* component of his monitor model, giving motivation a moderating role in language acquisition. In contrast to integrative motivation, instrumental motivation in language learning refers to the desire to learn a language for 'utilitarian, or practical purposes' (Krashen, 1981: 22) as a means to some other end, such as getting a job or gaining entrance to university.

Subsequent work drew attention to problematic aspects of these early approaches to language learning motivation. The concept of integrativeness was criticized for its implication of a desire for cultural assimilation, and doubt was cast on its ability to explain motivation in the context of globalized English, in which the idea of a 'target community' becomes very vague (Ushioda & Dörnyei, 2009: 2–3). Dörnyei (2009: 27) attempts to resolve many of these controversies by approaching the concept of integrativeness from the perspective of the psychological concept of possible selves. In the resulting L2 Motivational Self system, integrativeness is reformulated as 'the L2-specific facet of one's ideal self'. Individuals will appear to have an integrative orientation when their perception of the 'best they can be' (their ideal self) is a competent user of the target language.

Yashima (2009) expands the L2 Motivational Self system with the concept of *international posture*. In some senses a response to the criticism that integrativeness presupposes a specific target community, international posture recasts this as an alignment with a perceived global community, 'a tendency to relate oneself to the international community rather than any specific L2 group' (2009: 145). While Yashima does not explore the concept in relation to CMC, the communicative resources of the internet clearly have the potential to open individuals up to such an international audience.

The L2 Motivational Self system explicitly ties motivation to identity, or aspirational identity. This is also the case in the work of Bonny Norton (2013), who adopts a post-structuralist perspective to reformulate language learning-related phenomena previously conceptualized as motivation. She criticizes previous approaches to motivation as stemming from problematic ontological positions that regard identity as fixed and essential, and artificially separated from and contrasted with social context (Norton Peirce, 1995: 19). Instead, Norton draws on Bourdieu's (1977) economic metaphors in linguistic interaction to develop a notion of *investment* which she advocates in place of motivation.

A key factor in Norton's (2013: 43) analysis is that attitudes to language learning and use are moderated by 'inequitable relations of power between language learners and target language speakers'. She examines the case of Eva, a Polish immigrant to Canada. Eva's main potential opportunities for interaction in English were in her workplace, but she found that her anglophone colleagues were reluctant to engage with her: she reported overhearing comments such as 'I don't like working with people who aren't Canadian' (Norton, 2013: 100). Norton (2013: 101) describes this as a 'Catch-22' situation: 'She needed to have command of English in order to gain access to the social networks in the restaurant, but she couldn't develop fluency without access to these social networks'.

CMC has the potential to break this cycle, by providing a platform to develop an identity as a competent user of the target language, away from the inequitable power relations of the immediate physical context. Lowry *et al.* (2009: 181) observe a reduction in 'status effects' – verbal and non-verbal cues that help establish hierarchical social relations between interlocutors – in CMC compared with face-to-face interaction, while Montoya-Weiss *et al.* (1998: 717) note that the reduced visual cues of CMC can reduce communication apprehension (see Section 2.3.1). Lam (2000) examines the case of Almon, a teenager who had immigrated to the US from Hong Kong, and whose frustrations in trying to integrate and learn English had finally been overcome by his involvement in an English-speaking online community centered on Japanese pop music. Almon's CMC activities allowed him to establish himself as a competent communicator, a 'legitimate speaker' (Bourdieu, 1977: 650), in a way his schooling did not, and his English itself immediately began to improve. Almon's use of CMC to gain access to social capital is in marked contrast to the example of Norton's Eva.

The kind of personal 'reinvention' demonstrated by Almon is made possible by the relative anonymity of CMC interaction, and is therefore most effective between previously unacquainted interlocutors. Mention is often made in the literature of the famous cartoon in *The New Yorker*, captioned: 'on the Internet no one knows you're a dog'. The strategic presentation of the self online in such contexts has been the object of study of digital anthropologists such as Sherry Turkle (1995), whose seminal *Life On The Screen* explored the affordances of internet communication technologies for the expression of decentered, multiple identities. Similarly, Becker and Stamp (2005: 245) draw on the work of Goffman (1959) to study *impression management* in internet chat rooms, exploring participants' use of 'fictitious identit[ies]' in their online activities. While the internet undoubtedly provides the resources for such experimentation, there is no reason to assume this behavior is typical of CMC users. Pasfield-Neofitou (2012: 10) notes that 'users may choose not to make use of this potential', and cites boyd (2007) in observing that 'young people are more interested in communication with people they already know personally than with strangers' (Pasfield-Neofitou, 2012: 11). In relation to the current study, it is important to remember that CMC encompasses a broad range of contexts and configurations of interlocutors. Some might involve anonymity and deliberate experimentation with identity, others might involve well-acquainted interlocutors maintaining a pre-existing relationship.

Many of the attitudinal benefits of CMC discussed above rely in some way on the capacity of CMC to overcome the limitations of physical context. The next section discusses the concept of language learning context in more detail.

2.2.3 EL2 CMC and language learning context

Many approaches characterize exposure, or opportunities for exposure, as a function of the environment in which an individual is learning an L2. A common distinction is drawn between *naturalistic* or *informal* learning environments on the one hand, and *formal* learning environments on the other. In the former, language is encountered by the learner with little consideration for their non-expert status, and in the presence of an authentic communicative need. The language itself, as an abstract system, is subordinate to the uses to which it is put. In formal environments (such as the language classroom), on the other hand, the language itself is the object of study, and consequently it is presented to the learner in a controlled fashion. Spolsky (1989: 171) observes that the distinction is 'usually stated as a set of contrasting conditions', shown in Table 2.1.

The division of stereotypical conditions illustrated in Table 2.1 has subsequently contributed in large part to the crystallization of a dichotomy between the terms English as a foreign language (EFL) and English as a second language. This distinction is typified by this extract from the Wikipedia article 'English as a Second or Foreign Language':

> Technically, TEFL refers to English language teaching in a country where English is not the official language, TESL refers to teaching English to non-native English speakers in a native English-speaking country and TESOL covers both.[1]

EFL contexts are conflated with formal learning environments, and ESL contexts with informal environments, though in reality the two pairs of terms operate at different levels of abstraction, and both formal and informal environments will likely exist in both EFL and ESL contexts, albeit in differing degrees.

Exposure as the defining distinction between EFL and ESL contexts is also the underlying assumption behind academic research such as Yamashita and Jiang (2010), in which a comparison is made of the success with which study participants in EFL and ESL contexts learn English collocations. No discussion is entered into in the paper regarding the definition of, and distinction between, EFL and ESL, other than a brief reference to 'the increased amount of input' (Yamashita & Jiang, 2010: 653) of ESL settings. In the description of the research methodology, the contexts are described briefly and unproblematically: '...the ESL users were students, researchers or instructors at four Universities in the United States ... [the] EFL learners were students at a University in Japan' (Yamashita & Jiang, 2010: 654) (all participants were Japan-born Japanese native speakers). This description also highlights the fact that the terms EFL and ESL are often connected with the terms *learner* and *user*, respectively, reflecting the assumption of increased opportunities for language *use* in ESL contexts.

While this EFL/ESL distinction is a dominant paradigm in English language teaching literature and practice, Nayar (1997) provides a challenging critique of the use of the two terms in such an antithetical relationship. He demonstrates that the two terms originally arose independently of one another to refer to the teaching of English and were only later stitched together into a dichotomous pair. He notes the importance of exposure in delineating the positions, observing in the case of ESL contexts that '[t]he crucialness of environmental support is a repeated theme in the discourse' (Nayar, 1997: 17). Furthermore, he finds at least two quite different uses of the term ESL: one in which English is learned by newcomers to a context in which it is the dominant (often only) language, such as immigrants to the US, and another in which it is learned as a language of status or officialdom in a multilingual context such as India.[2] Nayar advocates redesignating the latter as English as an associate language (EAL) for clarity.

Siegel (2003: 179) presents a finer-grained analysis, recasting the typical ESL environment as one in which the target language is the dominant language in the geosocial context, such as is the case of immigrants from Spain learning English in the UK, for example. The EFL environment he characterizes is one in which the target language is external to the geosocial context in which it is learned, with little practical application immediately outside the classroom: South Korean learners learning English in South Korea, for example. To these two, Siegel adds other possibilities: contexts in which the target language has an institutional role, for example in post-colonial situations such as India where English is a lingua franca of administration and bureaucracy; contexts in which the target language co-exists with other primary languages, for example when situated in Switzerland learning one of the country's three official languages; and finally contexts in which the target language is a minority language in the geosocial context, such as in the case of English speakers learning Welsh in the UK.

Clearly there is an interplay between social context and exposure. However, all the approaches to classifying the social context of language learning examined above are ultimately based on geography. CMC has the potential to operate quite independently of the geographical or (offline) social settings in which a learner finds themselves, and thus disrupt traditional classificatory models.

Norton's (2013) critique demonstrates that target language exposure, and especially its interactional component, cannot be guaranteed or assumed even in so-called ESL (Siegel's 'dominant L2') contexts. This highlights the danger of operationalizing the EFL/ESL dichotomy as a tool for making inferences about a learner's needs in a particular context. The larger the scale of the context, the more such labels obscure heterogeneity and variety. To apply them at a national level, as is frequently done, is misleading and ineffective: Nayar (1997: 27) notes that South Africa and Zimbabwe could be categorized as EFL, ESL or native English contexts, depending on where one looks within the country. However, the enthusiastic adoption of the EFL/ESL dichotomy demonstrates an underlying awareness both of the importance of exposure to the target language for the process of learning it, and of the fact that opportunities for such exposure will vary greatly between learners, depending on the social context in which learning takes place.

It is exactly this exposure to language in authentic interaction that CMC has the potential to provide, regardless of the physical environment of the learner. Quite independently of which of Siegel's (2003) social contexts language learners find themselves in, the affordances of the internet provide them with the capability to interact with expert or non-expert speakers of their target language, anywhere in the world. Such interaction has many of the same benefits for language acquisition as face-to-face encounters (Pasfield-Neofitou, 2012: 12) and indeed the characteristics of

CMC can help overcome psychological and social barriers to expression sometimes encountered by learners using their L2 in person, as seen in the comparison between Almon and Eva in Section 2.3.2.

2.2.4 Learning context in a hyper-connected world

Given the potential for instant communication with target language speakers all over the world, regardless of physical location, it becomes tempting to suppose that learning context is an irrelevance, provided learners have a good internet connection. However, just as exposure is not guaranteed even in stereotypical 'ESL' learning contexts, neither does it automatically follow from access to an internet-enabled electronic device. Nayar (1997: 16 footnote) notes in passing a distinction between dominant language contexts in which the learner has an expectation of permanent residence, and those in which the sojourn is temporary, and integration into the L2 community may be less of a priority. In either of these variants, though perhaps especially in the latter, CMC has the potential to further isolate the learner from the L2 community around them, allowing them instead to remain in uninterrupted contact with friends, relatives and popular culture 'back home'. Pasfield-Neofitou (2012: 7) cites Miller and Slater (2000) in stressing the importance of considering not '*the* internet' as a monolithic entity, but an individual's 'internet', their network of connections and activities which may be quite different from that of another individual. This suggests that while it is perfectly possible that the technical affordances of the internet might allow for such empowerment as experienced by Almon, another CMC user's personal 'internet' might reinforce existing social networks and identities, and, where these are predominantly L1, hinder L2 development rather than facilitate it. For exposure to occur online, learners must, for whatever reason and with whatever motivation, engage with groups and activities online in which there is cause to use the target language.

2.2.5 Implications for language teaching

Pasfield-Neofitou (2012: 2) calls for CMC to be more closely integrated into language teaching: 'teachers cannot afford to ignore providing students with the basic skills and strategies they will need to deal with Internet use outside of the classroom'. If only for the sake of retaining relevance to the lives of learners, language teaching must understand the extent to which learners use their English outside the classroom, and incorporate and support it. Ushioda (2011: 203) concurs with this in relation to the concept of learners' *ideal selves*: 'how we engage our students' social identities in their L2 interactions within and beyond the classroom now would seem to have important consequences for how they visualize themselves as users of the L2 in the future'. Lamb and Arisandy (2019: 17) argue that to ignore learners' L2 CMC is to risk 'failing to acknowledge important elements in … learners' evolving L2-mediated identities', and that 'teachers have no choice but to acknowledge it and modify their classroom practice, if they wish to continue to serve their learners' long-term best interests'.

The degree of exposure to authentic language in contexts where learners engage in substantial EE activity increases the importance of the authenticity of materials used in the classroom. Henry *et al.* (2017: 7) note: 'Not only do students express the feeling of a difference between experiences speaking/using English in school and their "extramural English experiences"… but that school experiences lack the authenticity of leisure-time experiences'. While the difficulty of achieving true authenticity in classroom materials has been a matter of long debate (Widdowson, 1998), the need to create 'a sense of continuity between what [students] learn and do in the classroom, and who they are and what they are interested in doing in their lives outside the classroom' (Ushioda, 2011: 204) is greater than ever in the hyper-connected digital age.

Nevertheless, any appropriation of EL2 CMC activities in the classroom must be done with care, lest the original purposes of such interactions be clouded by a focus on learning. In a presentation at the 2018 Informal Second Language Learning Conference at the University of Oxford, Geoff Sockett facetiously glossed the integration of informal and formal learning as 'spoiling the fun'. In setting out a set of principles underlying the integration of classroom learning and autonomous out-of-class learning, Mercado (2015: 191, my emphasis) notes the importance of 'learner "buy-in" to autonomous learning practices', explaining that 'unless students see value in what is being asked of them, *especially if it will take up some of their valuable personal time*, positive affect and motivation may be lacking'. By definition, however, the activities under investigation in this book are those which already form an existing part of the individual's 'valuable personal time', rather than being imposed upon it by language education professionals. This must be preserved in any effort to augment the learning outcomes of such practices.

2.3 Complexity in Language Learning

This book is built on the premise that language learning is a holistic enterprise that extends far beyond the classroom into many different aspects of the life and identity of the individual learner. Extramural EL2 CMC activities should not be thought of as external to the learning process, but as an integral component of a wider system leading to learning outcomes. The ISLL field has emerged from a growing acknowledgement of the need to treat language learning, and indeed language itself, as a complex, contextually situated, sociocultural process (Beckner *et al.*, 2009). A narrow focus on the classroom and the cognitive processes of the individual learner cannot provide a full account of learning processes and of successful, or unsuccessful, outcomes. A dissatisfaction with cognitivist approaches to SLA that prioritized intrapersonal traits and processes (Firth & Wagner, 1997) led to efforts among researchers to explore and develop theories of language and language learning which situate the individual in their social and cultural contexts, treated not just as background variables, but as core formative components of the process. This 'growing sensitivity to complexity' (Mercer, 2016: 473) emphasizes the importance of understanding phenomena as interrelated components of larger systems, and of grounding any analysis of such phenomena in an acknowledgement of the wider contexts in which they are situated. Van Lier (2004: 4) characterizes this as an 'ecological approach', which takes 'account of the full complexity and interrelatedness of processes that combine to produce an environment'. Similarly, complex dynamic systems theory (CDST) (Beckner *et al.*, 2009; Larsen-Freeman & Cameron, 2008) has been used to analyze the multiple individual and contextual variables interacting in an individual's L2 development. CDST proposes that a system such as L2 development proceeds in a non-linear trajectory that is highly sensitive to the initial conditions of the variables, sometimes settling into stable states, and at other times transitioning to a qualitatively different developmental stage by means of transformative 'phase shifts'. CDST originated as a mathematical theory, and the question of whether L2 development can be regarded as such a system in a literal, mathematical sense, or whether the concept is applied analogously, is still open to debate (Cameron & Larsen-Freeman, 2007: 3).

Another key theoretical framework that emphasizes the cultural, social and historical situatedness of language learning is Vygotskian sociocultural theory (Lantolf & Thorne, 2006). Soviet psychologist Lev Vygotsky argued that the human mind emerges through a dialogical relationship with the cultural and social context in which it develops. Consequently, it is impossible to account for the psychology of the individual in isolation from his or her context (Kaptelinin & Nardi, 2006: 39). A central concept is that of mediation: humans rarely interact directly with the world around them, but usually do so with the aid of mediating artefacts, or tools (Inaba, 2019: 20). These may be material tools, such as a hammer, or psychological tools, such as maps, symbolic systems such as algebra, or language. The process of mediation by psychological tools distinguishes higher mental functions from natural mental functions, 'such as memory or perception with which every animal is born' (Kaptelinin & Nardi, 2006: 41). The study of human development, including L2 learning, is therefore the study of the mediated interactions between humans and their environment. In examining the interrelations between formal and incidental learning, this book adopts this complexity-oriented theoretical perspective, in the form of AT. This framework is described in the following sections, along with the rationale for its use.

2.4 Activity Theory

Vygotsky's ideas were developed by his student and colleague Antonin Leontiev, who expanded the social element, enlarging the perspective from individual-mediated action to viewing the individual subject within a complex, collective activity (Engeström, 2015: xiv). Activities minimally consist of a human subject, an object, which may be material or abstract, and a mediating artefact, and are undertaken in pursuit of some motive, which might be the acquisition of the object itself, or some more abstract state to which the object represents an intermediate step (Kaptelinin & Nardi, 2006: 31–32). On a lower level of analysis, activities are constituted by actions, which are directed toward a goal. The goal of the action may not always coincide with the object of the overall activity, but the action is nevertheless contributory to, and necessary for, the activity. Activity is therefore an abstraction, realized by concrete, goal-directed actions (Leontiev, 1978: 99–100).

AT was taken up and developed by Yrjö Engeström (2015), who incorporated more directly the social aspect of Vygotsky's thought. To the subject–tool–object triangle, he added further components representing the community in which the subject is situated, and in which certain rules will constrain the possibilities for action. Members of the community have specific roles to play in the activity (as, of course, does the subject), assigned according to the Marxist concept of the division of labor. Engeström's triangles-within-triangles model is reproduced in Figure 2.2.

Although the activity system is taken as the unit of analysis in AT, it is not intended to be considered in isolation, but as embedded within a network of neighbouring activity systems, linked activity systems (Lantolf & Thorne, 2006: 249; Russell & Yañez, 2003: 340). These neighbouring systems may share objects, or they may be interrelated with the

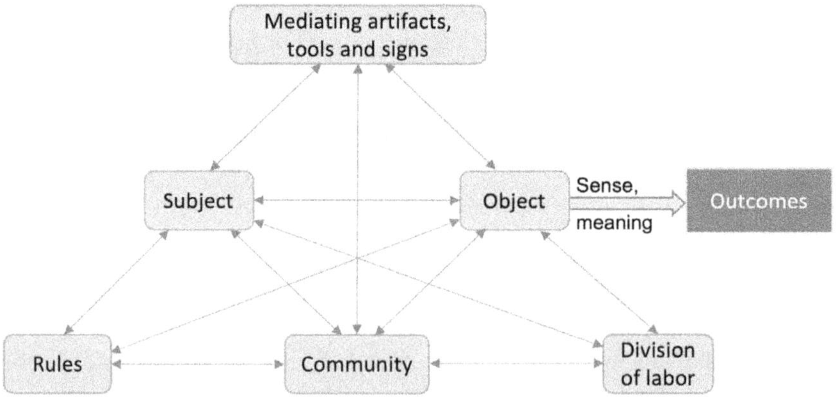

Figure 2.2 Engeström's activity system, adapted from Engeström (1987) with permission from Taylor and Francis

outcomes of one activity changing the components, and therefore outcomes, of another.

For present purposes, AT has a particular theoretical benefit in the explicit conceptual position given to the motive for the activity. As discussed earlier, a key characteristic of the type of learning process under investigation is whether or not the individual enters into an activity with the primary goal of learning the language. AT enables this to be addressed in the analysis, and for this reason the theory is adopted as the principle element of the theoretical framework used. In the next section, therefore, a number of central aspects of AT (including motive) will be discussed in more detail, in order to provide background to further discussion in subsequent chapters.

2.4.1 Subject

The subject is a living, intelligent entity with agency, which Kaptelinin and Nardi (2006: 33) define as 'the ability and the need to act'. A subject has needs, which can only be met through acting in the world, and this is the genesis of activity. Lantolf and Thorne (2006: 222–223) claim that the notion of the subject in prior work on AT is 'under-theorized', and suggest incorporating within it cognate notions that have arisen in applied linguistic research on social identity such as Kramsch (2013) and Norton (2013). This will be returned to in the subsequent chapters.

2.4.2 Objects, motives and outcomes

There is a certain ambiguity in the AT literature regarding the precise nature of these three components. Lantolf and Thorne (2006: 231, note 16), in a chapter endnote, acknowledge that '"Object" presents a special challenge within AT's nomenclature', and Inaba (2019: 23) cites Yamagata-Lynch (2010: 17) in noting that difficulties in translating original Russian source material into English have exacerbated the difficulties. The three are certainly closely related to one another: Leontiev (1978: 7) states that 'the object of activity is its motive', but this simple equivalence is qualified in later developments. This will be explored in a commentary on the five highlighted sections in the following passage, taken from Lantolf and Thorne (2006: 223, emphasis and numbering added, citations modified to fit current context):

> In alignment with A.N. Leont'ev, 'object' describes the orientation of the activity **and arises from the motive for an outcome or result** (1). Engeström explains that **the object 'refers to the "raw material" or "problem space" at which the activity is directed** (2) and which is molded or transformed into "outcomes" with the help of physical and symbolic, external and internal tools', which mediate the activity (1993, p. 67). Elsewhere, Engeström explains: '**An entity becomes an object of activity**

> **when it meets a human need** (3) … in this constructed, need-related capacity, the object gains motivating force that gives shape and direction to activity. The object determines the horizon of possible actions' (Engeström, 1999b, pp. 380–381). As we described in the explication of Leont'ev's use of the terms 'motive' and 'object', **the motive is the cultural-psychological-institutional impetus that guides human activity toward a particular object** (4). The projected outcome, off in the future, provides a conceptual web that temporally relates immediate action with 'important new, objectified meanings and relatively lasting new patterns of interaction. **It is this projection from the object to the outcome that, no matter how vaguely envisioned, functions as the motive of the activity** (5) and gives broader meaning to … actions' (Engeström, 1999a: 31).[3]

There is a degree of circuitousness here: the object arises from the motive (section 1), but the motive seems to arise from the object (section 5). However, section 5 also implies a space, 'this projection from the object to the outcome', which is echoed in Engeström's use of the term 'problem space' in section 2. The impression is of object not merely as concrete and inert (even in cases where it may be materially embodied), but as a dynamic interplay between a thing and the uses to which it may be put; indeed need-fulfilment is a crucial attribute of an object (section 3). This nebulousness around the exact nature of the object is acknowledged and indeed embraced by Engeström (2001: 134), who comments on the diagrammatic representation of his activity system model: 'The object is depicted with the help of an oval indicating that object-oriented actions are always, explicitly or implicitly, characterized by ambiguity, surprise, interpretation, sense making, and potential for change'.

The case of language learning as an activity system is a good example of the discussions above. Language learning is clearly directed toward the acquisition of a target language. However, it would be an oversimplification to claim that the language itself represents the object of language learning. Instead, the interplay between the language and the uses to which it may be put form a dynamic matrix of object, outcome and motive. For example: language for academic achievement, resulting in a motive of attaining a recognized qualification for university entrance; or language coupled with a notion of being a 'global citizen', resulting in a motive of engaging in online communities using the target language. These examples recognize the 'cultural-psychological-institutional' nature of the motive, highlighted in section 4 of the passage above.

A further facet of the concept of motive is its potential for multiplicity. Leontiev (1978: 169) asserts that activity 'responds simultaneously to two or more motives', and he differentiates between two types. 'Sense-forming motives' constitute the rationale for engaging in the activity, while 'motives-stimuli' provide 'stimulating factors (positive or negative), sometimes sharply emotional and affective'.

The two examples given in the preceding paragraph also highlight a fundamental aspect of the object (and, given that all activity is directed toward the object, of activity itself): the distinction between *use value* and *exchange value* (Engeström, 2015: 67). Language as a tool for communicative interaction is distinguished from language as a commodity that can be exchanged for professional (or indeed social) advancement. There are parallels between these concepts and the distinction between instrumental and integrative motivation.

2.4.3 Contradictions

Tension between the two types of value is regarded by Engeström (2015: 70) as a source of contradiction and conflict within the components of the activity system: indeed, he considers it the 'primary contradiction of activities in capitalist socioeconomic formations'. He identified three further levels of contradiction in activity systems. Secondary contradictions involve compatibility between different elements of the system, such as are seen when models of language teaching based around learner autonomy are implemented in Confucian heritage cultures. Tertiary contradictions occur upon the imposition of a 'culturally more advanced' form of the activity in question, or when subjects actively seek out such advanced forms of the activity. Engeström gives the example of the imposition by parents and teachers of serious study on a schoolchild who just wants to play with their friends, but another excellent example was encountered in Section 2.1.2 in the case of students finding learning-oriented interpersonal chats to be 'inauthentic' and 'boring'. Finally, quaternary contradictions occur in the interaction between the focal activity system and its neighbouring systems. An activity system's contradictions are the principle driving force behind its continual evolutionary change (Engeström, 2015: 73), as subjects find novel forms of practice that transcend the conditions that created such 'double binds' (Engeström, 2015: 112).

2.5 Conclusion

In this chapter, I have demonstrated that the focus of the book is on L2 computer-mediated interactions whose sense-forming motive is not, primarily, language learning. Such interactions are nevertheless of interest and relevance to any account of language learning that acknowledges the 'big picture' of an individual's development, allowing for incidental learning outcomes to result from use of the L2. There is strong theoretical and empirical evidence for these outcomes, and they are what I intend and refer to by the use of the term 'informal learning'.

I further outlined the use of AT as a means of conceptualizing and linking different language activities within the ecology of the contextualized individual. AT was chosen to provide the theoretical foundation of this book, in large part due to its formulation of the notion of the motive of an activity, something which was shown to be a key delineating characteristic of the object of study.

Chapter 3 provides an overview and high-level discussion of the methodological deliberations and decisions underlying the research design, and an account of the data collection process. The following chapters then turn to the research findings.

Notes

(1) https://en.wikipedia.org/wiki/English_as_a_second_or_foreign_language.
(2) Nayar (1997) also identifies a potential third variant of the term ESL, referring to Scandinavian contexts.
(3) This citation is incorrectly given as Engeström (1999b) in the text.

3 Research Methods

This chapter provides an account of the methodological decisions made during the research design phase of the project. Methodological deliberations began not with a commitment to a particular research paradigm, but with a consideration of the research goals and questions and an acknowledgement of the inherent complexity of language learning. Much prior work utilizing complex dynamic systems theory or sociocultural theory employs a qualitative, emic approach that explores the experience of the individuals from their own subjective perspective (e.g. Sockett, 2013). However, Toffoli (2020: 14) notes that, in the exploration of a complex system, 'quantitative approaches provide a valuable initial means to delineate the scope of a phenomenon, identify broad lines of practice or get a general idea of the perceptions of a particular audience on a subject', before arguing for the use of qualitative and quantitative methods in tandem. An 'initial means to delineate the scope of the phenomenon' is exactly what I had in mind in relation to second language (L2) English computer-mediated communication (CMC) (EL2 CMC). This pragmatist foundation led to a mixed-methods approach, as some aspects of the research were best tackled quantitatively, while others were best suited to qualitative analysis. The account provided here begins with a restatement of the research questions set out in Chapter 1, and a discussion of the methodological implications of them when considered together with the broader objectives. Following this discussion, an overview of the research design and data collection methods is given. This chapter deals with global aspects of research design. Subsequent chapters present further methodological detail specific to the analysis presented in those chapters, prior to the presentation of findings. As such, little mention is made here of the qualitative aspects of the research, or of the corpus linguistic methods used to address RQ3. For a full account of these, the reader is directed to Chapters 6 and 7 (Sections 6.3 and 7.3), respectively.

3.1 Research Questions

- RQ1: How widespread are L2 English CMC activities?

There are numerous examples in the literature (see Chapter 2, Section 2.1.2) of studies that have been conducted on small populations, often university student cohorts, exploring the extent and/or nature of their English language use online. To date, these have been predominantly qualitative in nature, using diaries and interviews to elicit rich insights into the ways that L2 users engage with English in their spare time. In order to provide a novel perspective to complement these prior studies, I wanted to survey behaviors on a larger scale than hitherto attempted. I envisioned this component of the research as quantitative in nature, collecting data attesting to the frequency of use of English in a range of different online communicative contexts.

- RQ2: What challenges do L2 English users face in online interactions?

I thought it most appropriate to approach the notion of communicative difficulties with an emic perspective, allowing research participants to tell me in their own words about their – potentially negative – experiences online. A quantitative approach to this question would have required the researcher – me – to second-guess participants' experiences and produce a closed list of items which would have little chance of covering everything that participants might want to say. This clearly was a case in which 'the [quantitative] researcher will only be able to get answers to questions she has thought of' (Holliday, 2015: 52), and so I determined to pursue this component of the research using qualitative methods.

However, in answering this question I also wanted to examine a singular, generic notion of communicative discomfort, effectively flipping the question around to become 'What kinds of online communicative activities do L2 users find most challenging?'. As with RQ1, the intention to investigate this on a large scale suggested taking a quantitative approach, asking research participants about their level of comfort in a given range of communicative activities.

- RQ3: How does the English language used in CMC differ from the language more generally? What kinds of language knowledge are important for learners in this regard?

Exploring the nature of language in a particular discourse domain is ideally addressed using corpus linguistics, utilizing both quantitative and qualitative analytical techniques. A discussion of corpus linguistics, including discussions of the particular corpora and analytical techniques used, can be found in Chapter 7 prior to the presentation of the findings.

- RQ4: How can L2 English CMC activities be supported and integrated in formal language learning?

The final research question was to be addressed through a synthesis of the findings of the preceding research phases, combined with prior research, within the given theoretical framework.

3.2 RQ1 and RQ2: A Survey-Based Approach

A potentially suitable data collection method was suggested by a recent project undertaken by colleagues at the University of Nottingham designed to elicit responses from L2 English users regarding their L2 'role models' (Muir *et al.*, 2019). This project, also undertaken in collaboration with Cambridge University Press (CUP), had utilized CUP's online dictionary to recruit respondents for a questionnaire. CUP's online dictionary is a specialist learner-oriented online dictionary, whose extensive global reach is attested, albeit informally, by its 2.32 million 'likes' on Facebook. Using this recruitment method, the project had garnered 8472 questionnaire responses. The decision was therefore taken to repeat this approach. Such a questionnaire would be ideally suited to addressing RQ1 and the quantitative component of RQ2, and the inclusion of a limited number of open text response items in the questionnaire would provide data that could be analyzed qualitatively for the emic component of RQ2. While this would result in a data set that was somewhat unusual for qualitative research, consisting of many short texts, rather than fewer, longer texts, it was envisioned as being somewhat similar to Twitter data, which has been subject to qualitative analysis in the literature (Ahmed *et al.*, 2019). The scale provided by such a method would, again, provide a novel perspective on the subject matter, compensating for the limitations of nuance and depth incurred by such short texts. Further discussion regarding the consequences of the questionnaire method can be found in Chapter 9 (Section 9.3).

The different approaches to the different questions were envisioned to complement one another, working together in a holistic, mixed-methods design. The quantitative approach to RQ1, along with the quantitative component of RQ2 would provide twin measures on frequency of use and level of comfort in communicative contexts and activities online. The two components of RQ2 would provide a mixed perspective on discomfort online: a ranking of activities most likely to cause discomfort along with personal accounts of some causative factors. Where these factors were language related, the corpus approach to RQ3 would provide evidence of such linguistic phenomena. Taken together, these would provide a detailed picture of EL2 CMC and the nature of language online, and these would provide a firm foundation for making recommendations for effective pedagogic practices in response to RQ4.

3.3 Questionnaire Design

The decision was therefore taken to conduct a survey using a questionnaire deployed on the Cambridge Dictionary website. The questionnaire was designed to provide data to address research questions 1 and 2, which in turn were further analyzed into the following study questions:

- SQ1: How comfortable do L2 English users feel when engaged in communicative activities online using English, and how does this compare to similar experiences offline?
- SQ2: In what text-based contexts, and with what degree of frequency, do L2 English speakers use their English to communicate with people online?
- SQ3: What forms or aspects of text-based online discourse do L2 English users find challenging?
- SQ4: To what extent do English learners demonstrate a desire to incorporate online discourse more directly in their language learning?

A component addressing each of these four questions was incorporated into the finished questionnaire, which was constructed iteratively in coordination with CUP, to ensure their priorities and requirements were met. A further component collected demographic data. These components structure the following chapters of this book. Chapter 4 reports on the component addressing SQ1, Chapter 5 on those addressing SQ2 and SQ4 and Chapter 6 on the component addressing SQ3. In each chapter, further detail and discussion are provided regarding methodological considerations specific to that component. What follows here is an overview of the design and deployment of the questionnaire as a whole. The questionnaire can be seen in full in Appendix A.

Questions were mostly single-item Likert-type arrays probing either frequency, agreement or level of comfort. Mindful of the advice that '[i]n questionnaire design less is often more' (Dörnyei & Taguchi, 2010: 12), Likert-type constructs were used rather than true Likert scales, as the multiple items needed to test each concept in a true Likert scale were felt to be too cumbersome and resulted in an overly lengthy questionnaire. The precise number of anchor points and their labels varied; full discussions of this aspect of the design can be found in subsequent chapters. These Likert-type questions elicited ordinal data, requiring non-parametric statistical tests to be used in their analysis.

Other questions asked for responses in the form of free text where discursive answers were required. These data were analyzed qualitatively. The questionnaire was designed and administered in English, as respondents' potential first languages (L1s) were unknown. Every effort was made to ensure that questionnaire items were worded simply and comprehensibly. This included using CUP's online text inspector tool[1] to ensure that as much of the question text as possible was rated as A1 or A2 level difficulty.

3.3.1 Demographic data

A further component of the questionnaire collected demographic data from respondents, in order to look for variation by age, language level and country of location. A brief rationale for each of these is given below.

3.3.1.1 Age

The relationship between chronological age and technology use has been studied in some detail, with most studies agreeing that there is a connection between the two. Prensky (2001) refers to *digital natives* and *digital immigrants*, not in a geographical sense, but in terms either of having been born into a technologically saturated world, or of having to adapt to one later in life. This distinction was later expanded to include a second generation of digital natives in response to the transition to Web 2.0 technologies (Helsper & Eynon, 2010: 507). Taipale (2016) shows that these second-generation digital natives prefer synchronous modes of communication, although these are limited in the study to instant messaging and internet telephony. Friemel (2016: 324) shows a drop off in internet use among 70+ year olds. Hauk *et al.* (2018: 309) find some evidence of a link between age and component variables of the technology acceptance model (TAM; Davis, 1989): increased age correlates with a decrease in the Perceived Ease of Use and Perceived Usefulness of technologies. Interestingly, however, the observed effect disappears when the technology in question is intended to facilitate 'social and emotionally meaningful goals' (Hauk *et al.*, 2018: 306). The type of technology matters, then, with older people more likely to accept technologies which help them remain socially active.

Age was probed using seven age groups, largely decade by decade (30–39, 40–49, etc.), but separating 18–21 from 22–29. This was done due to the significant life stage transition occurring for many 21–22 year olds as they leave education and enter employment. Under-18s were not permitted to complete the questionnaire for ethical reasons.

3.3.1.2 Language level

It seems likely that respondents reporting a higher level of proficiency with English will use their L2 in a wider variety of contexts, including forms of CMC, than lower-level L2 users. Certain characteristics of CMC in particular might be expected to be tied to language level: greater expectations of synchronicity, more complex participation structures, especially those involving a wider public audience, and more complex discursive forms such as writing blogs would seem likely to daunt lower-level users to a greater extent than those with a higher level.

3.3.1.3 Location

As discussed at some length in Chapter 2 (Section 2.2.3), a key aspect of the classification of the social context of L2 learning and use is the degree of exposure learners/users have to the target language in the world around them. Two potential effects are possible here. On the one hand, it might be expected that those respondents who frequently use their English in the offline world around them would develop the confidence and fluency to use English in CMC. This would be visible in the data as a higher degree of engagement with English CMC in high exposure contexts. On the other hand, the communicative resources of the internet are in themselves a potential source of exposure, and may compensate for deficiencies in the offline world in low exposure contexts. In this case, there may be no apparent difference between low exposure and high exposure contexts. To explore these possible implications of the learning context, the questionnaire data were coded using Siegel's (2003) taxonomy in a procedure described below.

3.4 Piloting and Modifications

The questionnaire underwent two pilot distributions, with respondents recruited manually, as the live link on the dictionary was only available for the final version. The first pilot resulted in 22 responses being received, from personal acquaintances of the author, L2 English speakers of varying levels, located in the UK, Spain and South Korea. Small changes were made to the question wording and length as a result of respondent feedback, and are mentioned in later methodological discussions. The second pilot study provided 10 complete responses. Respondents were recruited in the same manner as the first, but were not repeat participants. The changes that had been made were judged to have resulted in more satisfactory data. Unfortunately, neither pilot study revealed the problems of collecting nationality data in open text format, as discussed in the next section.

3.5 Data Collection and Processing

Respondents to the questionnaire were recruited solely by means of a banner placed on the home page of CUP's online English dictionary. This convenience sampling method presented limitations for the research, which are discussed in Chapter 9. This banner was added to the site on 7 March 2018, and removed on April 4 2018. During this time, 10,354 complete responses were collected. Initial inspection identified four of these as defective, and they were removed, leaving a total of 10,350 cases in the data set.

Following the conclusion of the collection period, the data were downloaded from onlinesurveys.ac.uk in the form of a single comma separated values (.csv) file, making use of the website's own functionality to generate and include a unique response number (URN) for each case, code responses (meaning Likert-type scales were represented numerically) and combine scale/rank values into a single column. This latter ensured that items tested on Likert-type scales were present in a single column containing a value corresponding to the respondents' choice; not choosing this option resulted in each item being presented with separate columns for all possible options, each containing a value of 0 or 1 indicating whether or not it had been chosen.

The data were visually inspected using Microsoft Excel and the programming language Python. A deficiency in the data was quickly identified: respondents had been asked for their nationality and country of location in the form of open text questions (rather than, for example, a drop-down selection list). This meant that there was a great deal of variation in answers: country names and demonyms, varieties of demonym, spelling mistakes, discursive answers ('I am from China'), non-Roman scripts and ethnonyms not corresponding easily to a nation state (e.g. 'Kurdish'). This was adjusted using Python script to standardize the values, though a few cases (<80) were unrecoverable.

Using the standardized nationality and location data, all cases were coded to indicate the type of English learning environment (on a national level) the respondent was located in. Following Siegel's (2003) taxonomy of language learning contexts, the position of English in each country in the data set was coded as follows:

- Dominant: these are countries in which English is the dominant language spoken by a large majority of the population.
- Co-existing: these are countries in which there are co-existing groups of native speakers of more than one language, such as Canada.
- Institutional: these are countries in which English has an official status and/or is used for commercial or bureaucratic purposes.
- External: these are countries which have no historical connection to English.

In each case, the judgement as to which category was appropriate was made based on quantitative and descriptive data obtained from three separate sources: Ethnologue,[2] Internet World Stats[3] and Katzner and Miller (2002: 337–368).

The final, clean data were exported to Statistical Package for the Social Sciences (SPSS) for quantitative analysis. The data can be seen at https://rdmc.nottingham.ac.uk/handle/internal/7021.

3.6 Initial Description of the Data

The data set resulting from the deployment of the questionnaire comprised 10,354 complete responses. Four of these were identified as defective and removed, leaving 10,350.

Respondents represented 167 different nationalities, and were located in 157 different countries, as visualized in Figures 3.1 and 3.2.

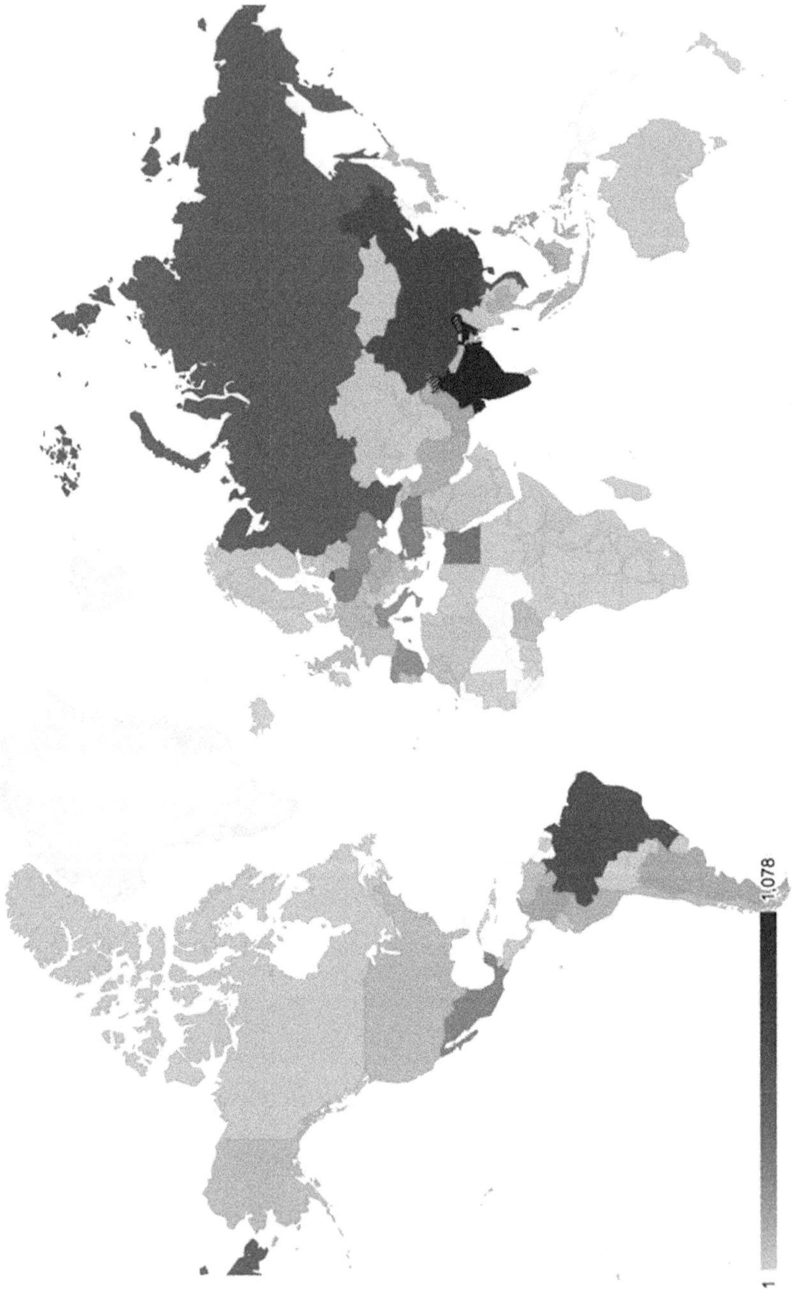

Figure 3.1 Distribution of respondents by country of nationality

Figure 3.2 Distribution of respondents by country of location

The composition of the data in regard to the four demographic variables being explored – age, level and location (social context) – is shown in Figures 3.3–3.5 respectively.

Over 78% of respondents were under the age of 40, with the oldest group – 70 or over – accounting for only 0.6% of the total (not labelled in Figure 3.3 due to space constraints). Despite the large overall size of the data set, this group still only contained 66 individuals. Also under-represented, though to a lesser extent, were respondents of a post-beginner level, while almost two-thirds of respondents considered their English level to be upper intermediate or above.

The data were even more strongly dominated by respondents in 'external' countries. This is unsurprising, as this type of country is by far the most numerous in the world, but it highlights the fact that the majority of L2 English users in the world are not located in English-speaking countries.

This chapter has provided an account of the methodological foundation of the research design, as well as an overview of the construction of the primary data collection instrument, and the data collection process. The next chapters present the results of the analyses that establish the extent of EL2 CMC in the life of the individual (Chapters 3 and 4), its

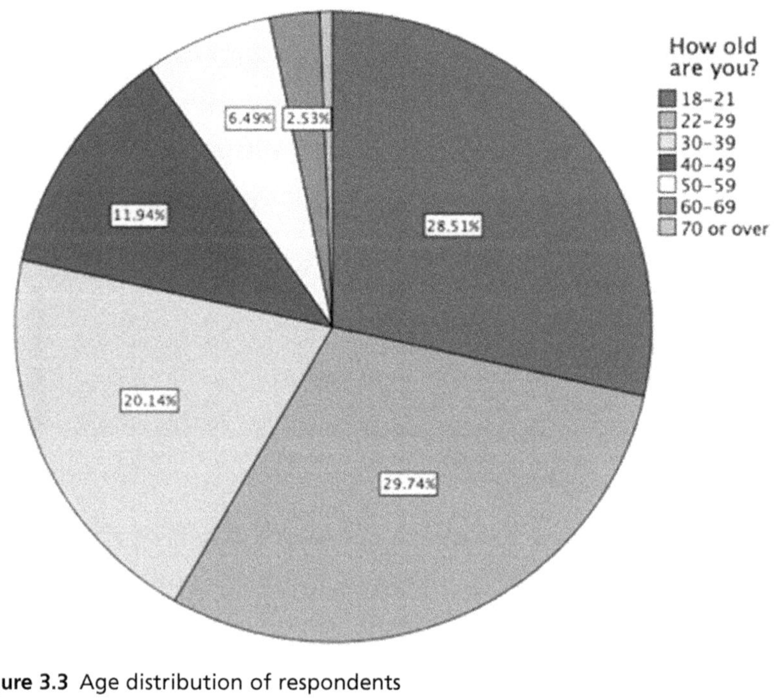

Figure 3.3 Age distribution of respondents

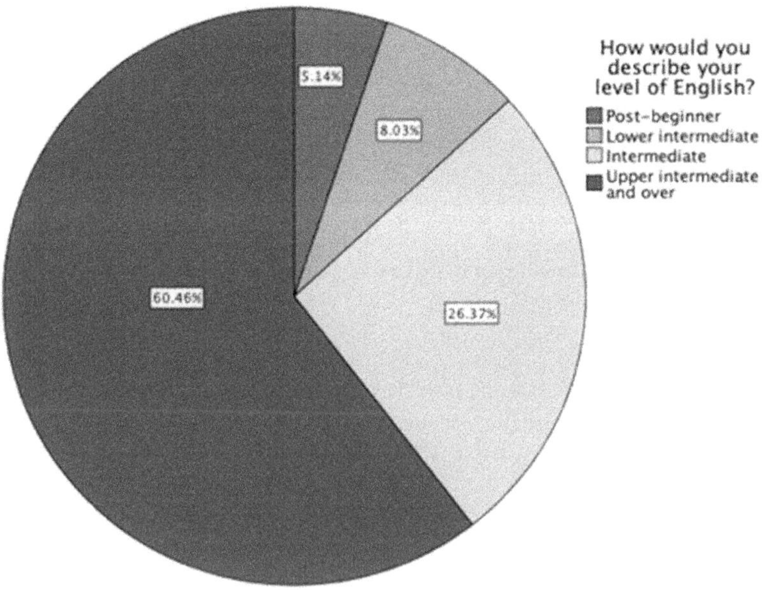

Figure 3.4 English-level distribution of respondents

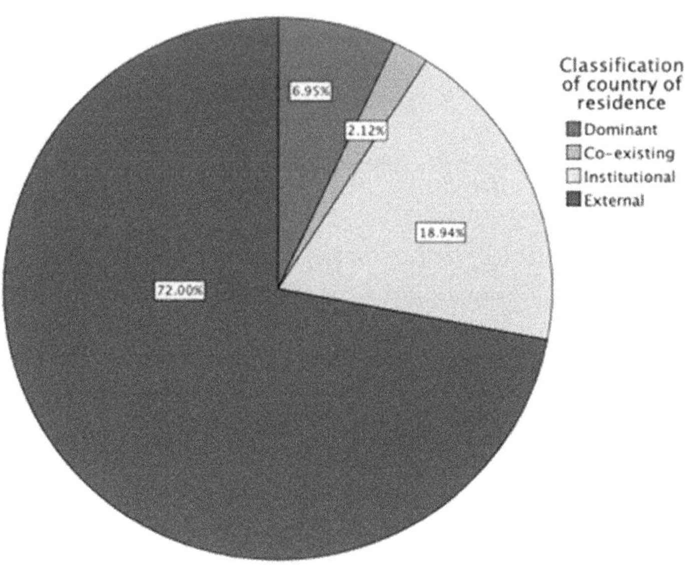

Figure 3.5 Classification of respondent location

challenges (Chapter 5) and the nature of language online (Chapter 6). These analyses are then brought together in Chapter 7 to consider how learners' EL2 CMC activities can be integrated into the language classroom.

Notes

(1) http://www.englishprofile.org/wordlists/text-inspector.
(2) www.ethnologue.com.
(3) https://www.internetworldstats.com/languages.htm.

4 EL2 CMC Activities and Communicative (Dis)Comfort

This chapter takes up the notion of language activities, using the concept of language functions to provide candidate motives for such activities. There then follows a discussion of affect in language learning, to provide a theoretical rationale for surveying second language (L2) users' level of comfort when engaging in functionally defined language activities online. An analysis of the findings of this survey is then presented, followed by a discussion of the implications for the intended integration of L2 English computer-mediated communication (EL2 CMC) and formal language learning.

4.1 Language Activities and Language Functions

In Chapter 1, I set out the object of study: L2 English interactions online through which incidental learning might be expected to occur. I also established activity theory (AT) as the theoretical framework guiding the exploration of these phenomena, entailing the use of the activity system, or systems, as the unit of analysis. However, the insistence on prioritizing activities whose primary motivation is not learning related requires finding some other way to characterize the object of study in the abstract. If it is not language learning, what is it?

The distinction between language learning and language use discussed in Chapter 2 (Section 2.1.1) raises the possibility of using the term 'language use activities' as a counterpart to language learning activities. However, this is to risk proposing a misleading dichotomy. Chapter 2 (Section 2.1) also discussed the difference of motive or intention in the two variants of the term 'informal': activities initiated with the intention to learn, and those not initiated with the intention to learn. This is not a dichotomy, but the presence or absence of a single characteristic. To suggest that the second category of activities is motivated by a desire to use the language maintains the assumption of a focus on form, of 'practicing' one's L2.

It is more satisfactory to characterize our target phenomena as interactions in which the individual is engaged in collaborative meaning-making, with the purpose of establishing some kind of shared understanding with interlocutors, all of whom are deploying linguistic and other semantic resources at their disposal to do so. This reconception of language use as something more akin to 'doing language' has been given the processual term *languaging* in a number of areas of research into language and interaction (Becker, 1991; Swain, 2006). Swain (2006: 95) situates the term in the Vygotskian tradition, utilizing the Soviet scholar's assertion that 'language is one of the most important mediating tools of the mind' to define languaging as 'a dynamic, never-ending process of using language to make meaning'. This might be elaborated to read: 'using language to *interactively co-create* meaning', in order to acknowledge the inherently dialogical nature of this process. Linell (2009: 222) notes that 'linguistic resources have meaning potentials, rather than meanings', and that these potentials crystallize into shared meaning only in situated interaction. Languaging, then, is a collaborative activity, ideally suited to analysis through the lens of AT.

In a moment, I will populate the activity system schema introduced in Chapter 2 for a hypothetical EL2 CMC languaging activity. For now, however, I want to focus on the AT category of motive. As discussed, EL2 CMC languaging activities are held to be those into which the subject enters without the intention to learn; that is, the motive of the activity is not learning. The individual is not simply using language for its own sake, they are aiming for some kind of interactional outcome, whether it be arranging the shipment of a product via email or getting other members of a WhatsApp group to laugh at a joke. We might characterize these as 'the kind of things people may *do* by means of language', and this indeed is the phrase used by Ek and Trim (1998: 23) to characterize the language functions around which their Council of Europe-commissioned *Threshold Level* language proficiency recognition framework is organized. Incorporating the notion of 'doing things' with language as the sense-forming motive of our prototype activity system necessitates a brief detour to discuss functional approaches to language.

4.2 Functional Approaches to Language

Functional approaches to the study of language view language not just as a set of abstract structures but as serving (indeed, as having evolved to serve) a number of interrelated functions in the life of the individual language user. Halliday (1973: 11–16) observes seven functions in the language of very young children; at this stage, functions are tied to specific syntactical forms, which serve only one of these functions at a time (Halliday, 1973: 34). By the time the child reaches adulthood, Halliday (1973: 37–42) argues that these functions have become compressed into three overarching macro-functions: *interpersonal*, *ideational* and *textual*, all of which are simultaneously present in the functionally complex utterances of adult language.

Functional approaches to language such as that elaborated by Halliday provided impetus for a shift from a focus on grammatical form to a focus on function and meaning within applied linguistics and English language teaching from the 1970s onwards. Hymes' (1972) seminal work on *communicative competence* introduced the idea that a proficient language learner was able to appropriately use language in the correct contexts to get things done. These ideas of activities carried out by means of language were developed and incorporated into language teaching by means of notional-functional syllabuses, which organized content around such principles rather than around grammatical forms (Wilkins, 1976). By the 1980s, functional approaches to language were dominant in the field of English language teaching: 'The power and influence of this new [functional] set of categories have been enormous, to the extent that it has become conventional for syllabus designers to take them as given' (White, 1988: 18).

Functional approaches to language have also been influential in language policy at national and international levels. A Council of Europe-commissioned initiative in the early 1970s resulted in the *Threshold Level* project, which aimed at the standardization of language teaching throughout Europe by means of a detailed specification of language functions. Such a framework could then be applied to any European language, enabling language skills to be quantified and recognized across the continent. The contemporary successor to *Threshold* is the Common European Framework of Reference (CEFR) for languages (Council of Europe, 2001), whose alphanumeric levels have become widely recognized indicators of language ability, with major examinations calibrated to test them. Through the CEFR, a functional perspective on language is now embedded in mainstream approaches to language teaching throughout Europe.

In spite of the functionalist origin of the CEFR, the descriptors of the framework use the term *communicative language activities*, rather than 'functions'. The term 'activity' is meant in a non-specialist sense, but nevertheless illustrates the possibility of reconceptualizing the 'kind of things people may *do* by means of language' using the concepts of AT (Engeström, 2015). I therefore use this notion of language function to provide hypothetical candidates for the primary sense-forming motive of a protoype EL2 CMC activity.

4.3 Outlining a Functionally Motivated Language Activity

We can now begin to elaborate such an activity system in terms of the AT framework. In this system, the subject is the individual language user. The description of the subject may be enriched using the concept of the individual's *psychobiography*, the 'development of the self along a series of evolutionary transitions' (Pasfield-Neofitou, 2012: 22). Incorporation of this element of Layder's (1997) domain theory enables differentiation of an activity's outcomes according to different subject characteristics.

The object of the activity is the potentiality for some form of collaboratively and dialogically produced meaning. As the '"raw material" or "problem space" at which the activity is directed' (Engeström, 1993: 67), this potentiality is shaped into intended meaning through languaging between subject and interlocutors. Once established, this meaning constitutes the outcome of the activity. Achieving this outcome will form the primary sense-forming motive. Learning-related motives may also be present in differing forms and degrees. Inaba (2019: 93) notes that learning outcomes may be present as sense-forming motives or motives stimuli, depending on the individual. As a motive-stimulus, learning outcomes may lead to feelings of satisfaction and pleasure without changing the nature of the activity itself. As a secondary sense-forming motive, the anticipation of learning outcomes may cause the subject to initiate the activity with them in mind. The motive-type of learning outcomes, and the possibility of their enhancement, is discussed further in Chapter 7.

A possible motive-stimulus is suggested in Yus' (2017: 71) discussion of *phatic effects* in WhatsApp interaction: 'feelings of connection, of sociability, of group membership, of friends' acknowledgement and awareness, etc.'. In particular, the concept of international posture discussed in Chapter 2 (Section 2.2.2) (Yashima, 2009) may be present as a motive of this sort. A final, negative motive-stimulus may be present in feelings of anxiety or symptoms of situational communication apprehension (CA; McCroskey, 1984; and see Chapter 2), which may reduce the likelihood of successful outcomes. Where the activity includes language learning motives, CA or language anxiety may act as an affective filter, impeding the process of acquisition (Krashen, 1982: 30).

The artefacts and tools in this case include the English language, along with any semiotic affordances that might be provided by the CMC platform being used, such as stickers, emoji or text formatting, and multimodal resources such as pictures. Technical facets such as synchronicity, persistence of transcript and size of message buffer may also provide meaning-making tools.

The rules of the activity are both socially and technologically determined. Socially derived rules include norms of interaction such as turn-taking (Schegloff, 2000) and Grice's (1975) conversational maxims, which are as applicable to face-to-face conversation as to CMC, as well as socially derived rules specific to the CMC platform, such as rules regarding what type of content is acceptable. Technologically derived 'rules' refer to patterns of discourse necessitated or engendered by the technical facets of the medium, such as the overlapping adjacency pairs common in synchronous platforms (Herring, 1999). Both these types of rules may double-up and serve as tools in the meaning-making activity, if the subject utilizes them tactically. Grice (1975: 49, *et passim*) discusses the different ways in which his conversational maxims may be broken by conversation participants, and the implicatures created by these transgressions. Lewis and Fabos (2005: 487) show how teenagers using instant messaging software manipulate the expectations of synchronicity inherent in the platform for the strategic presentation of self, deliberately waiting to respond to messages from others to create an appearance of being socially in demand.

4.4 Affective Barriers to Language Acquisition

Chapter 2 (Section 2.2.1) incorporated the ideas of Steven Krashen in developing a theoretical understanding of incidental learning. A key component of Krashen's (1981, 1982) monitor model of language acquisition was that of the *affective filter*. This term was used to represent the moderating effects on the conversion of input to the intake of a number of psychological states or traits, including motivation and attitudes to the language and the learning process. Two sources of negative affect particularly relevant to the study of EL2 CMC are *communication apprehension* (McCroskey, 1984) and *language anxiety* (Dörnyei, 2005: 198–201; MacIntyre & Gardner, 1994). The more general concept of CA refers to feelings of anxiety or fear that people sometimes feel in communicative situations. McCroskey differentiates *traitlike CA*, regarded as a stable personality trait akin to shyness, from *situational CA*, which may be experienced by anybody as a consequence of certain combinations of contextual variables. The L2-specific language anxiety refers to the 'worry and negative emotional reaction aroused when learning or using a second language' (MacIntyre, 1999: 27), and, in line with Krashen's (1981, 1982) affective filter hypothesis, has been frequently shown to have a negative impact on language learning and use (Dörnyei, 2005: 201). In terms of AT, feelings of anxiety or symptoms of situational CA can form a negative motive-stimulus, discouraging continued engagement with the activity and reducing the likelihood of successful outcomes.

It is not within the scope of this book to enter into an extended discussion of the above notions. However, they serve to demonstrate that feelings of discomfort in L2 communicative situations will impede potential incidental learning outcomes. Following this reasoning, attaining a better understanding of the kinds of EL2 CMC activities that are more likely to provoke feelings of discomfort will help to inform teaching practices that seek to support and integrate EL2 CMC.

4.5 Constructing the Questionnaire

Questionnaire respondents were asked to indicate their level of comfort when engaging in a range of language activities, which were derived from the CEFR to ensure relevance to current approaches to language teaching and learning. The CEFR utilizes an 'action-oriented' approach to language use, viewing language users as 'social agents' embedded in multiple social and cultural contexts which ultimately give full meaning to their linguistic utterances. Language is used to accomplish tasks, which may or may not be language related in themselves (Council of Europe, 2001: 9). These rather abstract 'tasks' are realized more concretely in the CEFR description scheme as *communicative language activities*, and, as discussed above, are therefore conceptualized as the primary units of analysis of the AT framework.

The CEFR differentiates *Interpersonal*, *Transactional* and *Evaluative* 'macro-functions' of language use (Council of Europe, 2018: 31). *Interpersonal* language involves the initiation and maintenance of relationships; *transactional* language is used to obtain goods and services and exchange information; and *evaluative* language facilitates discussion and decision-making. These three macro-functions are not mutually exclusive – there are many interpersonal factors involved in any group decision, for example. All three macro-functions were represented in the activities chosen for inclusion in the current study.

This theoretical structure appears very similar to Halliday's (1973) use of three co-existing metafunctions. However, while the foundations are similar, there are some key ontological differences. Perhaps most obviously, the three categories here – evaluative, transactional, interpersonal – do not map exactly onto Halliday's triad of experiential, interpersonal and textual. In Hallidayan systemic functional linguistics (SFL), evaluation (or appraisal) is a form of interpersonal meaning (Martin & White, 2005: 1) and therefore subsumed within it. Halliday's analysis is on the level of the utterance, while the three macro-functions here are on the level of activities, which may subsume a number of utterances in the pursuit of a communicative object. Halliday's triad represents types of meaning co-present within the utterance, while the present categories refer to primary sense-forming motives underlying the activity. As such, there is a degree of prioritization of one over another that is not present in Halliday's paradigm, as shown in Figure 4.1.

Items in the questionnaire were expressed as much as possible in everyday, high-frequency language in order to facilitate comprehension: thus 'initiating relationships' was expressed in personal terms as 'making friends' and in professional terms as 'finding new clients/customers'. Table 4.1 gives a full list of activities included in the questionnaire.

A four-point Likert-type scale was used, ranging from *Very uncomfortable* to *Very comfortable*, with a fifth option – *I don't do this* – included to allow for such a possibility. This fifth option was not regarded as being part of the scale to which the other four belong: it was not assumed that respondents would choose it as an extension of *Very uncomfortable*, for example. It exists as a 'not applicable option'. A four-point scale is a more restricted set of responses than is usual with Likert-type items, which frequently have five or seven response options

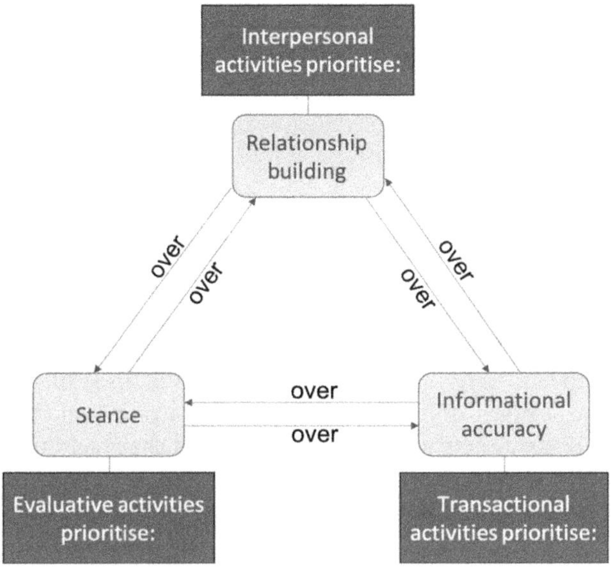

Figure 4.1 Prioritization of motives among macro-functions

Table 4.1 Activities included in questionnaire, categorized by macro-function

Macro-function	Activity
Interpersonal	Making new friends Keeping in touch with existing friends Finding new clients/customers Communicating with existing clients/customers
Transactional	Working together with others in a project or game Exchanging information with others Arranging to meet others face to face Communicating with buyers or sellers for shopping purposes Managing personal administrative matters such as banking or taxation
Evaluative	Stating your opinion in a discussion Defending your opinion in a discussion Agreeing or disagreeing Offering advice (including writing reviews)

(Ozok, 2007: 1160). The odd number is due to the presence of a neutral option, which in this case might have been 'Neither comfortable nor uncomfortable'. However, it was felt that the term 'Comfortable' was sufficiently neutral in its own right, so no further neutral option was used. The goal of the question was to identify online discourse functions that caused respondents discomfort, but a fine-grained grading of the level of discomfort, such as might have been provided by a larger set of response options, was not judged necessary for the analysis. The simple differentiation between 'Uncomfortable' and 'Very uncomfortable' was felt to provide a sufficient level of granularity, and so the four-point scale was used.

4.6 Comfort with L2 Use Online

The following sections present the findings of the analysis of the questionnaire data. The data are frequently presented visually, in charts and tables. The charts provide helpful visualization, while the tables, some of which are quite complex, are intended for the benefit of readers who wish to inspect the data for themselves. The key findings from the tables are discursively described in the body of the text, however, and readers who do not want to study them in detail should be able to follow the narrative without problems.

Figure 4.2 shows the distribution of responses across the 12 activities performed online. The data are presented as a divergent bar chart, with the 'I don't do this' answers in the middle. This is done in acknowledgement that the 'I don't do this' response is not a point on the same scale as the other response options: it is not assumed that respondents choose this as an extension of discomfort. Other options for the presentation of this information were considered, such as separating the 'I don't do this' responses and presenting them to one side, but the solution given here allows all the data to be viewed together.

The 12 activities are ranked in order of the aggregated percentage of the 'Uncomfortable' and 'Very uncomfortable' responses. It is noticeable that almost all activities show a substantial majority of responses in the 'Comfortable' or 'Very comfortable' categories. The only activity for which this is not the case is New Clients, but this is due to a larger amount of respondents choosing 'I don't do this', rather than indicating

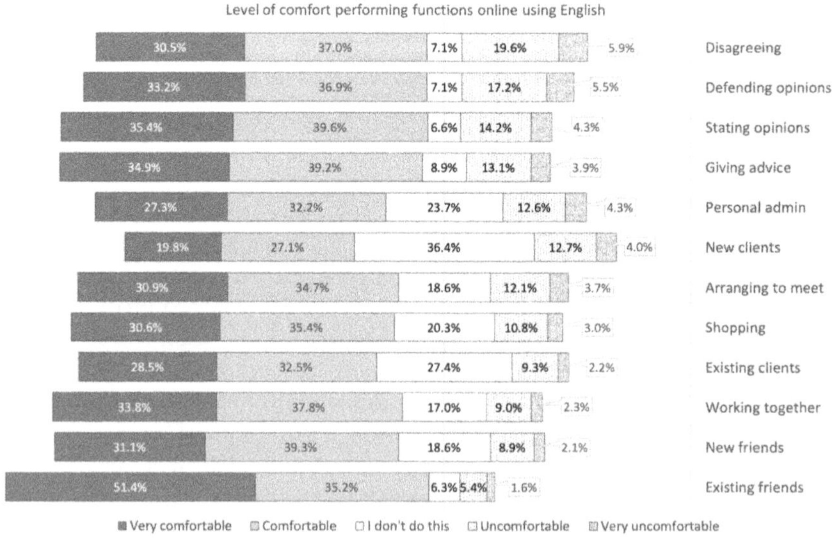

Figure 4.2 Divergent bar chart showing questionnaire responses regarding comfort level

discomfort. This high degree of comfort with English language activities online is indicative of the pervasiveness of digital communication in everyday life, and the unremarkableness of enacting basic activities online, even in an L2. It also suggests that most online activities should be conducive to language acquisition through incidental learning, given that affective filters caused by CA seem generally low.

The two activities involving communication with new or existing clients or customers receive the highest levels of 'I don't do this' responses, suggesting that English language CMC activities are more prevalent in personal spaces. This reflects analyses such as those by Yus (2017) and Lewis and Fabos (2005) regarding the inherent enjoyment of online communication being a large part of the motivation for taking part in it. Activities involving communication with friends have the lowest levels of discomfort, though Figure 4.2 shows that respondents are more likely simply not to make new friends online than to feel discomfort doing it. Activities with friends are likely to be low in the situational characteristics, including status effects, that stimulate CA.

A key finding from Figure 4.2 is that the four highest-ranked activities – *disagreeing, defending opinions, stating opinions* and *giving advice* – are all categorized as evaluative language activities in Table 4.1. These four also receive the lowest levels of 'I don't do this' responses after *keeping in touch with existing friends*. Clearly, these are common activities which nevertheless are most likely to provoke discomfort. Barton and Lee (2013: 87) discuss evaluative language functions in terms of *stance*, and note that '[s]tance-taking has become a key discursive act in online interaction'. The act of stance-taking, however, in turn opens up the language user to the attention and evaluation of others, both of which can lead to CA (McCroskey, 1984: 26). This is an important aspect of online language use in which language teaching practitioners need to support their learners, and it is discussed further below.

Evaluative language activities carry an inherent risk of infringing implicit rules of conversational interaction that tend toward cooperation and agreement. The avoidance of disagreement is codified in Leech's Politeness Principle – intended as an accompanying expansion of Grice's (1975) Cooperative Principle – as the Agreement Maxim: 'Minimize disagreement between self and other' (Leech, 1983: 132). Failure to adhere to politeness norms can lead to rudeness, even if this is unintentional (Yus, 2011: 264). Since politeness norms differ between cultures (Leech, 1983: 84; Yus, 2011: 255), such unintentional offence is an inherent danger of the kind of information-poor intercultural communication that is often a feature of CMC, and this is exacerbated in activities which are inherently face-threatening, such as a frank exchange of views. Thus, these communicative activities contain a fundamental tension between the communicative goal (the expression and defense of potentially contrary opinions) and the means for attaining it.

Table 4.2 Differences between online and offline data

	Very comfortable	Comfortable	Uncomfortable	Very uncomfortable	I don't do this
Making new friends	-3.75%	1.01%	-4.18%	-1.65%	8.57%
Existing friends	4.76%	-1.15%	-2.03%	-0.83%	-0.75%
Existing clients/customers	0.51%	2.11%	-0.74%	-0.26%	-1.61%
Finding new customers	-1.63%	1.86%	-0.59%	-0.18%	0.55%
Working together	-0.60%	1.85%	-1.78%	-0.66%	1.19%
Arranging to meet	-1.00%	0.65%	-0.50%	-0.31%	1.16%
Buying/selling	1.59%	2.22%	-1.74%	-0.77%	-1.30%
Personal admin	-0.14%	1.17%	-1.04%	-0.05%	0.07%
Stating opinions	-0.79%	1.86%	-0.49%	-0.38%	-0.20%
Defending opinions	-0.98%	0.48%	0.28%	0.08%	0.14%
Disagreeing	-1.85%	1.28%	0.86%	-0.21%	-0.08%
Offering advice	-1.00%	1.85%	-0.54%	-0.39%	0.09%

Note: The values are the result of calculating the online value as a proportion of the offline value, represented as a percentage difference. Positive scores, extending to the right of the axis, indicate higher scores in the online data; negative scores, extending to the left, indicate higher scores in the online data.

In order to look for differences in comfort levels online and offline, data from the questionnaire items probing comfort engaging in communicative activities online were compared with data from the items probing the same offline. This is presented in Table 4.2, which shows, for the most part, only small differences between the two sets. This suggests that the online nature of CMC interactions is not necessarily problematic in itself; indeed, the small but consistent increase in 'Comfortable' responses in the online data is consistent with the notion of the 'lean-medium' nature of CMC mitigating potential causes of discomfort.

The greatest differences between the online and offline scores (Table 4.2) were seen in the *making new friends* activity, in which respondents were substantially less likely to make new friends using English online than offline (a difference of 8.57% in the 'I don't do this' responses, with the higher value in the online data). *Keeping in touch with existing friends*, on the other hand, showed a 4.76% increase in 'Very comfortable' responses in the online data compared with the offline data, with this surplus distributed across the other four response types. These two findings are consistent with previous observations (boyd, 2007: 9–10; Lewis & Fabos, 2005: 482) that young people are more likely to use CMC technologies to maintain existing relationships than to initiate new ones.

4.6.1 Demographic analysis

4.6.1.1 Age

Respondent age has some effect on many of the activities, but this is most strongly seen in the *making new friends* activity. Younger

Table 4.3 Differences between online and offline data for the making new friends activity, stratified by age

		How old are you?						
		18-21	22-29	30-39	40-49	50-59	60-69	70 or over
Making new friends	Very comfortable	-2.50%	-1.50%	-4.30%	-6.70%	-10.20%	-6.50%	-9.10%
	Comfortable	7.60%	3.00%	-2.70%	-6.30%	-6.40%	-14.10%	-3.00%
	Uncomfortable	-5.60%	-4.60%	-3.00%	-3.80%	-2.90%	0.40%	1.50%
	Very uncomfortable	-2.40%	-2.00%	-1.10%	-0.70%	-1.10%	-1.50%	4.60%
	I don't do this	2.90%	5.10%	11.20%	17.40%	20.60%	21.80%	6.10%

Note: See Table 4.2 for a description of cell values and formatting.

respondents are more likely to engage in this activity than older respondents, with a peak in 'I don't do this' responses among 40–49 year olds. University-age respondents are most comfortable doing this, following by respondents in their twenties. Comparative analysis between online and offline scores (see Table 4.3) shows that the proportions of 'I don't do this' responses for this function are consistently higher in the online than the offline data. This effect is smallest among 18–21 year olds, rising to a difference of over 20% among respondents in their fifties and sixties. This again demonstrates, as noted in the previous section, that respondents in all age groups are less likely to make new friends using English online than offline, although young people are more comfortable than older people when making friends online.

There is a drop in university-age respondents talking to clients/customers consistent with the assumption that this age group is less likely to have entered the workforce, while respondents in their thirties to fifties are more likely to be very comfortable doing this.

Young people are more likely to be comfortable with collaborative working using English. While this is potentially an effect of increased online gaming among young people, a comparison with the offline data shows little difference between the two sets, suggesting that this group of respondents feels as comfortable collaborating in English offline as online. As respondent age increases, engagement with this activity decreases.

There are similar patterns in three of the transactional activities: *arranging to meet*, *communicating with buyers/sellers* and *managing personal admin* (see Table 4.4). University-age respondents are not comfortable or don't do them; this tendency begins to reverse among 22–29 year olds, rising to a moderately inflated proportion of 'Very comfortable' responses among respondents in their thirties to fifties. Respondents between 60 and 69 years are more likely not to engage in these activities.

A final noticeable trend in the age analysis is for 18–21 year olds to be more likely to report feeling 'Very comfortable' in all four of the evaluative language activities. This is consistent with discussions around the emergence of a second generation of so-called 'digital natives' (Helsper & Eynon, 2010: 507), who have grown up surrounded by

Table 4.4 Level of comfort with EL2 CMC activities, cross-tabulated with age

		How old are you?						
		18-21	22-29	30-39	40-49	50-59	60-69	70 or over
Making new friends	V comfortable	5.7	0.3	-2.1	-3.2	-1.6	-2.6	-0.4
	Comfortable	2.9	5.5	-1.3	-4.5	-4.5	-3.3	-3
	Uncomfortable	1.9	1.9	-0.9	-1.3	-2.5	-1.4	-1.7
	V uncomfortable	-0.7	-0.7	1.1	0.6	0.2	-2	3.1
	I don't do this	-11.6	-8.5	4.2	10.2	9.4	9.1	4.4
Keeping in touch with existing friends	V comfortable	-0.2	-2.3	0.4	1	2.4	0.5	0
	Comfortable	-1.2	3.3	1.3	-1.6	-3	-0.5	-2.4
	Uncomfortable	1.9	1.1	-1.6	-0.8	-0.6	-1.5	-0.9
	V uncomfortable	2	-1	-1.5	0.3	0.7	-0.6	-0.1
	I don't do this	0	-2.2	-1.1	1.7	1	1.6	5.5
Communicating with existing clients/customers	V comfortable	-7	-3.4	4.9	4.6	4.3	1.1	0.3
	Comfortable	-5.2	4.2	1.8	0.2	-0.6	-0.6	-1.2
	Uncomfortable	3.2	2	-0.2	-3.1	-2.3	-3.7	-1.3
	V uncomfortable	0.1	0.3	0.2	-0.1	0	-1.2	-0.4
	I don't do this	10.4	-2.4	-6.7	-2.7	-2.2	2.3	1.9
Finding new clients/customers	V comfortable	-2.2	-1.1	2.2	0.8	1.3	-0.3	0.9
	Comfortable	-2.5	2.4	1.2	-0.6	-0.5	-0.4	-0.8
	Uncomfortable	1.9	4.4	0.1	-3.4	-4	-3.4	-3.1
	V uncomfortable	-0.5	-1	2	-0.4	0.6	-1.1	0.2
	I don't do this	3.1	-4	-3.9	2.4	1.9	3.5	2
Working together with others in a project or game	V comfortable	4.9	-4.6	-0.4	0	2.1	-1.8	-2.2
	Comfortable	-1.8	5.5	0.2	-1.1	-4	-1.9	-1.8
	Uncomfortable	0.6	2.7	0.5	-2.7	-1.1	-2.6	-2.1
	V uncomfortable	1.3	-0.7	0.3	-0.8	0.2	-0.8	-0.4
	I don't do this	-4.9	-3.1	-0.2	3.8	3.3	7.1	6.8
Arranging to meet others face-to-face	V comfortable	-2.3	-3	3	1.8	3.6	-1.6	-0.1
	Comfortable	-5.7	4.2	1.7	0.2	-0.8	1.3	-1.8
	Uncomfortable	3.7	2.2	-1.3	-2.7	-2.7	-2.4	-2.6
	V uncomfortable	3.2	-0.5	-1.2	-0.7	-0.8	-2.2	0.4
	I don't do this	5	-3.1	-4	0.2	-0.7	3.4	4.4
Communicating with buyers/sellers for shopping purposes	V comfortable	-3	-1.8	3	0.8	3.1	-1.4	1.8
	Comfortable	-5.3	2.5	3.1	0.8	-0.7	0.2	-1.6
	Uncomfortable	4.4	2.5	-2.3	-2.2	-4	-1.9	-2
	V uncomfortable	1.2	-0.1	-1.2	-0.5	0.7	-0.7	0.8
	I don't do this	5.8	-2.8	-4.9	-0.1	0.2	3.1	1.1
Managing personal matters such as banking, energy suppliers, phone/internet suppliers, government administration	V comfortable	-3.7	-2.3	3	1.8	3	0.1	1.9
	Comfortable	-3.5	3	2	-0.6	-0.9	-0.2	-2.2
	Uncomfortable	0.2	4.2	-0.5	-2.6	-2.1	-2.1	-1.2
	V uncomfortable	4.3	0.6	-2.5	-1.8	-1.2	-1.9	-0.5
	I don't do this	5.5	-4.5	-3.8	1.6	0	2.7	1.6
Stating your opinion in a discussion	V comfortable	4.2	-3.6	-2	0	2.6	-0.6	0.2
	Comfortable	-1.6	3	0	-0.4	-1.8	-0.3	-0.5
	Uncomfortable	-0.6	3.1	1.3	-1.4	-2.8	-1.8	-2.6
	V uncomfortable	0.2	-0.5	1.4	-0.6	-0.5	-1	0.1
	I don't do this	-4.3	-2.9	0.8	3.3	2.9	5.3	4.3
Defending your opinion in a discussion	V comfortable	4.2	-4.3	-2.3	1.1	2.5	-0.1	0.5
	Comfortable	-2.1	2.1	0.9	-0.3	-1.2	0	-0.1
	Uncomfortable	-0.4	4.5	0.9	-2.7	-2.7	-2.7	-3.4
	V uncomfortable	1.1	0	0.4	-0.2	-1.4	-1.5	0.2
	I don't do this	-4.1	-2.6	0.7	2.8	2.9	5.4	4
Disagreeing with someone	V comfortable	4.1	-4	-1.1	0.4	1.8	-0.9	0
	Comfortable	-0.8	1.7	-0.5	-0.7	-0.7	0.9	0.7
	Uncomfortable	-1.5	4.3	0.9	-1.1	-2.6	-2.9	-2.8
	V uncomfortable	-0.4	0.6	0.9	0.4	-1.3	-1.2	-1
	I don't do this	-3.2	-3.2	0.9	1.9	3.1	5.5	4
Offering advice to others (including writing reviews)	V comfortable	4.8	-2.7	-2.1	-0.4	1.7	-2	-1.3
	Comfortable	-0.7	3.5	0.4	-1.8	-2.6	-1	-0.7
	Uncomfortable	-1.8	1.5	2.3	0.7	-1.7	-2.7	-2.1
	V uncomfortable	-1.3	-0.9	1.1	0.3	1	0.9	0.9
	I don't do this	-3.8	-2.7	-0.7	2.6	3	7.6	5.3

Note: The values are adjusted residuals calculated by SPSS, showing the difference between observed and expected values, adjusted to be comparable across cells. Positive values, extending to the right of the axis, are higher than would be expected if responses were evenly distributed across age groups; the opposite is true of the negative scores.

Web 2.0 technologies in which stance-taking functions are so integral (Barton & Lee, 2013). Older respondents, on the other hand, are increasingly likely not to engage in evaluative activities using English online.

4.6.1.2 Location

A stratification of the data by learning context (Table 4.5) reveals a sharp contrast in all functions between institutional contexts and external contexts. External countries, in which learners will have little exposure to English outside the formal language classroom, show elevated levels of 'I don't do this' responses, coupled with a sharp reduction in 'Very comfortable' responses. This pattern is inverted in institutional countries. The tendency for respondents in external contexts not to engage with these activities suggests that the low level of exposure to English inherent in these environments is reproduced in respondents' online networks. This is contrary to the intuitive possibility that internet access has the potential to mitigate differences in the degree of exposure between contexts.

The parallel effect in institutional countries is difficult to explain without further research in these contexts. Respondents in institutional countries are more likely to feel comfortable in all communicative functions surveyed. This is not due to a disproportionate level of higher-proficiency learners in this group: Figure 4.3 shows that the institutional sub-group actually reports the lowest levels of English proficiency. This is curious in itself: the level data are self-reported, and it might be symptomatic of a different subjective perspective on proficiency in these contexts. These EL2 users don't regard their proficiency as particularly good, but feel more comfortable actually using it. It may be that the institutional nature of English in these contexts means that there is a higher chance that speakers are using English to communicate with other non-native speakers, although equally it may represent an indictment of the tendency to consider English users in these contexts as non-native. By contrast, L2 users in dominant contexts may be more likely to interact with native speakers, and to perceive a status difference between themselves and their interlocutors. This speculation warrants further research to understand the role of English and the dynamics of its use, both online and offline, in institutional contexts.

In dominant contexts there is an increase in use and comfort level in a number of functions associated with offline interactions and institutions, particularly *arranging to meet others*, *communicating with buyers and sellers* and *managing personal admin*.

The tendency to make new friends offline rather than online is repeated in the location analysis, with the difference most pronounced in dominant contexts, and least pronounced in institutional contexts (see Table 4.6). This again seems to point to a unique pattern of engagement with English language CMC in these institutional countries.

Table 4.5 Level of comfort with EL2 CMC activities, cross-tabulated with classification of country of location

		Location Classification			
		Dominant	Co-existing	Institutional	External
Making new friends	Very comfortable	-0.9	0.9	12.2	-10.5
	Comfortable	0.5	0.4	-2.9	2.1
	Uncomfortable	0.9	-2	-1.8	1.7
	Very uncomfortable	-0.6	-0.3	0.2	0.2
	I don't do this	0	0.1	-9.7	8.4
Keeping in touch with existing friends	Very comfortable	2.4	0.9	9.3	-9.8
	Comfortable	0.8	1.3	-4.3	2.9
	Uncomfortable	-1.6	-1.8	-2.9	3.9
	Very uncomfortable	-2.9	0.3	-0.9	2.4
	I don't do this	-3.6	-2.8	-7.7	9.6
Communicating with existing clients/customers	Very comfortable	3.1	0.8	16.4	-16.4
	Comfortable	2.2	1.7	-2	0
	Uncomfortable	-1	-1	-5.2	5.5
	Very uncomfortable	-1.9	-0.9	-1	2.2
	I don't do this	-4.2	-1.7	-10.8	12.3
Finding new clients/customers	Very comfortable	3	1.5	15.6	-15.8
	Comfortable	0.2	0.4	3.3	-3.1
	Uncomfortable	0.5	0.6	-4.4	3.3
	Very uncomfortable	1.2	-0.6	-2.6	1.8
	I don't do this	-3.5	-1.8	-11.9	12.9
Working together with others in a project or game	Very comfortable	1.6	1.1	12.3	-12
	Comfortable	0	1.7	-2.9	2
	Uncomfortable	1.5	-2.1	-4.2	3.5
	Very uncomfortable	-0.9	-0.4	-0.3	0.9
	I don't do this	-2.8	-1.9	-8.4	9.6
Arranging to meet others face-to-face	Very comfortable	4.6	2.1	8.1	-10.3
	Comfortable	0.8	0.8	-1.1	0.2
	Uncomfortable	0.5	-2.2	-1.9	2.1
	Very uncomfortable	-1.3	-1.5	-1.7	2.7
	I don't do this	-6.2	-1	-5.9	9
Communicating with buyers/sellers for shopping purposes	Very comfortable	5.2	1.3	11.7	-13.6
	Comfortable	0.8	0.6	-1.1	0.3
	Uncomfortable	-0.1	-1	-3.3	3.3
	Very uncomfortable	-1	-1.4	-0.9	1.8
	I don't do this	-6.4	-0.9	-9.2	12
Managing personal matters such as banking, energy suppliers, phone/internet suppliers, government administration	Very comfortable	6.9	3.4	20	-22.4
	Comfortable	2.5	2.1	2.8	-4.5
	Uncomfortable	0.6	-1.4	-7.4	6.5
	Very uncomfortable	0.6	-2.2	-3.2	3.2
	I don't do this	-10.7	-3.8	-16.7	21.9
Stating your opinion in a discussion	Very comfortable	1.2	1.3	11.1	-10.7
	Comfortable	-1.7	-1.1	-4.5	5.3
	Uncomfortable	1.6	0	-3.9	2.6
	Very uncomfortable	-0.7	-0.5	-2.4	2.7
	I don't do this	-0.5	-0.1	-4.8	4.5
Defending your opinion in a discussion	Very comfortable	1.7	0.5	10.1	-10
	Comfortable	-3.1	0.7	-2.4	3.6
	Uncomfortable	2.3	-1.2	-4.8	3.3
	Very uncomfortable	0.3	-0.3	-3	2.6
	I don't do this	-1	-0.2	-4.3	4.4
Disagreeing with someone	Very comfortable	1.8	0.9	8.5	-8.7
	Comfortable	-2.5	0.1	-2.3	3.4
	Uncomfortable	1.7	-0.8	-4.1	2.9
	Very uncomfortable	0.4	0.3	-1.7	1.2
	I don't do this	-1.4	-0.9	-3	3.7
Offering advice to others (including writing reviews)	Very comfortable	1.9	1.4	11.8	-11.8
	Comfortable	-1.8	-1.2	-4.3	5.1
	Uncomfortable	1.1	0.4	-4.6	3.2
	Very uncomfortable	-0.2	-0.9	-1.1	1.4
	I don't do this	-1.2	-0.1	-6.2	6.2

Note: See Table 4.4 for a description of cell values and formatting.

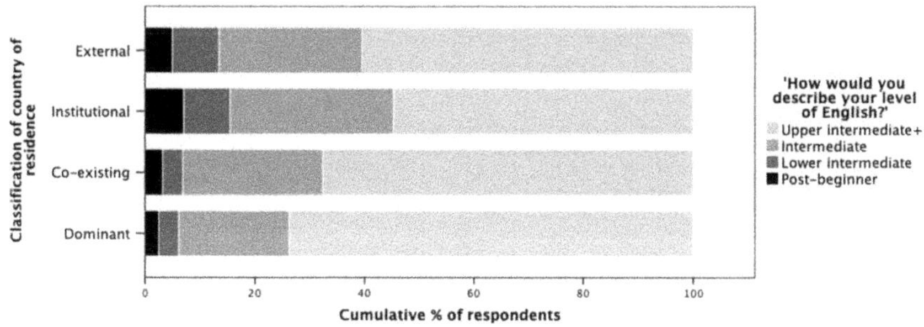

Figure 4.3 English proficiency level distribution across location types

Table 4.6 Differences between online and offline data for the making new friends activity, stratified by the classification of country of residence

		Classification of country of residence			
		Dominant	Co-existing	Institutional	External
Making new friends	Very comfortable	-9.90%	-4.60%	0.90%	-4.30%
	Comfortable	2.10%	0.40%	0.40%	1.10%
	Uncomfortable	-2.80%	10.50%	-4.60%	-4.00%
	Very uncomfortable	-2.10%	1.30%	-1.30%	-1.80%
	I don't do this	12.70%	13.20%	4.70%	9.10%

Note: See Table 4.2 for a description of cell values and formatting.

4.6.1.3 Level

There is a clear tendency for comfort level to increase with English proficiency in all functions (Table 4.7), culminating in a very pronounced increase in comfort among upper-intermediate-level respondents. Post-beginner respondents are more likely not to engage in most of the activities surveyed, and this is especially pronounced in the four evaluative functions, as well as *keeping in touch with existing friends*.

However, this picture is more nuanced in the comparison between online and offline data (see Table 4.8). This demonstrates a tendency for a small increase in the number of respondents choosing 'Comfortable' in the online data at post-beginner level. The effect is most pronounced (>3% more than the offline score) in *keeping in touch with existing friends*, *making new friends*, *communicating with existing clients/customers* and *working together with others in a project or game*. It is difficult to draw firm conclusions from this finding, but it suggests that CMC has the potential to provide a non-threatening alternative to face-to-face interaction for lower-level L2 users to interact in the target language, particularly in these substantially interpersonal activities. This corroborates previous research proposing a reduction in CA caused by the properties of digital media (Lowry *et al.*, 2009; Montoya-Weiss *et al.*, 1998), as well as a reduction in language anxiety in lower-level L2 users (Satar & Özdener, 2008).

Table 4.7 Level of comfort with EL2 CMC activities, cross-tabulated with classification of country of location

		How would you describe your level of English?			
		Post-beginner	Lower intermediate	Intermediate	Upper intermediate and over
Making new friends	Very comfortable	-2.4	-8.3	-11.3	15.8
	Comfortable	-4.9	-1.5	6.0	-2.4
	Uncomfortable	3.8	9.6	9.5	-15.7
	Very uncomfortable	10.4	7.1	1.9	-10.3
	I don't do this	2.3	2.0	-1.8	-0.6
Keeping in touch with existing friends	Very comfortable	-10.9	-16.2	-18.4	30.5
	Comfortable	-0.7	5.5	14.5	-15.8
	Uncomfortable	8.0	13.0	6.1	-16.4
	Very uncomfortable	10.0	6.2	1.2	-9.1
	I don't do this	11.0	7.2	3.0	-11.6
Communicating with existing clients/customers	Very comfortable	-4.5	-11.5	-14.9	21.9
	Comfortable	-5.3	-2.0	4.9	-0.9
	Uncomfortable	5.1	13.2	10.6	-19.2
	Very uncomfortable	13.6	7.7	1.5	-11.7
	I don't do this	2.3	2.6	2.6	-4.8
Finding new clients/customers	Very comfortable	-1.8	-7.3	-11.7	15.4
	Comfortable	-3.1	-4.6	0.0	3.9
	Uncomfortable	1.5	6.6	11.4	-14.7
	Very uncomfortable	9.0	9.9	2.5	-11.8
	I don't do this	-0.3	1.6	0.7	-1.4
Working together with others in a project or game	Very comfortable	-5.2	-11.0	-14.6	21.6
	Comfortable	-6.6	-2.0	6.0	-1.3
	Uncomfortable	3.4	11.7	9.1	-16.3
	Very uncomfortable	13.7	7.6	1.7	-11.9
	I don't do this	7.0	4.6	2.9	-8.4
Arranging to meet others face-to-face (including for non-personal reasons like accommodation, transportation, or buying/selling)	Very comfortable	-5.4	-12.0	-17.7	25.0
	Comfortable	-5.4	-3.2	3.8	0.8
	Uncomfortable	1.5	11.3	12.1	-17.8
	Very uncomfortable	12.5	9.4	3.7	-14.2
	I don't do this	5.7	4.2	4.5	-9.0
Communicating with buyers/sellers for shopping purposes	Very comfortable	-4.5	-10.7	-15.6	22.0
	Comfortable	-6.5	-0.4	4.9	-1.3
	Uncomfortable	4.3	8.9	10.1	-16.0
	Very uncomfortable	11.0	6.4	3.1	-11.4
	I don't do this	5.0	3.1	2.8	-6.5
Managing personal matters such as banking, energy suppliers, phone/internet suppliers, government administration	Very comfortable	-3.7	-11.2	-15.7	22.0
	Comfortable	-5.5	-1.1	2.7	0.7
	Uncomfortable	1.6	8.1	9.8	-14.1
	Very uncomfortable	10.1	8.8	5.1	-14.1
	I don't do this	3.9	2.4	3.3	-6.1
Stating your opinion in a discussion	Very comfortable	-6.0	-13.8	-19.5	28.0
	Comfortable	-7.5	-2.7	6.4	-0.9
	Uncomfortable	3.5	10.0	13.6	-19.4
	Very uncomfortable	12.0	13.7	4.9	-17.4
	I don't do this	11.7	6.8	1.8	-10.6
Defending your opinion in a discussion	Very comfortable	-6.0	-13.4	-19.4	27.7
	Comfortable	-7.1	-4.2	3.8	2.1
	Uncomfortable	1.1	8.2	14.1	-17.7
	Very uncomfortable	11.7	13.2	6.5	-18.5
	I don't do this	12.4	8.6	2.1	-12.3
Disagreeing with someone	Very comfortable	-6.7	-12.4	-18.3	26.3
	Comfortable	-7.2	-5.0	1.6	4.5
	Uncomfortable	2.0	7.2	14.2	-17.7
	Very uncomfortable	11.3	12.6	6.4	-17.9
	I don't do this	12.0	8.7	1.8	-11.9
Offering advice to others (including writing reviews)	Very comfortable	-5.9	-13.6	-18.7	27.1
	Comfortable	-7.7	-2.9	5.7	0.0
	Uncomfortable	4.0	8.9	14.5	-19.7
	Very uncomfortable	12.2	11.1	4.2	-15.5
	I don't do this	10.1	9.6	1.5	-11.3

Note: See Table 4.4 for a description of cell values and formatting.

Table 4.8 Differences between online and offline data, stratified by English level

		How would you describe your level of English?			
		Post-beginner	Lower intermediate	Intermediate	Upper intermediate and over
Making new friends	Very comfortable	0.20%	-0.70%	-1.90%	-5.30%
	Comfortable	3.30%	2.60%	2.50%	0.00%
	Uncomfortable	-1.90%	-2.80%	-4.80%	-4.30%
	Very uncomfortable	-2.00%	3.80%	-2.30%	-1.00%
	I don't do this	1.20%	4.70%	6.50%	10.60%
Keeping in touch with existing friends	Very comfortable	2.30%	1.80%	4.10%	5.70%
	Comfortable	4.10%	4.40%	0.50%	-3.00%
	Uncomfortable	-1.60%	-1.70%	-3.20%	-1.60%
	Very uncomfortable	-4.30%	-2.20%	-0.80%	-0.40%
	I don't do this	-0.30%	-2.40%	-0.80%	-0.60%
Communicating with existing clients/customers	Very comfortable	-1.20%	-0.50%	0.80%	0.70%
	Comfortable	3.60%	-0.10%	1.20%	2.70%
	Uncomfortable	-3.40%	3.00%	-0.40%	-1.10%
	Very uncomfortable	1.10%	-0.30%	-0.60%	0.20%
	I don't do this	-0.20%	-1.90%	-1.00%	-1.90%
Finding new clients/customers	Very comfortable	-0.80%	0.40%	-1.20%	-2.10%
	Comfortable	1.80%	-2.10%	0.00%	3.20%
	Uncomfortable	-2.50%	-2.00%	1.50%	-1.20%
	Very uncomfortable	0.20%	2.00%	-0.80%	-0.20%
	I don't do this	1.10%	1.80%	0.50%	0.30%
Working together with others in a project or game	Very comfortable	0.00%	1.90%	0.80%	-1.60%
	Comfortable	3.10%	-0.80%	2.30%	1.80%
	Uncomfortable	-3.20%	2.30%	-2.70%	-1.80%
	Very uncomfortable	-0.40%	-2.40%	-0.90%	-0.30%
	I don't do this	0.40%	-1.10%	0.50%	1.80%
Arranging to meet others face-to-face (including for non-personal reasons like accommodation, transportation, or buying/selling)	Very comfortable	1.30%	-0.40%	-1.70%	-1.00%
	Comfortable	1.50%	0.00%	0.60%	0.70%
	Uncomfortable	-3.60%	1.90%	0.80%	-1.10%
	Very uncomfortable	0.30%	-0.80%	-0.40%	-0.30%
	I don't do this	0.40%	-0.70%	0.50%	1.70%
Communicating with buyers/sellers for shopping purposes	Very comfortable	0.90%	2.00%	1.40%	1.70%
	Comfortable	1.90%	3.60%	2.10%	2.10%
	Uncomfortable	-0.10%	-2.40%	-1.50%	-1.90%
	Very uncomfortable	-3.20%	-1.60%	-1.20%	-0.30%
	I don't do this	0.60%	-1.70%	-0.90%	-1.60%
Managing personal matters such as banking, energy suppliers, phone/internet suppliers, government administration	Very comfortable	0.80%	0.50%	-0.40%	-0.20%
	Comfortable	0.90%	1.50%	0.20%	1.60%
	Uncomfortable	-2.90%	-0.50%	-0.60%	-1.10%
	Very uncomfortable	-0.50%	-0.60%	0.50%	-0.20%
	I don't do this	1.70%	-0.90%	0.40%	-0.10%
Stating your opinion in a discussion	Very comfortable	1.30%	0.50%	-1.40%	-0.90%
	Comfortable	2.90%	0.90%	2.70%	1.50%
	Uncomfortable	-1.10%	-0.10%	0.30%	-0.80%
	Very uncomfortable	1.20%	1.80%	-0.50%	-0.70%
	I don't do this	-4.10%	-3.10%	-1.20%	1.00%
Defending your opinion in a discussion	Very comfortable	1.80%	-1.30%	-0.90%	-1.20%
	Comfortable	-0.90%	-0.50%	-0.60%	1.20%
	Uncomfortable	-1.30%	1.60%	2.20%	-0.60%
	Very uncomfortable	1.90%	2.40%	0.20%	-0.50%
	I don't do this	-1.50%	-2.10%	-1.00%	1.00%
Disagreeing with someone	Very comfortable	-0.50%	-0.60%	-1.70%	-2.20%
	Comfortable	1.00%	0.40%	0.10%	2.00%
	Uncomfortable	1.10%	1.30%	2.50%	0.10%
	Very uncomfortable	-0.60%	2.30%	0.40%	-0.80%
	I don't do this	-1.00%	-3.30%	-1.20%	1.00%
Offering advice to others (including writing reviews)	Very comfortable	0.30%	-0.30%	-1.10%	-1.20%
	Comfortable	2.20%	2.50%	1.70%	1.90%
	Uncomfortable	-0.60%	-0.60%	0.60%	-1.10%
	Very uncomfortable	-1.10%	-0.20%	-0.20%	-0.50%
	I don't do this	-0.90%	-1.30%	-1.00%	0.90%

Source: See Table 4.2 for a description of cell values and formatting.

4.7 Conclusion

This chapter set out to investigate the degree of discomfort felt by L2 English users in online interactions. The data show that on the whole, L2 English users are largely comfortable with the range of activities surveyed, both online and offline. The broad similarity of the online and offline data is evidence in support of the notion that, increasingly, a marked compartmentalization between 'virtual' and 'real' worlds does not accurately reflect the experience of 21st-century life, and that this 'underlying dualism itself is becoming less significant' (Jordan, 2009: 182). Nevertheless, the data also provide evidence of digital communicative contexts providing lower-level L2 learners and users with 'a safe environment in which to practice and evaluate themselves' (Satar & Özdener, 2008: 608).

Stance-taking activities, necessitating the use of evaluative language, appear to provoke the highest degree of discomfort, but equally they appear to be some of the most commonly engaged with. Young people are less likely to feel this discomfort, a finding which supports the notion of a second generation of digital natives who are more accustomed to stance-taking activities online.

These findings, together with Barton and Lee's (2013) observation that this sort of language function is characteristic of online spaces, make a strong case for incorporating support for evaluative language online in formal language learning, whether supporting those learners who feel less comfortable engaging in evaluative language activities online, or encouraging those who feel more comfortable doing so to capitalize on the potential for informal learning in online discourse. Such learning material could focus on the available meaning-making resources in different online contexts, and potentially even use learners' own online interactions, captured by means of screenshots or chat logs, as authentic language texts for analysis and discussion in class.

A further major finding of the analysis is the unexpected pattern of responses given by respondents in institutional countries. Across the board, they are more likely to engage in all of the activities surveyed, and to feel a lower level of discomfort doing so. Further research is needed, exploring the use of English in these contexts, to better understand why these respondents seem so much more comfortable using English online, especially in relation to respondents in exposure-rich dominant countries. Such research would provide a valuable expansion of the discussions around the notion of language learning context, ensuring seminal models such as Kachru's (1985) circles and Siegel's (2003) taxonomy are updated to reflect the situation in our hyper-connected digital age.

This chapter has explored EL2 CMC from a functional perspective, using language functions as the sense-forming motive of language activities. Chapter 5 focuses on the rules and tools of EL2 CMC activities, exploring usage contexts defined socially and technically.

5 Contexts and Attitudes

The research reported in this book was prompted by a desire to understand the kinds of computer-mediated communication (CMC) activities commonly engaged with in second language (L2) English. This lay notion of 'kinds of activities' was approached in Chapter 2 from a functional perspective, understanding the motives and goals of communicative encounters. However, online interactions are always mediated by technological platforms providing affordances and constraints that shape the ensuing discourse. This is a non-deterministic process: users of technological systems appropriate affordances to find novel ways to express themselves and to circumvent constraints that might at first glance be thought to inhibit communication; in this process, novel forms of discourse emerge that the system designers might not have intended or anticipated (Kuutti & Bannon, 2014). Short messaging service (SMS) text messaging provides a good example of this: the combination of a short message buffer and the need to enter characters by repeated button presses did not inhibit its uptake, but led instead to a wildly popular novel form of abbreviated discourse (Crystal, 2008: 4).

Like any other form of discourse, CMC interaction is shaped by the social relationships between the participants. CMC adds an extra dimension to this contextual aspect by creating differing degrees of obfuscation of these relationships, through anonymity or the potential for highly selective self-presentation. Some CMC interactions may have strongly predefined social relationships, such as sending an email to a senior work colleague. In interaction in an anonymous chat room, however, social cues are gleaned from the language used by participants, and perhaps other resources such as user names, signatures and avatars.

Technological constraints and social norms can be analyzed within the activity theory (AT) framework under the *rules* component of the activity system, while technological affordances form part of the set of *tools* at the subject's disposal. Such rules should not be interpreted in the sense of explicit, codified proscriptions: they are more like conventionalized constraints that shape the discourse. As noted in Chapter 4, strategic appropriation and subversion of the rules of an activity can in itself provide an additional semiotic tool. The example of SMS messaging given above demonstrates the interaction between rules and tools in this way.

In this chapter, EL2 CMC interactions are approached from the perspective of the socially and technologically described contexts in which they take place, and which form integral aspects of their activity systems. Furthermore, L2 English users' attitudes to EL2 CMC and its place in their learning are reported.

In the following section, a brief discussion of classificatory frameworks of CMC is presented, in order to be able to formalize the lay notion of 'kinds of CMC'. This is followed by some methodological commentary regarding the construction of this component of the questionnaire. The findings of the analysis are presented in Section 5.3, followed by the findings of the questionnaire component probing a respondent's attitudes to EL2 CMC and learning in Section 5.4. Finally, the implications of these two areas for the book's overarching project of integrating EL2 CMC and formal learning are discussed in Section 5.5.

5.1 Classifying CMC

Efforts to classify forms of electronic communication have produced a range of classificatory frameworks of varying degrees of granularity. Baron (2008: 14) proposed a two-by-two matrix of electronic discourse types by pairing a dimension of synchronicity (synchronous/asynchronous) with one of the participant structure (one-to-one/one-to-many). Crystal (2006: 10) proposes five domains of 'e-discourse' with their own interactional characteristics: email, chat groups, divided into synchronous and asynchronous, virtual worlds and the world wide web. Frequently criticized for proposing 'Netspeak' as 'a single homogenous genre or communication type' (Herring, 2007: 2), unrepresentative of the linguistic diversity within CMD, Crystal (2006: 18) in fact invoked the term with regard to the observation that the existence of 'a type of language displaying features that are unique to the Internet, and encountered in all the above situations' was a 'widely held intuition'. Nevertheless, 15 years on, Crystal's classificatory scheme is insufficiently open-ended to describe the complexity of language use online, with social media and ubiquitous smartphone usage being especially notable absences. Baron's (2008) scheme remains useful to a point, but does not allow for consideration of media characteristics beyond her two given dimensions.

Herring (2007) proposes a broad and detailed classificatory system for CMD based on multiple, open-ended categories, which she refers to as 'facets'. These are divided first by the two basic influences on CMD: technological and social. Technological facets, known as medium factors, include synchronicity, reciprocity of transmission, persistence of transcript, size of message buffer, anonymity, privacy and quoting. Socially derived facets, or situation factors include: participation

Table 5.1 A summary of Herring's (2007) faceted classification scheme

Medium factors	Situation factors
Synchronicity	Participation structure
Message transmission	Participant characteristics
Persistence of transcript	Purpose
Size of message buffer	Topic or theme
Channels of communication	Tone
Anonymous messaging	Activity
Private messaging	Norms
Filtering	Code
Quoting	
Message format	

structure, participant characteristics, purpose, topic, tone, activity, norms and code. This is summarized in Table 5.1.

These lists are not exhaustive, but aim to allow a given CMD instance to be coded in such a way as to enable empirical analysis. It is based on this system that the 'technical characteristics' of online media are to be understood in this book. Herring's scheme does not account for contextual factors; Jones (2004) provides a detailed consideration of contextual factors around CMC practices, and the importance of redefining our notions of context in relation to CMC. This is particularly the case with regard to mobile forms of CMC, such as mobile instant messaging (IM), in which the physical and social contexts in which interlocutors may be located are virtually limitless.

5.1.1 Terminology

While Herring provides a detailed explanation of all these factors, she does not suggest any particular term with which to refer to instances of their combination. In order to provide this function, the term *socio-technical configurations* (STCs) is here proposed, and will be used throughout. This is adapted from Herring's (2007: 3) previous use of the term 'socio-technical modes' to approach more critically what had been commonly regarded as genres of CMC, recognizing that CMC contexts must be analyzed both technically and socially. Configuration is here preferred to mode, however, to emphasize the approach to CMC contexts as evanescent combinations of constituent facets, rather than as stable, enduring categories.

5.1.2 A word on synchronicity

The concept of synchronicity is frequently used as a fundamental categorical variable in classificatory frameworks of CMC, such as those of

Herring (2007) and Baron (2008). Although both authors adopt a binary division into synchronous and asynchronous, Baron (2008: 15) acknowledges that 'although it's common to speak of asynchronous versus synchronous communication as though the two were polar opposites, in actuality they fall along a continuum', and Herring (2007: 14) that 'CMC systems of intermediate synchronicity also exist'. Garcia and Jacobs (1999) point out that true synchronicity is only attainable when message production and message transmission are simultaneous, and that the majority of CMC platforms operate on a basis of quasi-synchronicity, in the sense that although interlocutors are co-present in time, messages are produced (typed) before they are transmitted (by pressing the 'enter' key or similar). True synchronicity, then, rests on the ability of interlocutors to have access to the composition of each other's conversational turns, what Jenks (2014: 79) refers to as turn monitor. In addition, it is usually possible to use apparently synchronous platforms for asynchronous interaction, something that has been frequently noted in the use of IM (Nardi *et al.*, 2000: 84). Furthermore, many of our assumptions of platform synchronicity stem from the metaphors we use – 'rooms' and 'messages' – to conceptualize technologies beyond our understanding, and there is often little difference in the technological architecture (Latzko-Toth, 2010: 363).

Dennis *et al.* (2008) therefore distinguish the higher-order concept of general synchronicity, defined as 'a state in which actions move at the same rate and exactly together', and which 'exists among individuals when they exhibit a shared pattern of coordinated synchronous behaviour with a common focus', from the more specific medium synchronicity: 'the extent to which the capabilities of a communication medium enable individuals to achieve synchronicity' (Dennis *et al.*, 2008: 581), and argue for the importance of considering not just the properties of the medium, but how those properties are appropriated and employed by users (Dennis *et al.*, 2008: 578). Similarly, Anderson *et al.* (2010: 5) discuss simultaneity as a property of interaction, compared to synchronicity as a technological medium property. Kalman and Rafaeli (2007: 1) argue that 'the level of synchronicity is not only a function of the medium being used, but also of decisions taken by users'. They discuss four factors which have led to a separation of the medium and the conversation in CMC: digitization, media convergence, 'always on' and portability. Interactions may move between devices and platforms, and the synchronicity element is best viewed as a dynamic property of the conversation, rather than a fixed property of individual media (Kalman & Rafaeli, 2007: 4), with values located along a continuum (2007: 9). Viewed in this way, synchronicity seems more usefully considered (in Herring's [2007] terms) as a situation factor, rather than a medium factor. Indeed, synchronicity shapes discourse less by means of technological capability, and more by means of the expectations engendered by subjective perceptions of the platform. An email may be sent in expectation of an asynchronous message exchange, while a WhatsApp message may anticipate an immediate response. In both cases, this expectation will affect the composition of the message.

5.2 Constructing the Questionnaire

Chapter 1 set out four study questions which the survey was designed to answer. The second of these asked 'In what text-based contexts, and with what degree of frequency, do L2 English speakers use their English to communicate with people online?'. To answer this, respondents were asked about the CMC contexts in which they use their L2 English. The goal was to obtain data that provide a fine-grained picture of the respondents' online EL2 interactions, and to this end this part of the questionnaire was designed to probe this feature in a finer degree of detail than is typical of surveys of information and communications technology (ICT) or internet use (e.g. Horrigan, 2007; OECD, 2015).

The questionnaire probed the frequency of English use in a variety of STCs of CMC. These were chosen to represent as comprehensive an overview of CMC discourse types as possible, derived initially from aspects of the 'Individual use of ICTs' section of the 2015 OECD Survey of ICT Access and Use (OECD, 2015: 22–30), and then further distinguishing between synchronous/asynchronous, personal/professional, public/private, creating/consuming (in the sense of writing or reading a blog) and one-to-one/one-to-many participant structures. Distinctions were made between personal and professional email, between public and private social media uses, between the creation of one's own blogs and the consumption of, and interaction with, those of others and between individual and group instant message exchanges. Airbnb and Couchsurfing were singled out as popular examples of *online social exchange networks* (Ikkala & Lampinen, 2014), environments that blend social and economic relationships, and online and offline interactions. Items were grouped for ease of completion into personal use, professional use, discussion activities, user-generated content and consumer activities. The final list of items can be seen in Table 5.2.

Two categories were taken from Herring (2007) to describe the STCs: those of 'synchronicity' and 'participant structure'. Following the elaboration of a theory of media synchronicity by Dennis *et al.* (2008), the term 'expectations of synchronicity' is here preferred over the traditional distinction between synchronous and asynchronous platforms. This indicates that what is relevant for participants is not the technical affordances of the platform for synchronous interaction, but the degree to which interlocutors are likely to expect an immediate response, based on the perceptions of synchronicity embedded in the platform. Values of *low*, *medium* and *high* are given for this. This definition also highlights

Table 5.2 Socio-technical configurations of CMC surveyed in the questionnaire

Category	Socio-technical configuration	Expectation of synchronicity	Participation structure	Gloss
Personal use	Writing/reading personal (not work-related) emails	Low	S-A	Personal email
	Writing public comments on social network sites like Facebook, Twitter, Instagram	Low	S-A-U-B	Social media
	Exchanging messages with an individual person on instant messaging apps like WhatsApp, Facebook Messenger, QQ, WeChat	Medium	S-A	Individual IM
	Exchanging messages in a group of people on instant messaging apps like WhatsApp, Facebook Messenger, QQ, WeChat	Medium-High	S-A-U	Group IM
Professional use	Writing/reading emails for work purposes	Low	S-A(-U)	Work email
	Using social network sites like Facebook for work purposes	Low	S-A-U-B	Work social media
	Using instant messaging Apps like WhatsApp for work purposes	Medium	S-A(-U)	Work IM
	Using professional networking sites like LinkedIn, Xing or Viadeo to communicate with professional acquaintances	Low	S-A-U-B	Professional networking
Leisure activities	In online forums or communities like Reddit	Low	S-A-U-B	Forums
	In real-time chat rooms	High	S-A-U-B	Chat room
	While playing online games	High	S-A-U-B	In-game chat
	Writing comments on photo or video sites like YouTube, Flickr, Tumblr	Low	S-A-U-B	Comment threads
Blogs	Writing blogs	Low	S-U-B	Writing blogs
	Reading and/or commenting on blogs	Low	S-A-U-B	Reading blogs

Consumer activities	Write reviews on websites like Tripadvisor, Amazon or Yelp	Low	S-A-U-B	Reviews
	Write/read emails to customer service representatives of companies such as banks, mobile phone companies, energy suppliers	Low	S-A	Consumer email
	Chat online with customer service representatives of companies such as banks, mobile phone companies, energy suppliers	Medium	S-A	Consumer chat
	Arrange to exchange services with people offline, on community websites such as Airbnb, Couchsurfing or Freecycle	Low	S-A	Service exchange

Note: As discussed in Section 5.2, the terminology of the 'Participation Structure' column refers to participant roles taken from Goffman (1981: 131–133): Speaker, Addressed recipient, Unaddressed recipient, Bystander. Parentheses are used to indicate non-essential, but possible, roles.

the role of synchronicity as an aspect of the *rules* of the activity of online interaction from an AT perspective. Although it is only one aspect among many of the rules of the activity, it is singled out here in recognition of its use as a fundamental classificatory characteristic of CMC in many taxonomies (e.g. Baron, 2008: 14).

The category 'participant structure', cognate with the AT component *division of labor*, was used to acknowledge the salience for the analysis of whether a configuration involved interaction in dyads, groups or a wider public arena. Terminology was taken from Goffman (1981: 131–133) whose work on the concept of *footing* introduces the terms *speaker*, *addressed participant*, *unaddressed participant(s)* and *bystander(s)* (coded in Table 5.2 as *S*, *A*, *Us* and *Bs*, respectively) to refer to participant roles in these contexts. This is used in place of designating STCs as *public* or *private*, as CMC technologies have blurred the boundaries between these terms (Pasfield-Neofitou, 2012: 162).

Throughout the book, the STCs chosen for inclusion in the survey will be referred to by a shortened gloss as indicated in the final column of Table 5.2. This gloss necessarily reduces the scope of activity implied under each STC however, and it should be remembered when the gloss is used that the broader description is being referenced.

Respondents were asked to indicate the frequency with which they use English in these configurations. A six-point Likert-type response set was chosen, the options being: 'Several times a day', 'Once a day', 'Several times a week', 'Once a week', 'Occasionally' and 'Never'.

The overall picture of responses to the questionnaire items probing frequency of online English use is shown in Figure 5.1, in which the STCs are ranked in order of the proportion of 'several times a day' answers. In general, the 'once a day', 'several times a week' and 'once a week' options tend to be comparatively underrepresented, with answers being instead polarized between the most and least frequent options, with, in addition, a considerable number of 'occasionally' responses. It may be that respondents found it difficult to precisely grade the frequency of their use, instead gravitating toward more vague 'all the time', 'sometimes' and 'never' categories. For this reason, the decision was taken to combine the values for 'Once a day', 'Several times a week' and 'Once a week' to produce four frequency categories, which were renamed according to Table 5.3.

The overall picture of the responses produced by this recoding of the data can be seen in Figure 5.2, again ranked by the 'Highly Frequent' category.

The decision was taken to regard the four categories as representing different types of engagement with the STCs in question, rather than as increments of frequency. This assumption requires the data to be treated as nominal, rather than ordinal, necessitating the use of the mode as the appropriate measure of central tendency.

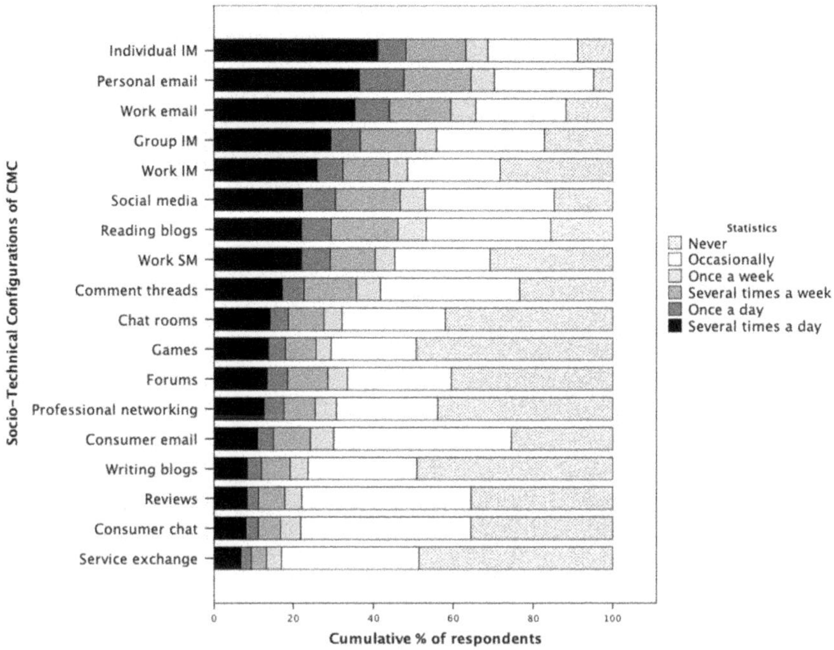

Figure 5.1 Frequency of English use in STCs

Table 5.3 Derivation of frequency categories from response options

Response option	Frequency category
Several times a day	Highly frequent
Once a day Several times a week Once a week	Habitual
Rarely	Occasional
Never	Unusual

To investigate the effect of the three demographic variables, the mean value of central tendency was used, calculated from the original six-point Likert data before the combination procedure described above. Although sometimes regarded as unsuitable for use with ordinal or nominal data, a robust defense of the use of the mean in this way can be found in Sullivan and Artino (2013: 541) and precedence of such use elsewhere in the literature (Lamb & Arisandy, 2019: 11). Given that the analysis sought only to make statements of comparative, rather than absolute frequency, the mean was regarded as both an acceptable and an optimal measure. It had the advantage of enabling a finer-grained level of analysis than the limited range of potential values presented by the mode analysis, and as it takes the proportions of all response categories into account, it is representative of the full spread of responses.

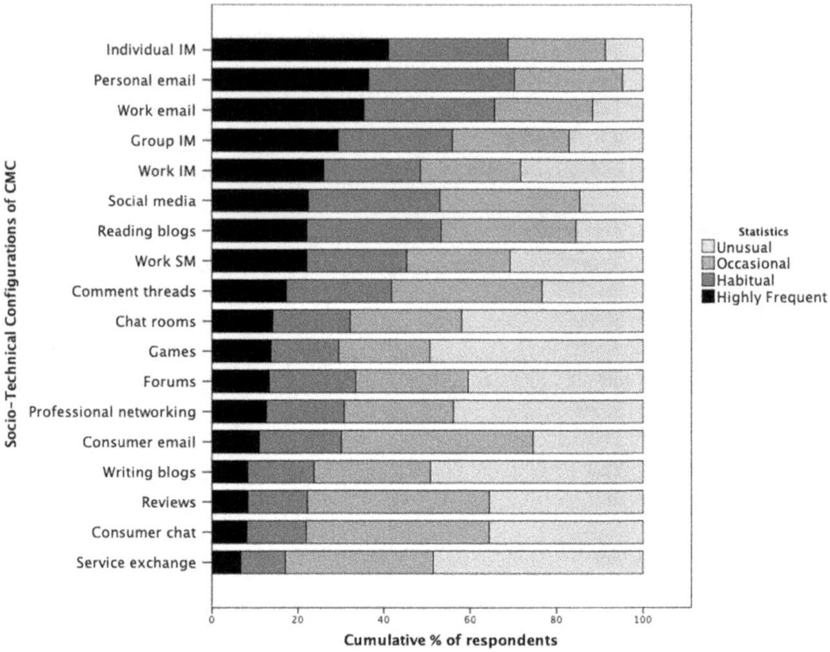

Figure 5.2 STCs ranked by 'Highly Frequent', following recoding

5.3 Surveying Socio-Technical Configurations of EL2 CMC Usage

Analysis of the mode values (Figure 5.3) showed that the STCs fall mainly into the categories of Highly Frequent, Occasional and Unusual, with *reading blogs* the only member of the Habitual category. Further inspection of the *reading blogs* STC showed that the margin between Habitual and Occasional responses for this STC is less than 1% (the smallest difference between two responses categories in the whole data set). Consequently, it was regarded as justifiable to include *reading blogs* in the Occasional category. The category with the largest membership is that associated with the lowest frequency of use (the Unusual STCs) and category membership grows progressively smaller as frequency of use increases (*reading blogs* being included in the Occasional category).

To refine the level of detail of the mode analysis, the response distributions of the STCs in each category were inspected to identify intragroup variation (see Figure 5.4). Sub-groupings were identified, and are discussed in the following paragraphs.

The Highly Frequent category contains forms of email and IM. These STCs are more intimate in nature than public-facing STCs such as social media, and do not incorporate *bystander* roles (see Table 5.2), meaning that users do not have to concern themselves with how their

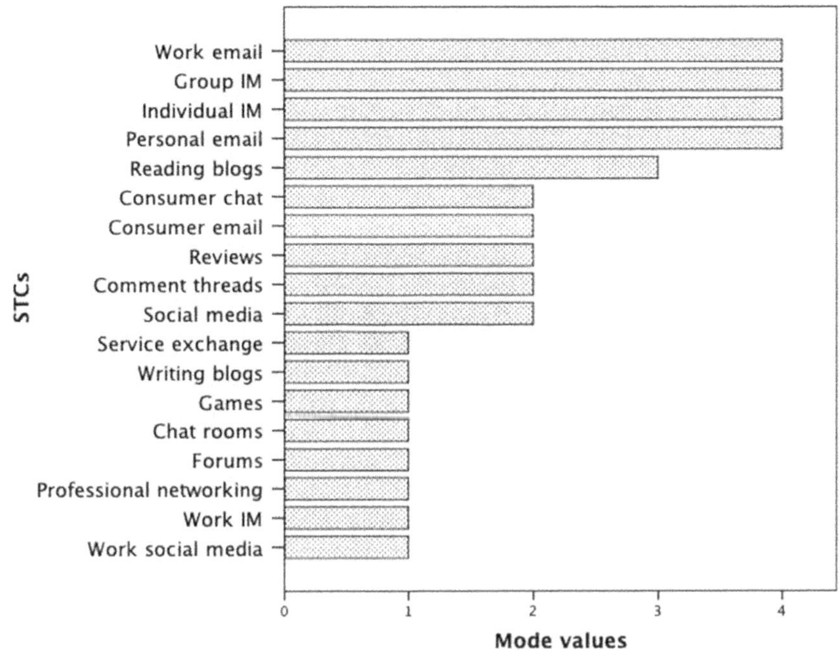

Figure 5.3 STC frequency mode values. The values 1–4 along the horizontal axis correspond to the frequency categories Unusual, Occasional, Habitual and Highly Frequent respectively

comments might be interpreted by unacquainted members of the public. Furthermore, these STCs engender only low or medium expectations of synchronicity, with the exception of *group IM*, which is classified as medium-high. Raised expectations of synchronicity may be expected to create a stressful environment for L2 users, who feel pressured to respond quickly and appropriately. The Highly Frequent STCs might further be characterized as constituting the essential maintenance of everyday life, socially and administratively.

The six STCs in the Occasional category (including *reading blogs*) may be separated into two sub-groups (see Figure 5.4). The first three, which have proportions of Occasional responses ranging from 42.3% to 44.4%, and whose second-largest proportion of responses was in the Unusual category, are likely to be tied to offline events: *reviews* will be left following a visit to a place or the purchase of an item, while *consumer chat* and *consumer email* will be in response to an interaction with a service provider of some sort. These are likely to be occasional by their very nature: few people will interact with their mobile phone provider with any kind of regularity. The STCs in this first sub-group have low or medium expectations of synchronicity. The second sub-group consists of public-facing social networking spaces, blog consumption and writing

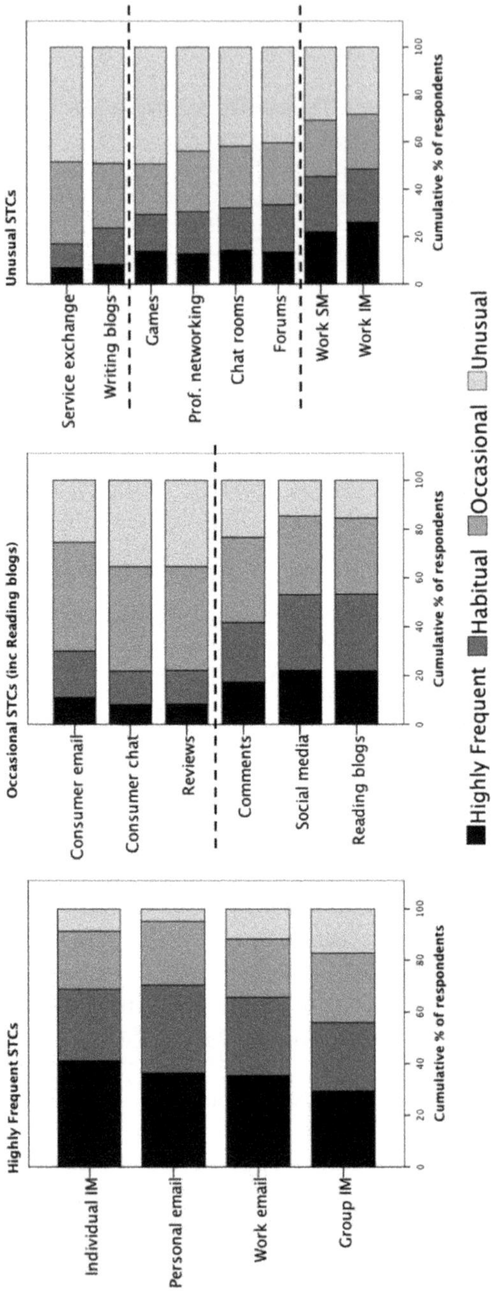

Figure 5.4 Breakdown of STC categories showing sub-groupings

on comment threads. These all have proportions of Occasional responses ranging from 31.1% to 34.8%, and their second-largest proportion of responses is in the Habitual category. These STCs all include *bystanders* in the participation structure (see Table 5.2): this public-facing aspect may be in part responsible for their presence in the Occasional category, rather than higher frequency categories.

The Unusual category contains the largest number of STCs. As with the Occasional category, however, visual inspection of the proportions of response types suggests a division into three sub-groups, based on their profiles of response types. *Writing blogs* and *service exchange* are dominated by Unusual and Occasional responses, with much smaller proportions of the two more frequent response types. Highly Frequent responses comprise only 6.8% of the total for *service exchange*, and 8.4% for *writing blogs*. Given the discursive complexity of writing the large blocks of text required in blog production, it is unsurprising that *writing blogs* should be so emphatically Unusual an STC.

The second sub-group comprises *games*, *professional networking*, *chat rooms* and *forums*, all of which receive proportions of Highly Frequent responses ranging from 12.7% to 14.2%. These STCs, while still dominated by Unusual responses, are nevertheless used Highly Frequently or Habitually by a substantial minority of respondents. *Chat rooms* and *games* both have high expectations of synchronicity (see Table 5.2), which may be intimidating for L2 English users.

The final sub-group consists of *work social media* and *work IM*. In these STCs, the four response categories are almost evenly represented, with the Unusual proportions gaining prominence only by a small margin. The balanced response profiles of these STCs suggest that, despite falling into the Unusual category overall, language teachers can expect considerable variety in the degree to which their learners engage with them.

5.3.1 Demographic analysis

Stratification of the STC data by demographic variables showed a number of different patterns, explored in the following sections.

5.3.1.1 Age

There was a statistically significant effect of respondent age on EL2 CMC use across all STCs. Kruskal–Wallis tests on all 18 STCs using age as the grouping variable showed significance (p) values of <0.001 for each.

As shown in Figure 5.5, English use in most STCs becomes progressively less frequent as age increases. This trend is most pronounced in *games* and *comment threads*; *games* in particular shows the sharpest

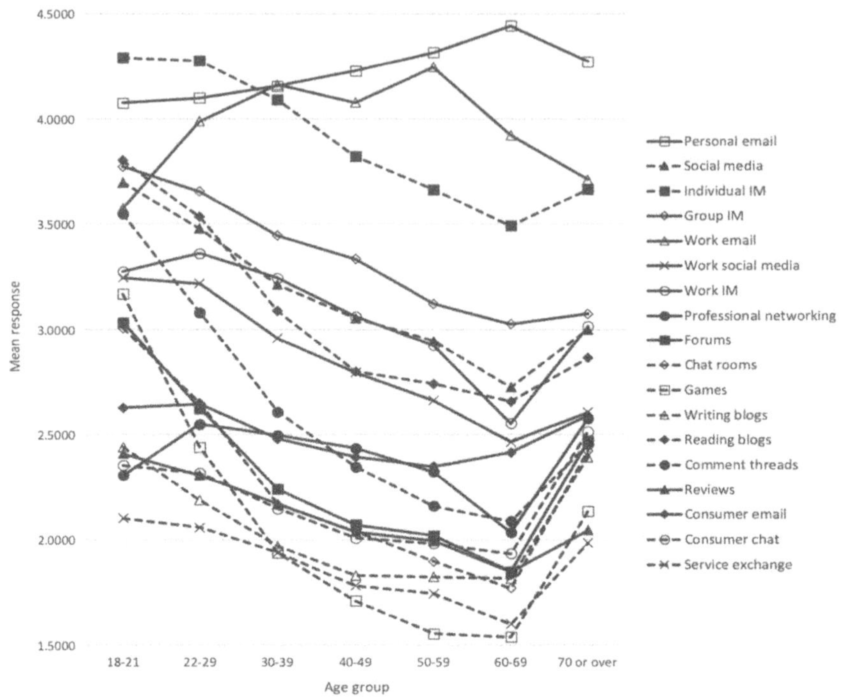

Figure 5.5 Mean frequency of STC use, stratified by age group. The integer values on the vertical axis correspond to the original response options in the questionnaire, in order of ascending frequency: higher values signify increased average frequency

drop in use between the two youngest age groups, and is the least frequently used STC from 40 years upwards. In other STCs such as chat rooms, individual IM and work SM, the drop in frequency of use is more pronounced after the 22–29 group. A few, such as work IM, consumer email and professional networking show an increase in frequency from the 18–21 group to the 22–29 group, before decreasing among subsequent age groups. A final subset, comprising personal email and work email, increase in frequency as age increases.

The 70+ age group appears to be anomalous to the trend described above, and seems to contradict previous research into the relationship between age and technology use (Friemel, 2016: 324). However, despite the large size of the data set overall, only 66 cases fall in the 70+ age group, and the effect observable in the data may be due to this small sample size. Further research would be required into this population before drawing firm conclusions in this regard.

Overall, the patterns shown in Figure 5.5 broadly support the conclusions of Taipale discussed earlier, regarding an increased preference for IM over email among younger people, for work-related as well as personal functions.

5.3.1.2 Level

Almost all STCs are significantly affected by English level. Kruskal–Wallis tests on all 18 STCs with English level as the grouping variable return significance (p) values of <0.001 in most cases. Consumer email shows $p = 0.020$, which is within the 0.05 minimum value accepted as indicating statistical significance. Forums and writing blogs both exceed this value, meaning there is no significant effect of English level on the use of English in these STCs.

An inverse trend paralleling that seen in the analysis of age groups can be observed in a breakdown by English level: the majority of STCs are used in L2 English more frequently as English level increases (Figure 5.6). The age and level variables themselves correlate only very weakly (Spearman's $r = 0.135$), so these effects can be regarded as independent of one another. Contrary to the overall trend, *games* and *chat rooms* show a decrease in frequency of L2 English use at the upper-intermediate level.

Curiously, however, in almost all STCs the general trend is interrupted at the lower-intermediate level by a drop in frequency. The cause of this is not entirely clear, although it may be related to differences in the number of respondents at each level: post-beginner level respondents account for only 5.1% of the total, although this still represents 532 people.

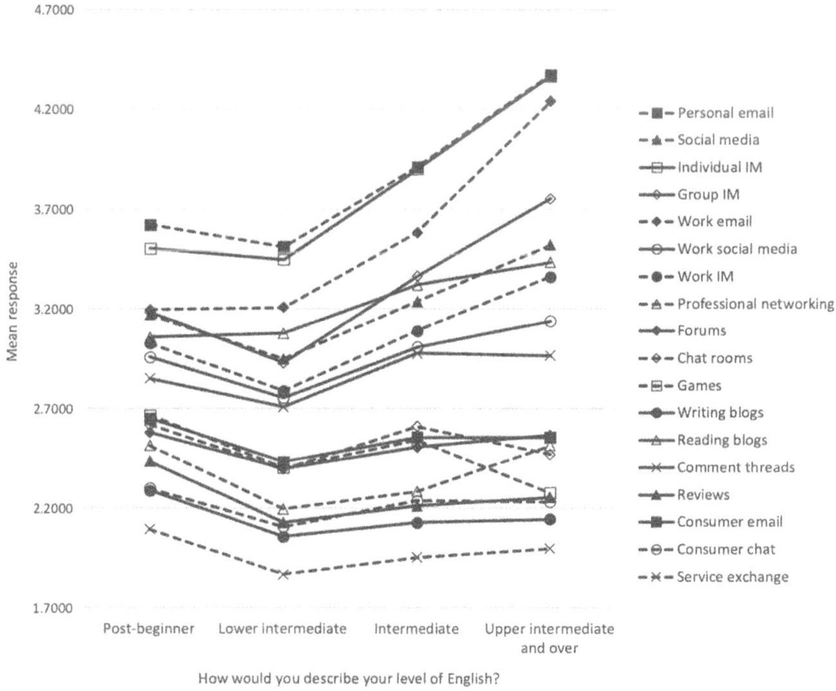

Figure 5.6 Mean frequency of STC use, stratified by English level

5.3.1.3 Location

Once again, there was a statistically significant effect of respondent age on EL2 CMC use across all STCs, with Kruskal–Wallis tests using age as the grouping variable showing significance (p) values of <0.001 for each. The discontinuity of the trends seen in a breakdown of the data by classification of country of location (see Figure 5.7) suggests that the four categories used do not represent a continuum, and that the data should be considered as nominal, rather than ordinal. Almost all STCs – the exceptions being personal and work email, and, by a small margin, service exchange – show more frequent L2 English use in countries classified as institutional. This seems to rule out the possibility of regarding the four levels of the location variable as related ordinally along a cline of exposure to English, unless they are rearranged to place institutional countries at the upper end of the scale, with dominant and co-existing countries in intermediate positions. However, it does not seem satisfactory to attribute a higher degree of English exposure in institutional countries than in dominant countries, given the largely monolingual-English nature of the latter. Furthermore, statistical analysis using Mann–Whitney *U*-tests shows there to be no significant differences between the co-existing and

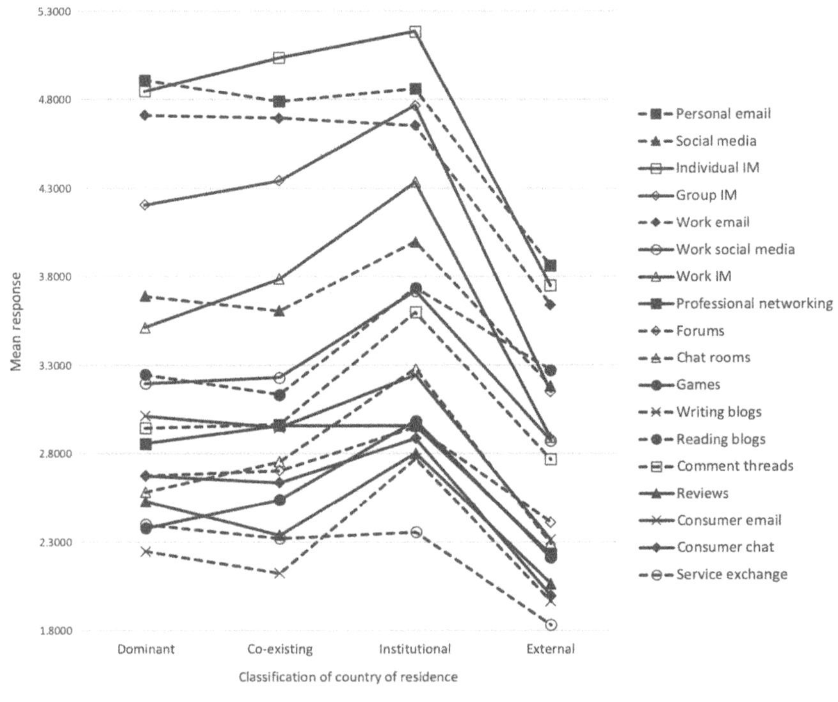

Figure 5.7 Mean frequency of STC use, stratified by classification of country of location

dominant sub-groups, suggesting that the moderate decline in frequency in most STCs from dominant to co-existing apparent in Figure 5.7 should not be interpreted as evidence of an ordinal relationship between them.

Nevertheless, the sharp and consistent contrasts between usage frequencies in dominant/co-existing, institutional and external countries does suggest a relationship between the role of English in these contexts and the degree to which it is used in online contexts. Precisely why institutional countries report comparatively high levels of EL2 CMC use across most STCs cannot be ascertained from the current data, and this would be a fruitful area for further research. The effect might be explained by the subset of respondents located in this type of context being disproportionately composed of those of a higher English proficiency level. This is not the case, however; as discussed in Chapter 4, quite the opposite is true.

Of particular note in the institutional sub-group is the relative positions of IM and email. IM-based STCs, especially work IM and group IM, show the most pronounced increase in frequency in comparison with dominant countries, while work email and personal email, as mentioned above, are two of only three STCs which are used less frequently in institutional countries than in dominant countries. For L2 English users and learners in these contexts, IM would appear to be replacing email.

5.3.2 Summary of findings and discussion

The extent of EL2 CMC use shows large variation depending on the type of CMC. There is a core group of four STCs – personal email, work email, individual IM and group IM – which might be considered the 'essentials' of online communication and can be characterized as being used habitually in L2 English. It is notable that these STCs do not involve a public audience, removing a potential source of discomfort for L2 users.

Six STCs are used, on average, occasionally. Three of these, which account for the STCs in the 'consumer activities' group with the exception of service exchange, may be described as intrinsically occasional in nature, while the remaining three, which are more social or recreational in nature, display greater variation between respondents. Teachers may well encounter substantial numbers of learners who use English in these STCs more frequently.

The remaining eight STCs are categorized as unusual. Of these the two work-related STCs – work IM and work social media – show greater variation between respondents, again suggesting that for many these belong in higher frequency categories. Of the STCs described as leisure or hobby related (*chat rooms*, *forums*, *games*, *comment threads*) only *comment threads* is not categorized as unusual. The other three all appear to be niche activities, little-used by the majority of respondents but reported as Highly Frequent or Habitual by about a quarter of respondents overall. *Writing blogs* and *service exchange* are the most reliably Unusual STCs in terms of their response distributions.

In general, trends were observed of EL2 CMC use increasing with language level and decreasing as age increased. With regard to learning context, it was concluded that the four classifications of context – dominant, co-existing, institutional and external – could not be said to exist on a scale of exposure to English and instead represented discrete categories. There was no statistical difference between dominant and co-existing countries, and while external countries displayed behaviors consistent with low levels of exposure to English, institutional countries did not represent an intermediate position between dominant/co-existing and external, but showed quite unique behaviors, with significantly higher levels of engagement with EL2 CMC than dominant/co-existing countries. A notable exception to this was in the case of forms of email, suggesting a preference for IM in these contexts.

The appropriation of what have been termed 'phatic technologies' (Wang & Tucker, 2016), such as social media and IM, for work purposes is limited to younger respondents, evidencing a generational shift toward the use of IM in both personal and professional domains.

5.4 EL2 CMC and Language Learning: Beliefs and Attitudes

This final part of the questionnaire elicited respondents' beliefs regarding the effect of EL2 CMC on their formal learning, and the degree to which they would like EL2 CMC to be addressed more directly in their English classes (SQ4). Respondents gave answers to four items relating to three areas of interest, each of which will be discussed in turn in relation to the data.

The four statements are restated below, and assigned numbers for ease of reference in the following discussion.

(1) Using English to communicate online has improved my English skills.
(2) I have more opportunities to use English online than offline.
(3) I would be interested in learning more about the kind of English I use online.
(4) I would like more content related to online English use in the English textbooks I use.

In the following discussion the term 'overall agreement' is used to refer to an aggregate of the response categories 'strongly agree', 'agree' and 'more agree than disagree', while 'strength' of agreement is used to refer to the proportion of overall agreement taken by the 'strongly agree' option. Figure 5.8 shows the overall response distribution of the four items.

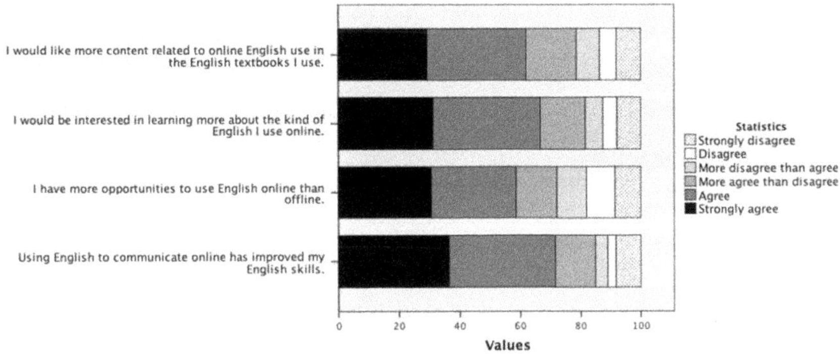

Figure 5.8 Overall response distribution to items in Question 26

5.4.1 The effect of EL2 CMC on learning

The first item in Q26 asked respondents to indicate their level of agreement with Statement 1. As shown in Figure 5.8, respondents demonstrated a high level of agreement with this statement. Almost 85% chose one of the three options indicating some level of agreement, with the most common response being 'strongly agree'. Of those who disagreed, 'strongly disagree' was the most common response, suggesting a degree of polarization. Nevertheless, this is clear evidence of the perceived benefits of EL2 CMC on the language learning process.

There are moderate, but statistically significant, effects of age, English level and country of location on the level of agreement with Statement 1. Agreement decreases somewhat as age increases, with 'strongly agree' responses dropping steadily from just over 40% among 18–21 year olds to just under 30% in the 60–69 group (see Figure 5.9). It sharply increases again to 37.9% among 70+ year olds, but the small sample size of this group suggests that this should be taken with a pinch of salt, and indeed a Mann–Whitney test of association shows that the difference between 60–69 year olds and 70+ year olds is not statistically significant ($p = 0.427$).

While 'strongly agree' responses are inversely associated with age, the same is true of 'strongly disagree' responses, though to a lesser extent. The 18–21 year old group return the highest proportion of this response type, with 9.3%; this then drops to 5.3% in the 60–69 group and 4.5% in the 70+ group. There are a number of possible interpretations of this effect. It may reflect a tendency toward choosing extreme response values that decrease with age, although there is evidence to the contrary in this regard elsewhere (Moors, 2008: 789).

The opposite is true of the data stratified by English level: an increase in 'strongly agree' responses in coordination with increasing language level corresponds with a decrease in 'strongly disagree' responses

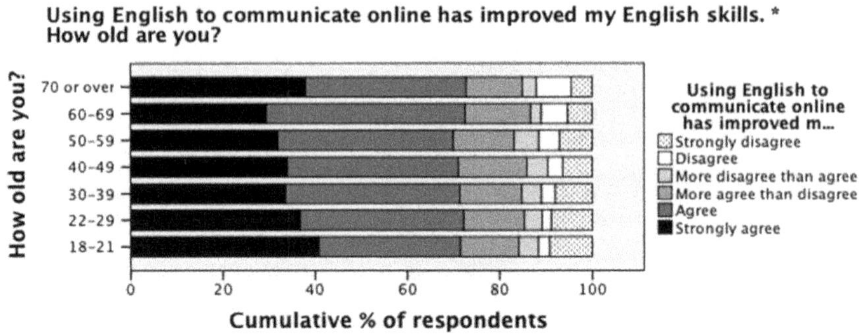

Figure 5.9 Questionnaire item 26.1 stratified by age

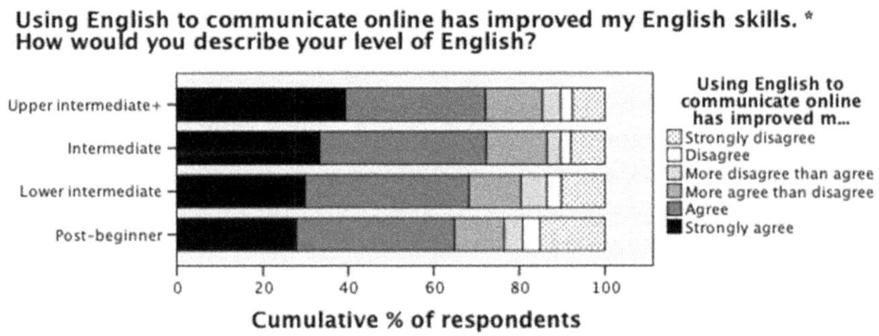

Figure 5.10 Questionnaire item 26.1 stratified by English proficiency level

(Figure 5.10). The positive association between English level and agreement with Statement 1 is unsurprising, as both relate to language proficiency.

The data stratified by classification of country of location show the same non-linear variation in response distribution seen in other analyses of this variable. Overall agreement is highest in external countries, while institutional countries show the greatest polarization, with the second-highest values for both 'strongly agree' and 'strongly disagree' (Figure 5.11).

5.4.2 The effect of EL2 CMC on exposure to English

The second item in Q26 asked respondents to indicate their level of agreement with Statement 2. As shown in Figure 5.8, this statement elicited the lowest level of overall agreement of the four, though at over 70%, agreement was still high.

As with the first item, age, English level and country of location all have statistically significant effects on response distribution. Overall agreement decreases slightly as age increases (see Figure 5.12), probably as a result of the lower engagement with EL2 CMC seen in higher age

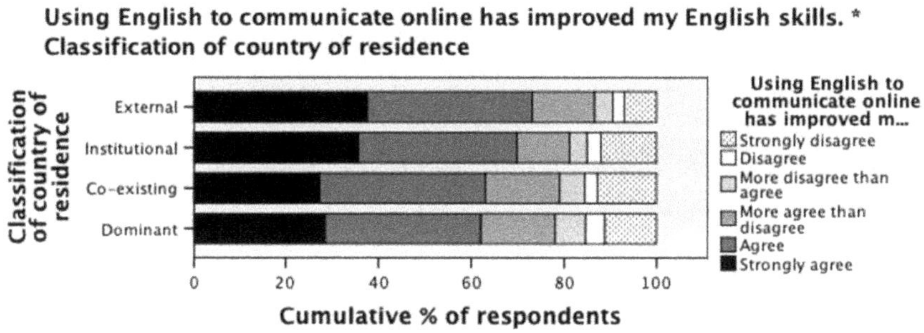

Figure 5.11 Questionnaire item 26.2 stratified by classification of country of residence

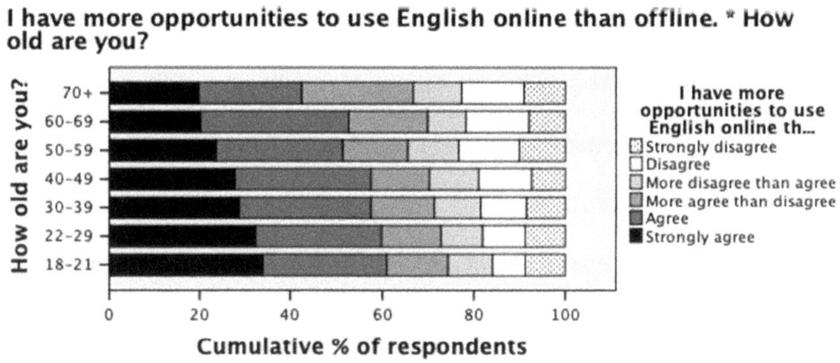

Figure 5.12 Questionnaire item 26.2 stratified by age

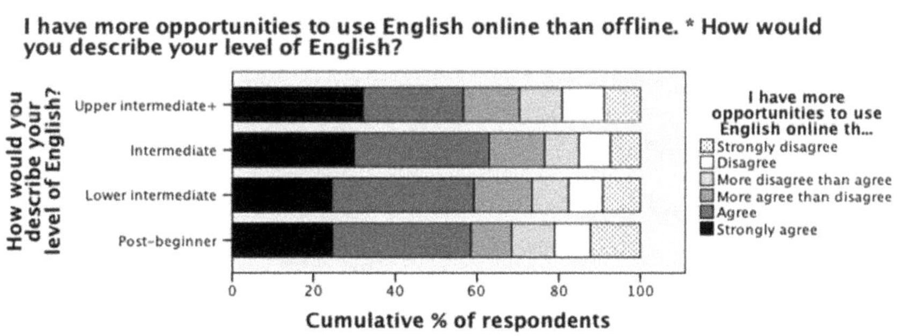

Figure 5.13 Questionnaire item 26.2 stratified by English proficiency level

brackets noted earlier. While overall agreement increases from post-beginner to intermediate level, it drops back at upper-intermediate level, in spite of a continued increase in the proportion of 'strongly agree' answers (see Figure 5.13).

The strongest effect is seen in the country of residence classification (Figure 5.14). 'Agree' and 'strongly agree' answers account for 60% of

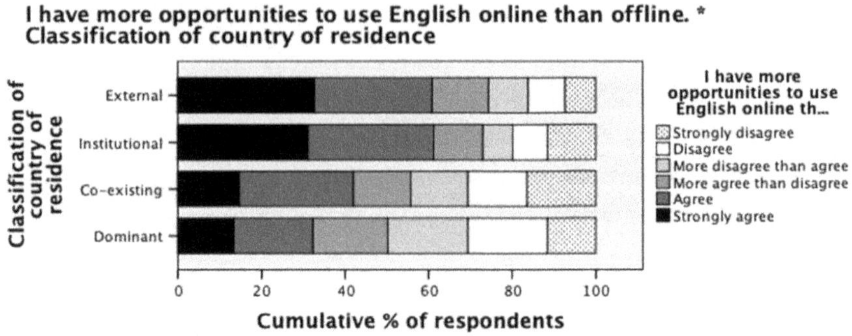

Figure 5.14 Questionnaire item 26.2 stratified by classification of country of residence

respondents in external and institutional countries, while responses from dominant countries are distributed close to evenly over the six response categories.[1] This is perhaps unsurprising given the contextual prominence of English in these countries, but it is a rebuttal of the idea that hyperconnectivity renders physical context irrelevant in regard to language exposure.

5.4.3 Interest in integration with formal learning and EL2 CMC-related learning materials

The third and fourth items in Q26 are closely related, asking respondents to indicate their level of agreement with Statements 3 and 4. The data from the two items correlate strongly (see Table 5.4) and they show near-identical patterns of response distribution, and so they are considered together, with data shown for Statement 3.

Table 5.4 Spearman correlation co-efficient, showing strong correlation between the two items from Question 26

			I would like more content related to online English use in the English textbooks I use	**I would be interested in learning more about the kind of English I use online**
Spearman's rho	I would like more content related to online English use in the English textbooks I use	Correlation coefficient	1.000	0.719**
		Sig. (two-tailed)		0.000
		n	10,350	10,350
	I would be interested in learning more about the kind of English I use online	Correlation coefficient	0.719**	1.000
		Sig. (two-tailed)	0.000	
		n	10,350	10,350

** Correlation is significant at the 0.01 level (two-tailed).

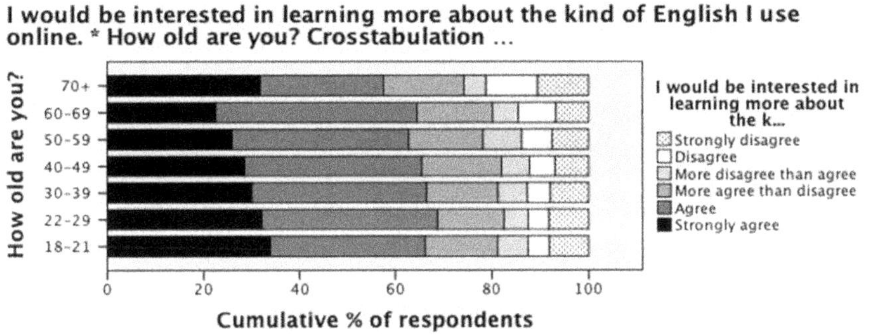

Figure 5.15 Questionnaire item 26.3 stratified by age

Overall agreement with these statements was very high, at a little under 80%. All four demographic variables show statistically significant effects on response distribution. While overall agreement remains largely constant as age increases, the strength of agreement becomes weaker. Some 34% of 18–21 year olds strongly agree with Statement 3 and 32.8% with Statement 4, compared with 22.5% and 19.8% of 60–69 year olds with Statements 3 and 4 respectively (see Figure 5.15).

As with the second item, overall agreement increases with English proficiency (see Figure 5.16), from around 77% at post-beginner level to around 82% at intermediate level. Overall agreement with both statements is slightly lower among learners of the highest level, at 80.9% for Statement 3 and 77.0% for Statement 4.

In the country of location data (Figure 5.17), the strongest overall agreement with Statement 3 is seen in external countries (82.9%), while the highest proportion of 'strongly agree' responses (37.6%) are from institutional countries. Respondents in dominant countries are a little less in agreement with the statement, with overall agreement at 68%. This pattern is almost identical for Statement 4.

5.4.4 Summary

Table 5.5 presents a brief summary of the main effects of each demographic variable in the response distribution for each statement. In general, the data suggest that learners believe EL2 CMC is beneficial for their English learning, and are interested in addressing it more directly in the classroom. There is less consensus regarding the potential for the internet to provide exposure to the language and reduce the disparity in exposure levels between contexts. The comparatively low level of agreement with Statement 2 among respondents from dominant countries shows that offline exposure is still salient in these contexts, suggesting that not all such L2 English users are as disempowered as Norton's (2013) Eva. Nevertheless, the 13.2% of respondents in dominant contexts who 'strongly

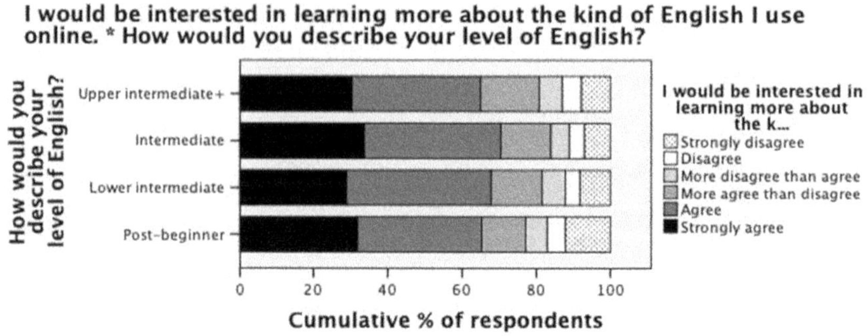

Figure 5.16 Questionnaire item 26.3 stratified by level

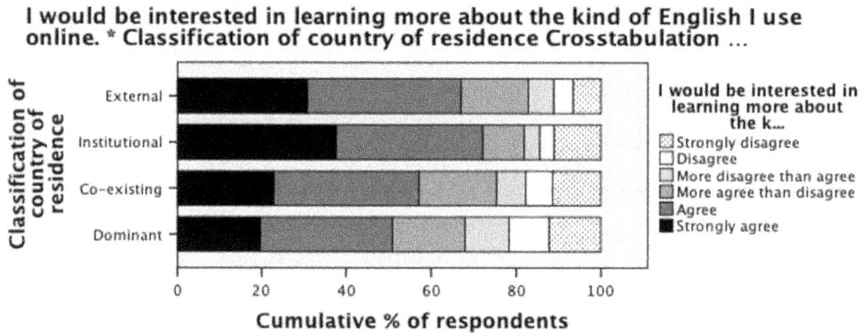

Figure 5.17 Questionnaire item 26.3 stratified by classification of country of residence

agree' with Statement 2 demonstrate that the internet can indeed be a rich source of exposure.

5.5 EL2 CMC, Informal Learning and the Language Classroom

It is clear from the findings that many L2 English users gain a significant amount of exposure to English through their CMC activities, and it is postulated, following the discussions in previous chapters, that substantial learning outcomes are l-ikely to result, through incidental learning processes. For language teaching practices not to engage with this area of learning would seem like a missed opportunity. On the other hand, drawing these practices into the classroom would risk compromising their 'extramural' nature, reappropriating them as new forms of class-related tasks. This is a delicate balance that any approach to the integration of formal learning and EL2 CMC practices must address and is discussed at length in Chapter 8.

Furthermore, the substantial amount of variation in the data suggests that, in a classroom setting, teachers may encounter a range of different

Table 5.5 Summaries of effects of demographic variables on agreement with statements in questionnaire items 26.1–26.4

Statement	Age	Location	Level
'Using English online has improved my English skills'.	While respondents generally agree with this, they do so less strongly as respondent age increases.	Respondents in low-exposure contexts (external countries) agree most and most strongly.	Overall agreement increases with level but plateaus after intermediate level. However, agreement is strongest in the highest level group.
'I have more opportunities to use English online than offline'.	Overall agreement decreases a little as age increases. Strength of agreement decreases rather more.	Agreement substantially lower and weaker in dominant countries.	Similar to the above, but the drop-off in overall agreement after intermediate level is more pronounced.
'I would be interested in learning more about the kind of English I use online'. 'I would like more content related to online English use in the English textbooks I use'.	As above.	Agreement is highest in external countries, strongest in institutional countries.	Similar to the above, but agreement strength also drops off at upper-intermediate level.

levels of engagement with EL2 CMC. Even in cases where the degree of this engagement may be low, the potential for learners to engage with online communities of other English users, whether native or non-native, expert or non-expert, is something that teachers can harness to enhance the learning experience. Nevertheless, care must be taken to ensure that any approach to integration is maximally relevant to the needs of all learners.

In the final section, the analysis demonstrated a widespread belief of the benefits of EL2 CMC in relation to overall language proficiency and a high level of interest among respondents in learning more about online language use.

In Chapter 6, a qualitative lens is turned on L2 users' experience of EL2 CMC and the kinds of difficulties in which they find themselves when interacting online.

Note

(1) As in other analyses, there is no significant difference between dominant and co-existing countries. Due to the small sample size of the latter, these responses are disregarded here.

6 Difficulties Encountered in EL2 CMC Interactions

Internet-based communication provides many opportunities for meaning-driven second language (L2) interaction with a multitudinous array of interlocutors. Such interactions are often entirely uncontrolled and unsupported, however, and potentially with little consideration given to an L2 user's non-expert status with the language.

In Chapter 4, I took a quantitative approach to investigating the online language activities most likely to provoke discomfort in L2 users. However, as discussed in Chapter 3, when planning the research underpinning this book, I was keen to incorporate a qualitative component, providing a means for respondents to outline in their own words their experiences of L2 English computer-mediated communication (EL2 CMC), with a particular focus on aspects of online interactions in English that they found difficult, challenging and possibly off-putting. This chapter presents the findings of this part of the questionnaire. I begin with a brief discussion of life in the 'digital wilds', before providing some methodological commentary in Sections 6.3 and 6.4.1, and finally presenting the analysis of the data.

6.1 Survival of the Fittest

A particular analogy that has proven popular in certain strands of research into L2 use and learning in uncontrolled digital environments is that of wildness, leading to the coining of such terms as the *digital wild* and *digital wilds* (Godwin-Jones, 2019; Sauro & Zourou, 2019; Thorne *et al.*, 2015). As a metaphor, it acknowledges the uncompromising nature of such interactions, the lack of support and the need for self-reliance on the part of L2 users. It also perhaps evokes semantically related concepts such as the 'survival of the fittest'. Zourou (2019) extends the metaphor by speaking of 'taming' such interactions by adapting them to a controlled, formal learning environment, and of the undesirability of doing so.

Participating in online discourse in the 'digital wilds' in an L2 can be a daunting prospect. Text-based forms of online discourse require users to present themselves entirely through the textual medium, and L2 users may feel under-equipped to adequately express themselves, or to keep up with the pace of discourse, especially in contexts with high expectations of synchronicity. As previously discussed, these challenges can lead to feelings of negative affect (Dörnyei, 2005: 198–201; MacIntyre & Gardner, 1994; McCroskey, 1984), which in turn can impede potential learning outcomes (Krashen, 1981: 22–23) and discourage participation (Yashima, 2002). Knowledge of the kinds of difficulties commonly encountered and consideration of their underlying causes will help to inform any approach to integrating EL2 CMC and formal learning, such as is presented in Chapter 8.

6.2 Systemic Contradictions

From an activity theory (AT) perspective, difficulties reported by questionnaire respondents may be symptomatic of contradictions of the activity system. Contradictions in the specific AT sense are more than mere difficulties, however: 'Contradictions are not the same as problems or conflicts. Contradictions are historically accumulating structural tensions within and between activity systems' (Engeström, 2001: 137). Systemic contradictions may place the subject in a 'double bind' situation, in which they are torn between opposing forces and have no clear course of action. When the subject so beleaguered finds a novel, creative course of action that transcends the contradiction, the activity enters a new and more sophisticated form. Respondent accounts will be examined for evidence of these double bind situations.

6.3 Methodology: Constructing this Section of the Questionnaire

The third study question set out in Chapter 3 asked: 'SQ3: What forms or aspects of text-based online discourse do L2 English users find challenging?'. As discussed in Chapter 3, this was envisioned as a qualitative endeavor, enabling respondents to relate their own experiences in their own words, though undertaken at a scale more commonly associated with quantitative methods. The intention was to provide rich insights into L2 communicative difficulties, both to stand in their own right and to complement the quantitative analysis of communicative discomfort in a manner similar to that described by Toffoli (2020: 14).

In order to accomplish this, the questionnaire included a component in which respondents were asked to rate the ease of use of a range of CMC technologies when using English. Four mandatory questions asked respondents to indicate how easy or difficult they found the use of English in four areas of CMC. The goal of these items was to filter respondents into an open text follow-up question, asking them to describe the difficulty they were thinking of. Due to this filtering function of the initial multiple-choice question, it was felt that a five- or seven-point Likert scale was unnecessary for these items, as they were not intended to capture nuanced information, but merely to act as a filter to reduce the number of open text responses received, and to avoid presenting respondents with a question that may not apply to them. Initially, therefore, a four-point Likert-type scale was used, from Very Easy to Very Difficult; where respondents chose Difficult or Very Difficult in any of the items, they were directed to a follow-up question asking them to describe, in a free text answer, what they found difficult about using English in the technology.

When the questionnaire was piloted, however, respondents seemed reluctant to choose either of the *difficult* options, with the consequence that only one open text answer was collected. It was postulated that this might be an effect of social desirability bias, the tendency for questionnaire respondents to answer questions in a way that represents an ideal image of themselves, coupled with a large psychological gap between *easy* and *difficult*. A fifth, intermediate option was therefore added: 'Quite easy but with some problems', in order to account for respondents who might have some difficulties but would not go so far as to characterize the experience as *difficult*. Further piloting suggested this change resulted in a more satisfactory distribution of responses.

The four items chosen for inclusion were: email, instant messaging (IM), discussing posts and real-time chat. These were chosen to be representative of a broader group of socio-technical configurations (STCs). Email was chosen to be representative of asynchronous communication mediating a range of potential discourse types and necessitating formulaic elements (such as openings and closings) and a consideration of levels of formality. IM was chosen to be representative of contexts in which synchronicity is possible but not always necessary, message lengths are likely to be shorter and contain higher levels of non-standard language forms. Discussing posts was designed to aggregate public social media use and comments threads on sites such as YouTube and on blogs posts. Common to these contexts are asynchronous sequential exchanges using evaluative language or exchanging opinions, very often with reference to an initial 'post' which provides the stimulus for the discussion. Barton and Lee (2013) refer to these activities as 'commenting', which they regard as 'an important act of positioning oneself and others', and a core literacy skill for online communication. Real-time chat is included to cover synchronous modes of communication including chat rooms and online games. Latzko-Toth (2010) observes that there is little difference on a technical level between chat and IM, but goes on to explore how they are conceptualized differently by their users. He uses the terms *conference* and *copresence* to differentiate the perceived functions of the two formats, with the former referring to the locational metaphor inherent in the idea of a chat 'room' (one of Latzko-Toth's [2010: 365] interviewees refers to it as a 'virtual water cooler'), and the latter referring to the sense of nearness created by IM platforms (Latzko-Toth, 2010: 369).

6.4 Difficulties of EL2 CMC Reported by L2 English Users

The analysis proceeded in two phases. As originally intended, the data were analyzed qualitatively in the first instance. However, the scale of responses received along with the functionalities of Nvivo meant that a secondary, quantitative phase was also possible. Each phase is presented in turn, with further methodological detail added before the presentation and discussion of findings.

6.4.1 Qualitative analysis

The qualitative phase utilized the procedures of thematic analysis (Braun & Clarke, 2006). As indicated by Braun and Clarke (2006: 87), the first step in a thematic analysis (indeed, any qualitative analysis) is to explore the data in depth, getting to know and understand them. As predicted at the outset (see Chapter 3), the data in this case were perhaps atypical for qualitative analysis, which often deals with a limited number of extended texts such as interview transcripts. This data set, by contrast, comprised a very large number of very short texts (9460 individual comments from 5030 respondents). These dimensions presented similarities to data sets gathered from the micro-blogging site Twitter. Twitter data sets have been subject to the kind of qualitative analysis undertaken here in a number of previous studies, such as Ahmed *et al.* (2019).

The dimensions of the data set required a consideration of the concept of prevalence with regard to emerging codes. Braun and Clarke (2006: 82) stress the qualitative nature of thematic analysis and argue that the importance of a theme should not be determined by quantification: 'It is not the case that if it was present in 50% of one's data items, it would be a theme, but if it was present only in 47%, then it would not be a theme'. They further argue that the decision to pursue a theme should be based 'on whether it captures something important in relation to the overall research question' (Braun & Clarke, 2006).

The data were first explored using the functionalities of Nvivo, particularly the text search and word frequency queries to explore the usages of prominent words. These techniques were used to suggest potential themes and areas to focus on. Manual coding of the data was still approached inductively, allowing themes to emerge from the data. However, this was guided to an extent by the presence of certain terms in the word frequency list, such as 'understand', 'find', 'time', 'express', 'formal', 'slang', 'native', 'real' and 'proper'.

Coding was undertaken iteratively, with periodic revisions of already-coded data to ensure that the evolving codebook was applied consistently and uniformly. Texts were multiply coded for all relevant codes. At this stage these were semantic codes, based on specific language used by respondents. Based on the discussion of prevalence above, codes were chosen that reflected some particular communicative difficulty, especially in relation to the component concepts of AT.

When all data were coded semantically, a process of sorting and grouping codes under larger latent themes began. The resulting codebook was broad, with a total of 23 top-level themes. It can be seen in full in Appendix B, including a selection of 'think-aloud' comments documenting the coding process. The discussion of the themes identified is organized around the components of AT. In keeping with the qualitative approach and with Braun and Clarke's (2006: 83) recommendations, the precise number of instances of a theme is not considered relevant. Themes are not given weight in this way, and the reporting of themes does not provide quantitative measures of prevalence for them. Multiple examples are provided in each case to demonstrate how the theme is represented by the respondents.

6.4.2 Findings

The analysis of the difficulties data will be presented grouped around the categories of AT. Throughout the analysis, examples will be provided from the data, indexed to the Nvivo file.[1] The indexing system uses a code consisting of two letters indicating the particular sub-file (email, chat, instant messaging and discussing posts: EM, CH, IM and PO respectively), followed by a number corresponding to an ID number within the file. Respondents' original words, including any language errors, are reproduced in the examples.

6.4.3 Activity – object – motive

As discussed in Chapter 4 (Section 4.3), the object and motive of an activity are highly context specific, and as such they are not easily analyzed in general terms with regard to a prototype activity system. However, it is possible to consider some properties that the object is likely to have. As discussed in Chapter 2, the activities of interest in this book are those with a genuine communicative need, including, by extension, some kind of outcome. Any activity that seeks outcomes from linguistic interaction with other individuals must have as (part of) its object some form of dialogically established meaning, whether that is the formation of a new relationship or the agreement to participate in a commercial transaction. This meaning-under-construction constitutes the object of the activity; when satisfactorily established between interlocutors it becomes the outcome. There may well be more tangible outcomes, such as the successful completion of a project or a successfully booked holiday, but these will be dependent on the initial motive of establishing meaning. Respondents clearly have difficulty participating in this activity of meaning-generation, reporting difficulties conveying 'the precise feeling or information I want to say' (CH.2), and complaining that 'I can't express my real meaning in English' (EM.326). Different types of meaning are distinguished, with thoughts, ideas, emotions and opinions (see below) all mentioned frequently in the data. This failure to achieve the intended outcome of the activity is evidence of tensions and contradictions throughout the activity system, many of which are attested in the questionnaire data, and which are discussed in the following analysis.

As discussed in Section 4.5, a number of common activities require the taking of an evaluative position as a primary feature of the meaning being produced (see Figure 4.1). This 'stance-taking' (Barton & Lee, 2013) is an important characteristic of online communication, but comments from respondents echo the finding in Section 4.6 that this is a challenging aspect of L2 English use. Several comments allude to the idea of hedging, in order to avoid being unduly face-threatening: 'Sometimes when I try to comment on a feed about politics. Its hard for me to comment using passive words so I won't hurt anyone' (IM.997), 'Because you have to say what you think but in a way that don't affect others' (PO.1244), 'Using certain words or your own ideas without hurt someone else' (PO.1398). Others feel they don't have a wide enough vocabulary to show the nuance of their position: 'I am not fluent enough to express strongly my point of view' (PO.1542), 'I don't know how to describe my viewpoint' (PO.2214), 'Don't find proper words to describe my view' (PO.2445).

Further motives are mentioned in the data, with their own problems. Alongside comments attesting to problems achieving the kinds of meanings discussed above, others suggest difficulties with a more abstract form of meaning in which English users are simply trying to 'be themselves': 'I do not know how to express myself correctly' (CH.867), 'Hard to express myself fully' (PO.221). To express oneself has a conventional sense of articulating an intended meaning; however, a more literal reading of the phrase implies projecting the identity of the speaker. Work on self-presentation which adopts a 'performative lens' (Orsatti & Riemer, 2012) regards the intention to mean as a fundamental principle of identity, and language-mediated activities of meaning-generation and stance-taking as integral processes through which identity emerges (Bucholtz & Hall, 2005: 588). From this perspective, message and identity are bound together, although this is not to suggest that people are unaware of the image they are projecting, and often seek consciously to affect it: 'It's hard to tune your message in a way it appears to the other person like I intended' (IM.1386), 'I have to be carefull with ortography and grammar. I would like to be appreciated as an intelligent person and that puts me under pressure' (PO.2524). One respondent discusses this at some length, demonstrating that CMC users can approach the construction of a desired self-image quite consciously and deliberately:

> i prefer to use a different kind of grammar to talk, my vocabulary and sentence structure is very different from that of the feneral population.

> i wish to continue to learn proper british english but since american is ubiquitous it has become difficult to learn by myself. i cant trust google for the exact meaning of words in british english which is why i use cambridge dictionary. i have played dark souls and the english in that game is the kind of the language i want to speak. i even read all of the dialogues of that game to see how late modern english was like. i would like to learn more similar language. (IM.1288)

This respondent appears to be engaged in deliberate self-presentation in parallel with any other form of meaning they are engaged in producing. The minimal sense-forming motive for any EL2 CMC activity might therefore be regarded as 'establishing desired meaning whilst projecting desired self-image', both aspects of which can be problematic.

Language learning motives are also mentioned in the data, and it is clear that some EL2 users, at least, are aware of the learning benefits of their online interactions, and exploit them, developing strategies to maximize their learning. These include using their interlocutor as a source of language knowledge: 'Sometimes a native speaker use an advance vocabulary so I ask for their help in order to keep to conversation going on and improve my vocabulary' (CH.450), or looking for unfamiliar language in a dictionary: 'When I find a new word on Reddit, for example, I use an online dictionary to look it up and most of the times I successfully understand the meaning of the word' (PO.256). Conversely, others suggest that being unable to turn to resources such as dictionaries during fast-paced interaction is beneficial for learning: '[I]t is not possible to use fast a dictionary, as on the Internet chat, so it is difficult. But!!! Because of this, real-time chat is more interesting and it develops the language better!!' (CH.2461).

Common to the first two examples above is the concept of noticing, which is clearly taking place, and which triggers a secondary activity of language acquisition, in which the object of the system is a linguistic item. These language-directed activities are, according to McCafferty *et al.* (2001: 293), more conducive to retention and acquisition of language forms than more passive forms of exposure. The third example, on the other hand, suggests that such secondary activities may be disruptive. This is a subject that has been debated at length in language teaching research in relation to corrective feedback given to learners with the competing goals of accuracy and fluency (Lyster *et al.*, 2013). The potential for enhancing noticing without disrupting the flow of interaction is discussed in Chapter 8.

As discussed in Section 2.4.2, Leontiev (1978: 169) asserts that affective motive-stimuli can be negative as well as positive, and in Section 4.4, the potential was discussed for communication apprehension to act as a negative motive-stimulus, discouraging the subject from engaging in the activity. There is evidence of this in the data, in which a number of comments demonstrate non-participation and its causes. Responses such as 'I'm afraod to be misunderstood than I avoid discussing posts' (PO.1077) and 'I am very conscious on my grammar. That is why sometimes hold back commenting on discussion threads' (PO.1552) clearly show the link between CA and non-participation. Others suggest a more generalized frustration with the tools at their disposal: 'Lacking vocabulary makes me sometimes not to do/write things that I just want so' (EM.332). These comments, coded as 'Choose not to participate', are most common in the data from Question 23, regarding activities characterized as 'discussing posts'. This links to earlier findings (see Section 4.6) and discussions in the literature regarding the particular difficulty of evaluative language use.

6.4.4 Tools

The subject's activity toward the object of meaning creation is mediated by a range of mediating tools and artefacts. Those mentioned most prominently by questionnaire respondents are the English language, and language support resources such as online or offline dictionaries, online translation, internet search, grammar-checking tools and auto correct. Each of these are discussed in turn.

6.4.4.1 L2

Many respondents simply feel that their English is not good enough to participate fully in online interactions. Comments such as 'My level of English makes it difficult to make sentence quickly and grammatically correct' (CH.2582) and 'My English is too weak. Innocent people suffers of my efforts' (EM.1802) attest to this. Traditional linguistic categories such as vocabulary and grammar are frequently invoked as problematic aspects of L2 interaction, often without further elaboration. The prevalence of these categories is not surprising, given that they present perennial problems for L2 users in any situation. They are less interesting with regard to the current research questions and are not discussed in detail here. Prominent among the data are problems related to orthography, and mentions of spelling in particular: 'To make sure that a word spelled correctly without loosing a meaning. Like "knight" and "night"' (CH.487). This demonstrates the inherently written nature of language online, and the renewed importance of orthographic aspects of language. However, with the exception of email discourse, this is of a different nature to what has traditionally been regarded as writing. As discussed in greater depth in Chapter 7 (Sections 7.1 and 7.2), the equivalence of text-based online discourse to writing in its more traditional conceptualizations has been a topic of continued debate within the literature on and around CMC. There is now a general consensus that text-based language online is a form of 'oralized written text' (Yus, 2011: 174), incorporating many features of conversational-spoken language. However, the data here show that while this may be the case, text-based CMC nevertheless carries with it the orthographic difficulties of written discourse.

6.4.4.2 Production

A number of problematic aspects of producing English utterances are mentioned by respondents. Precision in word selection comes up frequently, often in connection with the idea of conveying intended meaning discussed above. It is most frequently characterized using the verb *find*, though *choose* and *remember* are often used as well: 'Find right word to express the meaning of what I am thinking' (CH.109), 'It's hard to choose the right adjective in short time' (CH.1159), 'Sometimes in a moment I can't remember the perfect word I wanted to use' (CH.588). Concern with the fluency, complexity and coherence of L2 utterances is frequently voiced. Finally, the cognitive load generated by EL2 interaction is mentioned. This is particularly the case in STCs with higher expectations of synchronicity, in which users feel under pressure to respond quickly. In these contexts there are many mentions of a lack of time to think and to prepare: 'I usually feel like I have no time to think about how it sounds and how I could writw my menssages in a better way in English' (IM.235).

6.4.4.3 Non-standard language

A commonality among the L2-related themes is the repeated concern with the non-standard nature of language online. There has been considerable debate in this regard in the literature, with some approaches being labelled by critics as 'technologically deterministic', for implying that the technical characteristics of the medium cause certain types of language to emerge. This tends not to be discussed in terms of a specific variety of English, though there are a few mentions of 'urban Internet vocabulary' (IM.300) or 'network language' (IM.1146), but in terms of deviation from norms.

This theme began to develop during coding for the concept of register, and its sub-component tenor (which was later subsumed in the theme sociolinguistic competence), in relation to mentions of formality or informality. It quickly became apparent, however, that many instances of the latter did not in fact refer to tenor in the sense of politeness, but to standardization of language or lack thereof. It is often paralleled with other designations of non-standard language such as slang, for example: 'lack of informal/slang vocabulary' (CH.1512). The concept of formality in the data seems to index two interrelated, but separate, concepts. On the one hand, it refers to politeness, but on the other, to the degree to which language encountered online conforms to or deviates from language norms which respondents have been taught: 'they don't write in formal English, what is hard to understand because we learn the formal one' (CH.323). Irvine (1979: 774) notes the distinction between these two sense of the word, noting that the first is a property of the social situation, while the second is a property of the code itself. This maps on to the current distinction between rules and tools in the activity. Formality as it pertains to the rules of the activity is discussed in Section 6.4.6.

The non-standardization of language encountered online is conceptualized in different ways throughout the data set. It is variously referred to as 'colloquial', 'common', 'daily', 'spoken', 'standard' and 'urban'. It is often mentioned as, or together with, abbreviation, which is a well-documented characteristic of language in conversational text-based formats such as short messaging service (SMS) text messaging (Knight *et al.*, 2014: 51). It is even described as 'bad' or 'broken', reinforcing the idea that this is not 'proper' language use. It is often linked to native speakers, and creates a sense that non-standard language use online is natural for native speakers, but difficult to learn for others: 'They usually use abbreviated expressions, able to be understood by native speakers only' (IM.1483). While certain types of abbreviation might be more easily decoded by native speakers, especially phonetically derived ones such as 'r u mad?', other types, such as initialisms (LOL, ROFL, AFK, BRB), are as alien to native speakers not familiar with certain online practices as to non-native speakers. Nevertheless, the data show a strong sense that online discourse is the domain of native speakers, to which those who consider themselves non-natives struggle to gain access. 'I find difficult to understand the meaning of some words that are commonly used only by native speakers' (CH.751), 'Like not sure how to say things in English or actually saying things but that's not how English-people would normally say and having them confused' (CH.524), 'I'm not so sure if some terms I use can fit into native speakers' idea' (EM.1330).

This is an aspect of language use online, and indeed more widely, that can be addressed in formal language instruction. Encouraging learners to challenge ideas of what it means to be a native speaker and instead to consider less essentialist paradigms is discussed further below.

This preoccupation with 'informal' language online is a symptom of the blurring of the distinction between written and spoken language online. Language online has the visual nature of written language, but it often displays attributes of conversationalness typically associated with speech. Yus (2011: 163) refers to this as 'oralized written text', and speculates as to whether 'users "hear" their own voices while they are typing their messages'. The visual aspect of CMC, which also incorporates its permanence (as opposed to the evanescent nature of speech), means that non-standard aspects of language are more noticeable. This is noted by Pasfield-Neofitou (2012), who in fact regards this as a potential facilitator of language acquisition. Questionnaire respondents, on the other hand, seem rather bewildered and disempowered by this aspect of language.

Some respondents are aware of the spoken/written hybridity: 'spoken language is different from written language and yet instant messaging is "chatty"' (IM.444), 'I want to type words the way real English is spoken rather than using old fashioned English from the books' (IM.544).

This latter comment also illustrates another theme, that of a perceived disjuncture between English use online and formal English instruction. Comments like 'english I learned is from text book, not the real english' (CH.193), 'they use words we don't learn at school' (CH.1081) and 'I am learning formal English' (CH.1834) suggest that, for such learners, classroom English and 'real-world' English are two different things. This is nothing new, and the debate around the authenticity of input in L2 teaching has been ongoing for a number of years. Widdowson (1998: 711) argues that using authentic language in the classroom is, in fact, impossible, due to the necessity of removing such language from its original context, from which it derived essential elements of meaning that are then unrecoverable. Widdowson (1998: 709) also argues that the greater the extent to which meaning is carried by context, the higher the level of shared knowledge between interlocutors, the more fragmentary and 'incomplete' the actual language use is likely to be, so that it is useless as input for learning.

However, the extent of exposure to authentic language-in-use facilitated by EL2 CMC brings a risk of an 'authenticity gap' (Henry, 2013) if some attempt is not made to acknowledge the authenticity of learners' interactions, and the comments above are evidence of just such a phenomenon. The difficulties of the use of authentic materials discussed by Widdowson are mitigated to an extent in the case of online discourse, for a number of reasons. Text-based online interactions are more dependent on language, due to the lack of other channels of information transmission, and context is more easily recoverable due to the permanence of the visual record of such interactions. While it remains true that authentic 'used' language is fundamentally decontextualized by bringing it into the language classroom, the ability to preserve much of that context and bring it along can mitigate this shortcoming.

Another aspect of the debate with regard to authenticity of materials is the question of which models are to be regarded as authentic and on what basis to select materials deemed 'authentic' (Gilmore, 2007). The recordable nature of CMC raises the possibility of side-stepping this debate by using such language as is encountered by the learners themselves as the source of authentic input. This approach would need to proceed in tandem with a language awareness approach, encouraging learners to assess the language they are being exposed to, to understand how it relates to its context and then develop their own models for its appropriate use. This is discussed further in Chapter 8.

Nevertheless, comments such as those above suggest that the gap between 'real' language and textbook language remains, and is a source of some frustration for language learners.

The potential for target language exposure made possible by the internet brings with it an increased awareness of the 'authenticity gap' and, as noted above, the permanence of the text makes it all the more noticeable. However, it also facilitates the preservation of the interaction, including the immediate context, and this presents the possibility of addressing such language in the classroom, as authentic episodes of language-in-use.

This is a clear example of Engeström's (2001) primary contradiction within the formal learning activity system, and of a quaternary contradiction in the interaction between the formal learning and EL2 CMC systems. Language in the English language teaching (ELT) classroom is inherently commodified, packaged for consumption in the form of textbooks and curricula, particularly in the lucrative market of English teaching. Language as taught in formal settings can be measured and assessed, leading to qualifications that can lead to personal advancement. This is the *exchange value* of English. Language as it is *used* in real-world interaction is dynamic and evanescent, especially in online contexts in which language plays an integral part in the interaction. The tension between the need to develop a closed set of forms for teaching and the limitless creativity of language-in-use is an inherent, primary contradiction in most language teaching practices, especially those closely linked to published materials. Exchange value language is what is meant by 'textbookish', and when it is embedded in the EL2 CMC system as a tool for use in the real world, it creates a quaternary contradiction between the two systems.

6.4.4.4 L1

In addition to the meaning-making tools provided by the English language, EL2 CMC users have at their disposal the affordances of their first language (L1) (Inaba, 2019: 24). This may be apparent in code-switching practices that utilize semiotic affordances from the L1 in combination or alternation with the L2: 'Sometimes we can't describe what we want to say in English. We tend to use english in combination with our respective languages' (IM.1332). The L1 is also involved in communicative activity in the sense of translation, and many questionnaire respondents reported thinking in L1 before translating into L2: 'The main difficulty is that first i think the sentence in my Native language which is Haryanvi (Belongs to Haryana state of India), and then i translate it in English and its take some time' (CH.571), 'I think in turkish and then try to translate in english. It is difficult to find the correct word and then I pause always while i am speaking or give up the sentence that I try to complete' (CH.665). This translation is frequently not a simple transfer: the term *language mapping* was used when respondents complained that there was a particular term or aspect of meaning in one language that didn't seem to have an easy equivalent in English: 'Very special meaning that exists in mother Language but not English' (CH.1135), 'sometimes it's difficult to find English equivalent or Russian figures of speech' (EM.1535).

In the analysis of the questionnaire data, all codes referring to interactions between languages were grouped under the theme of *translanguaging*. While this was methodologically convenient for grouping such ideas, its use does not adequately represent, or claim to invoke, the depth and complexity of the discussions around the use of the term (García & Li, 2014: 20; Wagner, 2018: 99).

6.4.4.5 Language support resources

Respondents mention a variety of external resources on which they can draw in order to support their online use of English. However, the use of these can present its own difficulties and barriers to successful interaction. Resources include digital and print dictionaries, assistive language technologies such as grammar and spelling checking software, machine translation tools such as Google Translate, as well as strategic practices such as using an internet search to provide examples of language in use: 'In order to be clear and brief, sometimes i get stucked on how to make a sentence sound better. I can just past the sentence into search line in Google trying to find any coincidence to be sure am writing well' (PO.1178).

Use of external resources such as dictionaries is an example of reliance on external artefacts that have not yet become internalized, like a musician who has not yet committed the music to memory and instead reads from the sheet music (Kaptelinin & Nardi, 2006: 47). In EL2 CMC activities that take place in contexts with high expectations of synchronicity, the need to consult external resources can lead to a secondary contradiction between the tools available to the subject and the rules of the activity, which require a rapid response: 'It is like oral communication but in writing – you have to react and produce utterances fast and at the same time get the spelling correct (no time to 'use the dictionary')'. Even in low-synchronicity contexts such as email, in which the pressure to respond is much lower or non-existent, the time-consuming nature of consulting external resources can be frustrating, leading to feelings of negative affect and producing a negative motive-stimulus: 'When I read or write an email I always use dictionary, it takes a lot of time' (EM.2669).

Other respondents mention the increased cognitive load and inconvenience caused by the multitasking necessary to switch between CMC apps and external resources: 'I often have to look up words or proper spelling which means I have to open a separate app like google then go back to the messenger app which can be a hassle' (IM.1209), creating an internal contradiction within the tools component of the activity system:

tools for fluency vs tools for accuracy. A further internal contradiction is present in the use of machine translation tools, with a few respondents demonstrating an awareness of the potential for this delegation of sense-forming to remove the subject from the meaning-making activity: 'And I generally use translate, but it's not usuful, because the translate couldn't the direction of phrase' (CH.386), 'APP can translate it for me, but it is not accurate' (IM.272).

Use of external resources can also reproduce the primary contradiction between the use value and exchange value of the language (see Section 2.4.3), with some respondents noting the inadequacy of their dictionaries, which were unable to help them with the non-standard language they encountered online: 'People in real-time chat possibly use words that are either slang or informal. Sometimes it's difficult for me to look up these words in dictionaries' (CH.814), 'It depends on topic discussed. There appear often spoken/slang expression which don't exist in online/printed dictionaries' (PO.1944).

6.4.5 Community

Respondents reported a number of problematic aspects related to the interlocutors with whom they interacted in online spaces. Native English speakers were often mentioned in a number of contexts. This was frequently in relation to non-standard language: 'sometimes people use slang that only the native speakers understand/know' (CH.113). However, there was also evidence of a perception of native-speaker competence as an ideal and of native speakers as guardians of the language: 'I'm not sure whether the way I express my ideas in English is acceptable with native speakers' (EM.603). This has the effect of disempowering L2 users, and the feeling of evaluation it implies is a cause of situational communication apprehension (McCroskey, 1984: 26). This is one of numerous interconnections between the community aspect of AT and the division of labor within that community, which Engeström (1993: 67) regards as including 'both the horizontal division of tasks between the members of the community and... the vertical division of power and status'.

The power differential created by the perception that native speakers are authorities over the language and models to which non-native speakers should aspire, naturally casts L2 users as subordinate participants. The discourses that perpetuate these power relations must be challenged in language teaching. While it is undeniable that there is a difference between languages acquired during the processes of primary socialization (Berger & Luckmann, 1966: 77) and those learned subsequently, teaching practices should challenge conceptions of automatic disadvantage conferred by non-native speakers status and encourage learners to look for other explanations for phenomena such as online slang. Online communities often develop linguistic markers of group membership that are intentionally opaque to non-members (Yus, 2011: 152), whatever their native language might be. Teaching approaches that encourage critical reflection on the origin of difficult language encountered online can help to assuage the assumption that failure to understand inscrutable language items is an inevitable consequence of birth.

The difficulties of establishing shared meaning with English speakers from other cultures is frequently mentioned: 'Like we if we are not well aware of people' specific culture, festivals, slang and some particular words and expressions which carry a different meanings within their folds' (CH.1155). As this example demonstrates well, co-creating meaning is made more difficult when participants do not share points of reference.

A handful of respondents suggest that the L1 of interlocutors can be a barrier to establishing understanding: 'Some people don't understand because of their primary language is problem' (CH.2229), 'Some time the people are from different language the translate is difficult' (CH.2538). Rather more respondents report that the English language proficiency level of other community members can be problematic, whether higher or lower than their own: 'Many of them do not have good skill of English as a medium of Communication' (CH.892), 'No just I speak general english cause my level is level 2 in amideast so when I try to speak with a level that more than mine I cant find the words' (CH.2014).

For some respondents, the communities in which they undertake communicative activities online tend not to include English users, meaning that they lack opportunities to engage in EL2 CMC: 'Actually, I just using my first language in Facebook. I have never used Facebook in English' (IM.401), 'Most my friends are Chinese, they don't understand the post if I write in English' (IM.1207), 'i am a filipino and some post that i mostly read is pilipino so I rather say/write my comment in my language so others can understand too' (PO.1723). The internet is not monolithic and people's subjective experience of it will depend on their particular networks. Connectivity does not guarantee target language exposure, and for some English users or learners, predominantly L1 networks can preclude it. Comments such as those above explicitly mention online networks, but others simply refer to friends or colleagues without specifying the context: 'Malayalam is the language common here so no need to use english' (CH.1049), 'because my social and work circle are Spanish speakers' (EM.1921), 'I don't have a lot of friends use English-language' (PO.2324). As discussed in the analysis in Section 4.6, and in Section 2.2.2, maintaining existing relationships is a more common online activity than initiating new ones, so offline networks can have a strong effect on those online.

6.4.6 Rules

As mentioned previously, the rules of an EL2 CMC activity may be considered from both technological and social perspectives. Technologically generated rules stem from the technical characteristics of the CMC platform being used, which shape interaction and place constraints on the ways in which meaning can be constructed. This is not a form of technological determinism, but an observation that patterns of discourse will be influenced by, for example, the maximum permitted message length, or the capacity for multiple interlocutors. As discussed by Kuutti and Bannon (2014: 3549), users of a platform will appropriate its technological characteristics and idiosyncratic forms of discourse will emerge. Most of the comments in the data relating to technologically influenced patterns of discourse focus on the difficulties of interaction in STCs with high expectations of synchronicity and/or multiple interlocutors. Speed and pressure to respond are prominent themes, especially in the responses to the question probing synchronous chat. Linked to both of these is the theme of multi-party interaction and interaction flow. This latter refers to the unfolding of a group discussion and the difficulty for respondents of maintaining their participation as the conversation shifts quickly from one topic to another, and different exchanges overlap with one another.

Most of the comments regarding socially derived rules of linguistic interaction relate to rules which apply as equally to face-to-face encounters as to online encounters. There are a number of prominent attributes which respondents regard as desirable, and a group of these – brevity, accuracy, clarity – demonstrate an implicit awareness of Grice's (1975) conversational maxims. There are also many references to 'appropriate' or 'suitable' language, which may be taken as evidence of an awareness, similarly implicit, of the sociolinguistic component of communicative competence. This long-established applied linguistic concept (Canale, 1983) comprises grammatical competence, sociolinguistic competence, discourse competence and strategic competence. Of these, sociolinguistic competence refers to awareness of the 'sociocultural rules of [language] use' (Canale, 1983: 7) and 'addresses the extent to which utterances are produced and understood *appropriately* in different sociolinguistic contexts' (Canale, 1983, original emphasis). This is clearly demonstrated in comments such as: 'Difficult to find proper words for the situation or the topic. Sometimes familiar words would not fit in that situation' (EM.1237) and 'Using appropriate vocabularies and responding to the context' (CH.256).

Instances of content coded as sociolinguistic competence in the data are found disproportionately frequently in the question probing difficulties of email use. A word frequency analysis of these responses show that the word 'formal' is especially prominent: 'I find it difficult writing the a formal email and sometimes I am insecure of sending an important email in English' (EM.419). This is further evidence of the distinction noted previously between two different senses of the concept of formality: on the one hand, it references a sense of politeness, and on the other, the degree of standardization of the language. These two might be differentiated as *formality* and *formalization*, respectively. It seems that, in regard to email communication, formality, in the sense of politeness, is more important than in other forms of CMC.

6.4.7 Division of labor

The concept of division of labor is closely related to those of community and rules. The activity of interpersonal interaction is distributed among the roles of speaker, addressed participant(s), unaddressed participant(s) and bystanders, with the expected duties of each role embedded in the socially generated rules of interaction, as discussed in previous sections. When community members fail to fulfil their roles according to the rules, the stability and success of the activity are threatened. This is manifest in the data in the form of comments relating to behavior on the part of interlocutors. Many comments reference aggressive or antisocial behavior, such as 'People are rude, and I don't know how to swear in English' (PO.140), 'Normaly the haters say a lot of bad words' (PO.331), 'Often illegible and abusive language' (PO.4260), 'some people like using violent words' (PO.2571). Others refer to uncooperative interlocutors: 'Not everyone takes the talk seriously' (CH.1888), 'some of my friends in online is grammar nazzi' (CH.1699). The possibility of encountering such behaviors is clearly a source of communication apprehension, with respondents commenting 'i afraid that I may use the wrong grammar and they will laugh at me' (IM.986), 'I'm afraid of making mistakes and others will ridicule me' (CH.2187).

6.5 Quantitative Analysis

Following the qualitative analysis, the coded data were then used for quantitative analysis. The participant characteristics of age, English level and country of location were incorporated into the Nvivo data set by autocoding the data to treat all respondents as individual cases tagged with the above data as attribute values. This produced a total of 5030 case nodes, corresponding to the number of questionnaire respondents who had provided data on at least one of the four questions.

With the data prepared in this way, cross-tabulation queries were then run to show the distribution of problem codes across the levels of the four demographic variables. A matrix coding query was used to show the distribution of problem codes across the four different files representing the different CMC modes. Nvivo's internal functionality allows for the results of cross-tabulation queries to be displayed as the number of coding references, or as the number of cases coded. The latter option was chosen, as the coding references option produces duplication when a respondent is given the same code in more than one file. This was felt to distort the accuracy of the results. The cases coded option shows the number of people who reported a problem, rather than the number of times a problem was reported, and this was felt to be a more representative value. A consequence of this choice was that the column totals for each level of the variable were the total of unique respondents, and were not equal to a manual summation of the column. This was not a problem for the subsequent analysis, however. The results of these cross-tabulation queries were exported to Microsoft Excel, where a number of operations were carried out. First, expected values for each cell were calculated by multiplying the row and column totals and dividing by the grand total. Then, these two values (observed and expected) were used to calculate adjusted standardized residuals, following a formula taken from an online source.[2]

The effect of these calculations is to produce a value which indicates the extent to which the observed value differs from that which would be expected if there were no effect of the variable. While it is possible to do this by simply subtracting the observed value from the expected value, producing a raw residual score, this does not allow for easy comparison with other cells as it gives no indication of the relationship of the residual value to the observed value. A raw residual of 10 is proportionally much larger if the observed value is 50, than if it is 500. Use of adjusted standardized residuals rectifies this by incorporating a weighting of the value against all others in the same column and same row, allowing values to be comparable.

The operations were slightly different on the result of the matrix coding query showing the distribution of problems across the different files. This was not possible as a cross-tabulation, but Nvivo does not offer the possibility of showing matrix coding query results as cases coded. Coding frequency was therefore used. The higher totals that this produced meant that it was not possible to calculate expected values in the same way as described above. Instead, expected totals were calculated using the proportion of total responses present in each of the four files. For each problem code, the total number of instances was multiplied by the proportion of the total data in each file to produce an expected value for each file. However, it was still possible to calculate adjusted standardized residuals as described above, as this relies on the ratio of the column totals to each other, rather than the column total values themselves.

Cross-tabulation of themes (denoted using italic font in the following sections) with respondent characteristics and CMC types shows how these variables interact with the different types of problems reported. In the following sections, these analyses are presented, starting with the four CMC types differentiated in the data collection: synchronous chat, email, IM and discussion forums (DFs). Subsequent sections deal with similar analyses of three demographic variables: age, English level and geosocial learning context.

6.5.1 CMC types

Table 6.1 presents a breakdown of the 23 top-level themes, listed for each form of CMC by their degree of prominence, determined by how disproportionately common the theme is in the sub-group (calculated as described above). Each form is discussed in the following paragraphs.

6.5.1.1 Synchronous chat

Unsurprisingly, problems relating to speed and pressure predominate in this mode. High positive residual scores for *discourse dynamics*, which includes *speed*, *pressure to respond* and *multi-party interaction* demonstrates how challenging these high-speed environments are for EL2 CMC users. This difficulty is reflected in the high positive residual of the theme *cognitive load* in the synchronous chat responses, and perhaps also by the prominence of the *don't do it* theme, though the data cannot speak to causality. *Non-standard language* is also high on the list. At the other end of the scale, respondents are much less likely to report problems related to communicative competence, whether grammatical or sociolinguistic, in synchronous chat contexts.

6.5.1.2 Email

The email data are a mirror image of the synchronous chat data. There is an unsurprising lack of concern with speed or fluid discourse dynamics, and also *non-standard language* has a strong negative residual, suggesting that emails tend to contain more standardized language forms. The most disproportionately common theme is *sociolinguistic competence*. This is probably in large part due to concern with formal email elements and structures, which were a commonly voiced issue. The need for longer discursive forms of writing in email along with the potentially high-stakes nature of some email interaction is perhaps behind the concern with *grammatical competence*, while *discourse competence* incorporates difficulties with coherence and cohesion. The position of the *production* theme is due in large part to a preoccupation with *form* (in the sense of discourse structure), a sub-theme within *production* which has a positive residual of 12.18 in email. Many respondents reported difficulty with the structural aspects of email writing.

6.5.1.3 Instant messaging

Respondents are most concerned with *non-standard language* in IM interaction, even more so than in chat rooms. This may be due to a higher level of non-standard language in IM in comparison with chat

Table 6.1 Problem themes, listed by degree of prominence in each form of CMC surveyed

Chat		Email		IM		Discussing posts	
Discourse dynamics	14.33	Sociolinguistic competence	19.35	Non-standard language	7.53	Conveying meaning	7.35
Don't do it	9.08	Grammatical competence	9.52	Lack of exposure	4.29	Topic	6.77
Cognitive load	6.93	Vocabulary	3.70	Not difficult	3.75	Impression management	4.50
Non-standard language	3.86	Discourse competence	3.09	Technical issues	2.56	Comprehension	3.66
Intrapersonal issues	2.89	Production	2.89	Resources	2.18	Intrapersonal issues	2.90
Comprehension	1.99	Orthography	1.41	Orthography	2.17	Native-speaker advantage	2.04
Strategic competence	0.91	Lack of exposure	0.77	Language learning	1.85	Vocabulary	1.66
Technical issues	0.70	Technical issues	-0.09	Don't do it	1.15	Non-standard language	1.55
Language learning	0.55	Translanguaging	-0.11	Strategic competence	1.09	Resources	1.25
Translanguaging	0.25	Topic	-0.15	Native-speaker advantage	0.77	Discourse competence	0.97
Production	0.04	Resources	-0.46	Translanguaging	0.56	Production	-0.12
Native-speaker advantage	-0.26	Strategic competence	-1.34	Discourse dynamics	0.56	Not difficult	-0.32
Lack of exposure	-0.35	Language learning	-1.42	Cognitive load	0.51	Strategic competence	-0.48
Orthography	-0.60	Not difficult	-1.77	Vocabulary	0.14	Translanguaging	-0.54
Not difficult	-0.92	Native-speaker advantage	-2.44	Conveying meaning	-0.23	Language learning	-0.56
Impression management	-1.33	Conveying meaning	-2.55	Impression management	-0.75	Grammatical competence	-0.62
Resources	-2.52	Impression management	-3.15	Discourse competence	-2.27	Don't do it	-1.38
Discourse competence	-3.22	Comprehension	-3.68	Grammatical competence	-2.43	Orthography	-2.56
Topic	-3.76	Intrapersonal issues	-4.28	Intrapersonal issues	-2.45	Technical issues	-2.73
Conveying meaning	-5.08	Cognitive load	-4.44	Comprehension	-2.83	Cognitive load	-3.88
Vocabulary	-5.74	Don't do it	-9.77	Production	-4.09	Lack of exposure	-3.93
Grammatical competence	-8.06	Non-standard language	-11.61	Sociolinguistic competence	-4.99	Discourse dynamics	-4.24
Sociolinguistic competence	-12.89	Discourse dynamics	-12.87	Topic	-5.13	Sociolinguistic competence	-6.29

Note: Values are adjusted standardized residuals, showing the difference of the observed value from that which would be expected if themes were distributed uniformly across files.

rooms, or it may be due to chat room users being more comfortable with such language. *Lack of exposure* is also disproportionately represented, suggesting that, of the four modes, IM is most likely to be used to keep in touch with acquaintances in offline networks, in which respondents' L1 may predominate. This hypothesis is supported by the notable unimportance in the IM data of sociolinguistic competence, which suggests that respondents' IM interactions tend to be with acquainted interlocutors, with low levels of social distance. *Technical issues* is more likely to be mentioned in IM than the other three modes. Closer inspection shows that this is due to the prominence of the sub-theme *auto-correct* (positive residual 5.32), which potentially suggests that IM is more likely to be used on mobile devices. It is notable that issues of *discourse dynamics* are not of great importance in the IM data, having a modest negative residual score. This suggests that IM is a less pressurized context than chat, despite both being generally regarded as synchronous modes of CMC, and it supports the decision taken in this book to speak of *expectations of synchronicity*, rather than simply classifying according to technical affordance.

6.5.1.4 Discussion forums

It is in these discursive contexts that problems of conveying precise meanings are most commonly found. The themes of *conveying meaning* and *topic* are prevalent here, suggesting users in these spaces are trying to accurately make their point, and that background knowledge is important. Within *conveying meaning*, *stance* is a particularly prominent sub-theme (positive residual 7.36), attesting to the evaluative nature of these forums. The position of *impression management* and *intrapersonal issues* is indicative of the public-facing nature of these spaces, in which the participant structure includes 'bystanders', who are not directly involved in the interaction but nevertheless are witness to it (Goffman, 1981: 132). Respondents seem to feel their identities are an integral component of interaction in these spaces.

In summary, there are predictable types of variation between CMC modes: the difficulty of email writing lies in structure and complexity, while that of synchronous chat is more concerned with keeping pace with a rapidly unfolding discussion. Other forms of variation confirm findings from previous research, such as the observation that IM seems to be used predominantly to maintain existing relationships, rather than communicate with strangers. Other forms of variation are less predictable: IM is less pressurized than chat, with speed being less of a factor, despite technological equivalence between the two. Finally, comment threads and DFs seem to be where respondents feel most keenly the desire to convey very precisely their intended meanings, and in which their very identities are at stake.

6.5.2 Demographic variables

6.5.2.1 Age

There are few strong effects of age on the distribution of problem types (see Table 6.2). There appears to be a spike in concerns with communicative, especially sociolinguistic, competence among 22–29 year olds, with a corresponding drop among older respondents. This is curious for not being present at all in the 18–21 group. Possibly, it is related to entry into the workforce, and the corresponding introduction to electronic communication in which appropriate formality becomes important. This corroborates a finding discussed in Chapter 4, that work email and work IM are frequently engaged with in the 22–29 age group, and that, while work email remains frequent in higher age groups, work IM drops to lower frequency from age 30 onwards. Taken together, these findings may be indicative of an increase in EL2 CMC used for work purposes, with younger people more likely adopters.

There is an increasing positive residual score for the theme *don't do it* as age increases, paralleling similar findings elsewhere. There is a moderate negative residual score for *spelling* among 18–21 year olds, potentially reflecting the more informal contexts in which younger respondents use their English.

Table 6.2 Problem themes across age groups

	Respondent Age						
	18-21	22-29	30-39	40-49	50-59	60-69	70-79
Cognitive load	-0.10	1.82	-1.78	0.70	-0.68	-1.42	-1.11
Comprehension	-0.21	0.79	-0.51	0.79	-1.00	-0.55	-1.29
Conveying meaning	-0.87	1.18	1.29	-1.71	-0.96	-0.16	-0.81
Discourse competence	0.22	1.07	-0.39	-0.26	-0.51	-1.88	-0.60
Discourse dynamics	-1.53	0.25	0.26	1.96	-0.39	0.33	-0.34
Don't do it	-4.10	-4.61	1.56	4.70	5.83	7.14	7.25
Grammatical competence	-1.97	1.90	0.72	1.37	-2.44	-1.41	-0.53
Impression management	-0.56	0.15	0.66	-0.81	1.34	0.20	-0.88
Intrapersonal issues	0.21	0.36	-0.93	-0.20	-0.52	1.18	-0.64
Lack of exposure	-0.98	0.57	-0.71	1.60	-0.56	-0.67	3.90
Language learning	1.61	0.11	-1.37	-0.30	0.48	-1.74	-0.56
Native-speaker advantage	-1.47	0.79	0.66	0.09	0.43	0.07	-0.95
Non-standard language	-1.94	-0.09	1.73	0.26	-0.31	1.84	-0.63
Not difficult	0.01	-0.26	0.39	0.11	-0.51	-0.28	1.07
Orthography	-2.91	-0.40	2.11	2.25	0.73	-0.03	1.22
Production	0.20	1.25	0.00	-1.83	-1.24	0.24	-1.87
Resources	-1.15	1.07	-0.96	0.61	2.12	-0.64	0.82
Sociolinguistic competence	0.20	3.37	0.29	-2.36	-3.34	-3.36	-2.11
Strategic competence	0.84	-0.38	-1.37	0.01	2.06	-0.05	-0.33
Technical issues	-0.59	-1.07	-0.23	1.42	1.28	1.13	2.30
Topic	-0.97	1.31	-0.46	-0.14	-0.57	0.38	0.08
Translanguaging	-0.30	-0.81	0.81	0.76	1.81	-0.93	-0.24
Vocabulary	0.86	-0.40	-0.83	0.75	-0.87	0.74	-1.76

Note: See Table 6.1 for a description of cell values.

Table 6.3 Problem themes across language proficiency levels (listed in order of prominence at post-beginner level)

	Respondent English level (self-reported)			
	Post-beginner	Lower Intermediate	Intermediate	Upper Intermediate +
Vocabulary	8.93	7.69	2.38	-8.91
Grammatical competence	4.26	5.66	1.50	-5.85
Translanguaging	3.74	2.09	0.18	-2.85
Lack of exposure	3.49	3.47	-0.23	-3.16
Comprehension	3.32	3.53	-0.73	-2.38
Don't do it	2.36	2.58	-1.45	-0.90
Resources	0.84	1.08	0.83	-1.75
Technical issues	0.63	-0.96	-0.80	0.97
Intrapersonal issues	0.54	0.68	0.95	-1.51
Not difficult	0.45	3.32	-0.22	-1.94
Strategic competence	0.42	0.77	-1.08	0.39
Discourse dynamics	-0.32	1.28	0.24	-0.78
Discourse competence	-0.42	-1.59	1.46	-0.50
Language learning	-0.59	0.13	-0.16	0.30
Cognitive load	-0.66	1.58	-0.86	0.22
Conveying meaning	-0.67	1.38	2.30	-2.69
Orthography	-0.69	-0.62	-0.15	0.73
Impression management	-1.36	-0.37	-0.75	1.38
Native-speaker advantage	-1.78	-2.50	0.64	1.31
Production	-1.84	-0.78	1.17	0.01
Topic	-2.71	0.55	0.92	-0.15
Non-standard language	-3.45	-2.50	-1.32	3.89
Sociolinguistic competence	-3.95	-2.93	0.19	2.96

6.5.2.2 Level

There is a clear tendency for lower-level learners to be preoccupied by concerns with basic language skills and grammatical competence, and much less likely to report problems related to sociolinguistic competence. The inverse is true of high-level learners (see Table 6.3).

6.5.2.3 Location

The largest effects of location are seen in dominant and institutional countries (see Table 6.4). The former are more likely to report problems associated with non-standard language, orthography/spelling and an awareness of their audience. Respondents located in institutional contexts are much less concerned with these aspects of interaction and are more likely to report problems relating to grammatical competence.

Table 6.4 Problem themes, listed by degree of prominence in each geosocial language learning context

Dominant		Co-existing		Institutional		External	
Non-standard language	3.88	Impression management	1.24	Grammatical competence	4.20	Lack of exposure	1.65
Orthography	3.51	Discourse competence	0.94	Vocabulary	3.53	Discourse dynamics	1.13
Don't do it	2.91	Grammatical competence	0.93	Production	1.60	Sociolinguistic competence	0.87
Technical issues	1.89	Orthography	0.76	Technical issues	1.04	Resources	0.87
Sociolinguistic competence	1.05	Translanguaging	0.75	Strategic competence	0.65	Non-standard language	0.65
Impression management	1.01	Intrapersonal issues	0.31	Orthography	0.54	Language learning	0.64
Topic	0.86	Native-speaker advantage	0.26	Intrapersonal issues	0.38	Native-speaker advantage	0.58
Comprehension	0.54	Not difficult	-0.04	Conveying meaning	0.07	Don't do it	0.51
Discourse dynamics	0.49	Comprehension	-0.11	Comprehension	-0.23	Not difficult	0.50
Grammatical competence	0.30	Technical issues	-0.29	Impression management	-0.41	Discourse competence	0.50
Cognitive load	0.20	Conveying meaning	-0.36	Language learning	-0.71	Cognitive load	0.45
Native-speaker advantage	0.15	Discourse dynamics	-0.44	Topic	-0.71	Translanguaging	0.41
Discourse competence	-0.11	Production	-0.49	Not difficult	-0.76	Conveying meaning	0.14
Intrapersonal issues	-0.34	Strategic competence	-0.56	Translanguaging	-0.80	Topic	0.12
Conveying meaning	-0.54	Topic	-0.62	Cognitive load	-1.00	Strategic competence	0.07
Translanguaging	-0.95	Don't do it	-0.67	Resources	-1.38	Comprehension	-0.03
Not difficult	-1.07	Lack of exposure	-0.73	Discourse competence	-1.72	Intrapersonal issues	-0.09
Strategic competence	-1.12	Sociolinguistic competence	-0.91	Native-speaker advantage	-1.89	Production	-0.22
Resources	-1.18	Non-standard language	-0.94	Sociolinguistic competence	-2.81	Impression management	-0.22
Production	-1.23	Language learning	-0.94	Lack of exposure	-2.87	Vocabulary	-0.23
Language learning	-1.37	Resources	-1.26	Don't do it	-3.13	Technical issues	-0.80
Lack of exposure	-2.84	Cognitive load	-1.34	Discourse dynamics	-3.39	Orthography	-1.09
Vocabulary	-2.90	Vocabulary	-2.45	Non-standard language	-3.92	Grammatical competence	-1.61

6.6 Summary: Difficulties Encountered in EL2 CMC

This part of the questionnaire was designed to answer SQ3:

- SQ3: What forms or aspects of text-based online discourse do L2 English users find challenging?

This section has constructed EL2 CMC as a prototype activity system, and analyzed data provided by questionnaire respondents to show how the difficulties they report encountering when using their English online correspond to the different components of the system. The analysis has shown how these difficulties are symptomatic of contradictions that exist within and between activity system components.

The primary sense-forming motive of EL2 CMC interaction has been identified as the achievement of a form of co-constructed meaning, with respondents sensitive to the need for precision on their part to achieve this as intended, and the difficulty of using their L2 for this. This meaning is likely to include an element of stance, particularly in DF-type contexts in which stance may be the dominant form of meaning. This can be particularly problematic and indeed intimidating for EL2 users. Motives-stimuli include self-presentation, and, in a negative capacity, communication apprehension.

Language-learning motives are also present for some respondents, though whether these are to be regarded as sense-forming motives or motives-stimuli is debatable. The difference between the two types of motives is probably related to aspects of awareness and intentionality discussed in Chapter 2: sense-forming motives are the overt reason for the activity, while motives-stimuli provide affective feedback responses. Where EL2 users have no intention of engaging in learning, but nevertheless become aware of encountering and possibly retaining new language, this might be regarded as a motive-stimulus. Where EL2 users enter into interaction with the possibility of learning in mind, the learning might then be considered a sense-forming motive, secondary to the primary motive of meaning creation. Chapter 7 will discuss the possibilities for formal language learning to shift the learning motives of EL2 CMC from motives-stimuli to sense-forming.

The tools available to EL2 CMC users include L2, L1, language support resources and semiotic platform affordances. Respondents report difficulties with the difference between L2 as encountered in the digital wilds and L2 as taught in the classroom. This is a fundamental contradiction of linked activity systems which incorporate both learning activities and use activities, and overcoming it presents the possibility of more closely integrated systems which directly approach the contradiction and break down the barrier between 'authentic' language and 'classroom' language. This is discussed further in Chapter 8.

EL2 CMC users have a number of language support resources available to them, including print and digital dictionaries, spelling and grammar checkers, machine translation software and the web itself as an archive of language examples. However, contradictions sometimes exist between the use of these resources and adherence to the rules of interaction, especially where such rules require immediacy. It may be that formal learning can support EL2 users in these interactions by weaning them off such resources where they impede fluency, in much the same way that communicative approaches to language teaching might discourage the use of dictionaries in face-to-face conversation, promoting strategic alternatives.

The communities that EL2 CMC users find themselves in might consist of a wide variety of individuals, from many different geographical locations and sociocultural backgrounds. Interlocutors may be native or non-native users of English, and there seems to be a perception that native speakers 'know best', and an assumption that people who use unknown or opaque terms are native speakers to whom such usage comes naturally. The effect is to position EL2 users as subordinate members of the community, and this disempowerment can act as a negative motive-stimulus. Formal language teaching is in a position to help counter this by promoting alternative frameworks to the native/non-native dichotomy, and helping learners to explore other reasons for the emergence of non-standard language forms, beyond the idea that they are the domain of the native.

Community members interact within rules that are both technological and social. The social rules may be navigated with the help of sociolinguistic competence, and formal learning can help to equip EL2 users with strategies for inferring sociocultural norms in reduced cues environments. However, a contradiction may exist in various permutations within or between the rules, tools, community and division of labor, by which community members are enabled or perhaps even encouraged by technological affordances to flout socially derived rules of conduct, and refuse to cooperate in the co-construction of meaning.

The analysis presented in this chapter provides a valuable insight into the concerns of L2 users as they go about their digital business. These insights will be returned to in Chapter 8, in a discussion of the integration of EL2 CMC and formal language learning. Before that, and following on from many of the observations noted above regarding the difficulties of non-standard language, Chapter 7 explores the nature of language online, in a bid to understand how it may best be, if not tamed, then at least grabbed by the horns, in the classroom.

Notes

(1) Available at http://doi.org/10.17639/nott.7014

(2) https://www.statisticshowto.datasciencecentral.com/what-is-a-standardized-residuals/

7 Language Online: A Corpus Study

Language used online is multifaceted and dynamic. It resists attempts to define it in monolithic terms and shows the same degree of variation as does 'offline' language. Although statements can be, and have been, made regarding 'e-language' more broadly, an analysis which aims to support second language (L2) English users in specific contexts needs to examine the variation between computer-mediated communication (CMC) forms in closer detail, in order to understand the kinds of variation from standard language forms that EL2 CMC users might expect to encounter in a range of online situations.

Chapter 6 discussed the experiences of L2 English users in digital communication, noting the frustrations that many felt when trying to use their English online, due to the nature of the language they encountered in these spaces. Many survey respondents felt that their formal learning had not equipped them with the kinds of linguistic resources they needed to negotiate digital discourse domains. The goal of this book is to better understand how these L2 English users might be supported through formal learning, and prepared for life in the 'digital wilds'. Chapters 4 and 5 explored the communicative language activities of L2 English users online and drew conclusions regarding their learning needs. This chapter examines the (English) language itself used in online contexts, in order to understand how it differs from English more generally, and how it varies between different forms of CMC. In doing so, insights gained will be used to consider potential strategies that L2 English users can be taught to employ when using their English online, in order to maximize not only their potential for communicative interaction, but also the potential learning benefits arising from such encounters.

This chapter begins with an overview of computer-mediated discourse (CMD) analysis, with a particular focus on the ways in which online language has been compared in the past to spoken or written language. The approach to studying online language using corpus linguistics is then outlined in Sections 7.3–7.5, including a description of the corpora used for the analysis and their characteristics. Two phases of analysis are then presented in Sections 7.6 and 7.7, providing two different perspectives on the nature of language online. The final three sections discuss the findings in relation to instant messaging (IM), revisit the spoken/written dichotomy and conclude the chapter.

7.1 Computer-Mediated Discourse Analysis

The language of the internet has been a subject of research for several decades. Online language use has been investigated for its unique characteristics and its relationship to traditional forms of discourse, leading to the emergence of terms such as 'e-language' (Knight, 2015) and 'Netspeak' (Crystal, 2001). Herring (2001) coined the term computer-mediated discourse, revisiting it more recently to expand its scope to cover mobile devices (Herring & Androutsopoulos, 2015). The study of CMD is described as:

> a specialization within the broader interdisciplinary study of computer-mediated communication (CMC), distinguished by its focus on language and language use and by its use of methods of discourse analysis to address that focus.
>
> (Herring & Androutsopoulos, 2015: 127)

A particular question that has preoccupied researchers is whether CMD more closely resembles written or spoken language. Crystal (2001: 47) concludes that it 'has far more properties linking it to writing than to speech'; Baron (2010: 6) cites her own previous work in describing CMD in the 1990s as 'essentially a mixed modality', before the results of her empirical study of IM reveal 'a more spoken than written style' (Baron, 2010: 21) in her IM corpus. However, I would argue that this preoccupation with the spoken/written paradigm misses a key characteristic of language online and fails to acknowledge a key assumption behind the use of the term 'spoken'.

7.2 Digital Conversation: Speech, Writing or Something Else?

Developments in corpus linguistics in the 1980s and 1990s enabled the analysis of large data sets of naturally occurring speech, and the detailed description of the grammatical features of spoken language (Biber *et al.*, 1999; Carter & McCarthy, 2006). Some early work in this area is careful not to treat speech and writing dichotomously, allowing for register variation within each, and observing that some forms of writing have more in common with some forms of spoken language than with other written forms (Biber, 1988). However, as observed by Rühlemann (2006: 386), other prominent work in this field does not critically explore the nature of speech itself, and since it utilizes corpora composed mainly of *conversational* speech, the authors essentially conflate speech and conversation.

Carter and McCarthy (2015) acknowledge this critique, and accept that the form of language use they are concerned with describing is more precisely designated as 'conversation'. They further regard 'the global ubiquity of real-time, face-to-face conversations as the benchmark for a grammar of speaking' (Carter & McCarthy, 2015: 5).

Research into CMC has often explored whether language online bears more resemblance to spoken or written norms. Crystal (2006: 26) considers this 'the heart of the matter' in understanding the language of CMC. With a few exceptions, this research tends to reproduce the conflation of speech and conversation. Yates (1996: 33), for example, briefly notes that '[s]peech is produced "on the fly" and is intended to be consumed, heard, in the same rapid and dynamic manner'. Likewise, Baron (1998: 137) does not discuss what kind of speech she is referring to, but the list of its characteristics she proposes ('face to face', 'interpersonal', 'dialogue') clearly show it to be conversation.

The conflation of speech and conversation is understandable, given that, historically, conversation has always taken place through speech (with the important exception of sign languages), and that many other forms of speech that may be considered (wedding speech, lecture, television news report) involve a degree of planning, preparation and indeed scripting that renders them less archetypally 'spoken' (i.e. conversational). But that is the crucial point: it is not the orality of so-called spoken language that accounts for its grammatical variation, but its interactional dynamic – its conversationalness. Furthermore, technological developments have led us to the point at which speech is no longer the only available mode of conversation. We have reached the age of the written conversation.

Having established conversation, rather than orally produced language *per se*, as the object of interest in the spoken–written discussion, it is possible to revisit descriptions of 'spoken language' (i.e. conversational interaction) and apply them directly to CMC situations. A number of studies of spoken and written language provide descriptions of the characteristics of the two from a top-down perspective, theoretically considering the relevant interactional dynamics, which are then often compared with bottom-up analyses of corpus data to explore associated linguistic patterns. It is useful to revisit some of these frameworks to consider what they imply with regard to conversation without speech. Three frameworks are compared and synthesized, taken from Baron (1998: 137), Biber *et al.* (1999: 1038–1052) and Crystal (2006: 28–30). Baron and Crystal list dichotomous pairings of characteristics attributed to 'speech' and 'writing', with Baron's categorized into 'social dynamics', 'format', 'grammar' and 'style'. Biber *et al.* present their framework more discursively, with sections headed by statements of the form 'Conversation is…'. This format is reproduced in the following synthesis. The three works will be referred to by author's name only, to avoid excessive repetition, though in the case of Biber *et al.* page numbers are also provided, as the framework is spread across several pages.

7.2.1 Conversation is co-present

The three authors agree that conversation takes place between co-present, or face to face, interlocutors. Crystal (2006) qualifies this as 'usually present', which might be seen as a modification of Biber *et al.*'s (1999: 1042) assertion of a shared 'immediate physical context of time and space'. Telephony technologies removed the requirement of a shared context of space, and while the removal of visual cues reduces the richness of the information communicated, a conversation by telephone is still very much a conversation. Co-presence, then, refers most fundamentally to co-presence in time. Co-presence in time enables immediate feedback between interlocutors, which in turn increases the amount of knowledge that the speaker can assume is shared by their interlocutor. If this is over-estimated by the speaker, it can be quickly rectified by requests for clarification. Indeed, it is likely that speakers will err on the side of over-estimation rather than under-estimation, as the latter can result in appearing pedantic or patronizing. A further consequence of co-presence in time is that propositions can be presented in a linear, additive fashion, with the relationships between them clarified *post hoc*. The inability to do this in non-co-present communication necessitates a more careful structuring of information, which is achieved through the use of complex grammar and syntax.

7.2.2 Conversation is synchronous

An important consequence of interlocutors being co-present in time – indeed, a bald restatement of it – is that the interaction takes place in 'real time' (Biber *et al.*), with 'no time-lag between production and reception' (Crystal), in a 'spontaneous' format (Baron). All three frameworks use non-technical vocabulary to refer to this characteristic, but a suitable technical term might be found in *synchronicity*. It is informative to consider this designation in light of its widespread use as a categorical variable in the classification of forms of CMC. Chapter 2 discussed the use of synchronicity as a categorical variable in classificatory frameworks of CMC, and highlighted the inadequacy of treating it as a concrete, technologically determined platform characteristic. However, it might be considered a defining characteristic of conversationalness.

Bieswanger (2016: 281) shows differing levels of synchronicity at different phases of interactions on the same platform and, like Kalman and Rafaeli (2007), argues for the idea of 'synchronicity of use' rather than 'synchronicity of mode'. His analysis draws attention to the parallels between synchronous interaction online and spoken language. Many linguistic features considered typical of one, are in other research strands, considered typical of the other (Bieswanger, 2016: 286–287). If, as discussed above, the orality of spoken language is disregarded as its defining characteristic, then it becomes apparent that spoken language and synchronous chat are differently mediated manifestations of the same underlying process: conversational interaction. Synchronous online discourse is not 'spoken-like', it *is* spoken, in the sense that 'spoken' is conflated with 'conversational'. Synchronicity, like the spoken–written debate, becomes a matter of the degree to which any given interaction approaches the characteristics of conversation, because synchronicity is in itself an inherent characteristic of conversation.

Synchronicity goes beyond the 'togetherness-in-time' which is an aspect of co-presence. It is, as demonstrated by the definitions of general synchronicity described above, a coordinated movement through time with a 'common focus'. This movement through time gives rise to many other observed aspects of conversation: its linearity and ephemerality (Baron), the lack of time for planning and editing utterances (Crystal) and its flexible structuring.

7.2.3 Conversation is interactive

Given interlocutors co-located in (at least) time and acting in synchrony, a further related characteristic of conversation is that it is created by the interactivity between two or more people (what Baron [1998] refers to as 'dialogue'). The communicative act of a conversation cannot be produced by one person acting alone, as could the communicative act of, say, writing a newspaper article. The acknowledgement of this underlies Grice's (1975: 45) Cooperative Principle: that conversation is dependent on interlocutors acting together in good faith. A consequence of this interactivity in association with the time pressure of synchronicity creates a need for systems to manage the distribution of utterances through time, such as turn-taking (Sacks *et al.*, 1974). Interactivity is dependent on the characteristic of co-presence, as one interlocutor cannot cooperate with another if he or she is not present, or if there is some obstacle impeding the perception of his or her presence.

7.2.4 Conversation is contextually embedded

Another key characteristic of conversation is that it is 'contextualized' (Baron, 1998), taking place within a 'shared context' (Biber *et al.*, 1999: 1042). This context is present in the interaction as 'a large amount of specific social, cultural and institutional knowledge' (Biber *et al.*, 1999), which interlocutors can each assume the other has access to. This extends to objects apparent to all interlocutors, which can therefore be indicated gesturally, or using deictic language such as 'this' and 'that'; to people, who can be referred to with pronouns without respecifying the referent every time; and to places, which can become 'here' and 'there'. Perhaps the most fundamental aspect of context is the interlocutors themselves, who become 'I' or 'we' and 'you'. This accounts for another of Biber *et al.*'s (1999: 1044) characteristics: 'Conversation avoids elaboration or specification of meaning'. This is a result of being contextually embedded, together with a tendency toward parsimony: verbally elaborating something that is available contextually would be a violation of one of Grice's (1975: 45) maxims of quantity: 'Do not make your contribution more informative than is required'.

7.2.5 Conversation is interpersonal

The three frameworks all note the propensity of conversation to be expressive of interpersonal matters (Baron), social relationships (Crystal) or 'politeness, emotion, and attitude' (Biber *et al.*, 1999: 1047). Crystal's (2006: 29) observation that '[s]peech is very suited to social or "phatic" functions' might also be included under this characteristic. In a sense, however, the interpersonal nature of conversation is a function of its contextual embeddedness, in that it can respond quickly to the contextually provided shared information regarding the interlocutors and the situation. Interlocutors always know something about one another, and even when this knowledge is extremely minimal (such as merely: 'you work in this bank'), it functions to shape the interaction. The politeness aspect is a result of co-presence, with interlocutors anticipating potential threats to face (Brown & Levinson, 1987).

7.2.6 Speechless: Conversation in CMC

In spite of their focus on conversation rather than speech, the very first characteristic of conversation in Biber *et al.* (1999: 1041) is 'Conversation takes place in the spoken medium', which they regard as 'so obvious that it does not need labouring'. Although the goal in the present analysis is to dissociate speech from conversation in order to explore one without the other, it is not denied that the orality of speech is an important aspect in the understanding of transcriptions of spoken conversation. Intonation, stress, prosody, rate of speech, loudness and timbre all carry information in a spoken conversation (Biber *et al.*, 1999).

These functions of orality are not available to interlocutors in text-based conversations. For this reason, CMC is often regarded as a 'lean medium', less informationally rich than its spoken counterpart (Tanis & Postmes, 2003: 677). However, CMC has its own unique resource that face-to-face conversation does not: visual text. CMC users have proven to be enormously creative in the ways they manipulate written text to color their messages (Crystal, 2006, 2008). This is explored in detail in this chapter.

The extent to which the other characteristics of conversation are enabled by CMC platforms depends on their technological affordances.

Temporal co-presence and synchronicity are usually possible in most online forms of communication, assuming a good internet connection. Co-presence can be further enhanced by the use of feedback features seen in IM platforms in particular, including notifications that a message has been sent, received and read, and dynamic indicators showing that the other person is composing a message. These facilitate legitimate interactivity in CMC.

Just as in spoken conversation, the depth of contextually provided shared knowledge varies. In cases where interlocutors are unacquainted (such as chat rooms, or in text interaction with a customer services agent), it is true that the level of such knowledge is low. It is perhaps the lack of such knowledge, particularly knowledge of the interlocutors themselves, that leads to the notorious tendency for online interactions to be aggressive and antisocial in certain circumstances (Arminen *et al.*, 2016: 291).

This section has demonstrated that the concept of speech as it is present in many of the discussions that have taken place in the literature regarding the distinction between spoken and written language is more accurately described as conversation, with an assumption that conversation must be enacted through speech. Consequently, CMC, and particularly those forms of CMC that are regarded technologically as synchronous, is often described as 'speech-like'. However, if speech and conversation are dissociated, and speech regarded as just one possible medium by which to engage in conversational interaction, then it becomes possible to consider CMC to be an alternative to speech when engaging in conversation. The question then becomes not whether a given form of CMC is 'speech-like', but whether it facilitates, and is used for, conversational interaction. This is explored in the following analysis.

7.3 Corpus Analysis

The second research phase of the project sought to address RQ3 (see Section 1.6), exploring the nature of language used and encountered in CMC. The goal was to identify differences in the use of common language items in CMC as compared to the English language more generally, as well as to identify forms of typographic variance from general English use. The findings will subsequently be used in the discussion in Chapter 8 to suggest strategies with which EL2 CMC users can approach online interaction that maximize their participation in digital domains of discourse, and enhance the potential learning outcomes.

The corpus analysis aims to answer the following study questions:

- SQ5: In what ways are standard linguistic forms used differently in CMC than in general English?
- SQ6: What differences in language use can be observed between different forms of CMC?

- SQ7: What forms of non-standard typography are used in online discourse?

7.3.1 A brief introduction to corpora and corpus studies

Corpus approaches to the study of language enable researchers to examine features of language use across large volumes of text. Language corpora, in modern parlance, are digitized collections of pre-existing texts, often taken from a wide range of sources. Consequently, they can provide evidence of language as it has been used by real people, allowing researchers to move beyond personal intuition or small-scale observation when investigating language use. Corpus approaches do not seek to answer questions regarding what it is possible to say in a language, but rather what is, or has been, said by real language users. In consequence, sampling and representativeness are an important consideration in the compilation of a corpus and they carry implications for the kinds of conclusions that can be drawn from them.

As noted by Hunston (2002), a corpus itself is of little use, being nothing more than a collection of text files on a computer. Specialist computer software provides the capacity to interrogate the corpus and examine patterns of language use. This is made more sophisticated through the practice of annotation, adding metadata to the corpus files. Annotation may refer to the practices of *tagging* and *parsing*. Tagging refers to the inclusion of classifying data to the corpus files. These data can be of many kinds, such as the source of the data or the characteristics of the language users (Hunston, 2002: 18). Parsing refers to the practice of analyzing text into its constituent parts, such as clauses, phrases and words, along with parts of speech such as nouns, verbs, adjectives and adverbs, all which information can then be added to the text, at the level of the individual word. This can be done quickly and easily through the use of computerized algorithms whose accuracy is constantly being improved: the current benchmarks are around 97% accuracy.[1]

Corpus software provides two main kinds of functionality. The first is statistical analysis, based on the frequency of occurrence of words, word types or combinations of either. Ambiguities in the precise meaning of the term 'word' have led to a preference in statistical corpus studies for the term 'token' to apply to the smallest unit of a corpus.[2] Contracted forms such as *don't*, *I'll* are counted as two tokens. Corpora typically therefore contain more tokens than words, and tokens are used in statistical operations. The frequency of occurrence of any given item queried by the researcher can be normalized against the size of the corpus, given as the total number of tokens, and this value of relative frequency can be used as a point of comparison between different corpora or parts of the same corpus. Further statistical processes can quantify the tendency of words to occur together, a phenomenon known as collocation. However, these operations are not used in the current analysis, so are not discussed further here. Statistical corpus procedures enable corpora to be used for quantitative analysis.

The second major form of functionality of corpus software is to display instances of a given language form, in the limited context of the text immediately preceding and following it. These are referred to as concordance lines, and allow researchers to perform qualitative analysis of the language in the corpus, observing the patterns of use. This has led to the development of descriptions of language based on such usage patterns, for example the concept of pattern grammar (Hunston & Francis, 2000).

7.3.2 The corpora

An initial question faced by any corpus-based study is whether to construct a new, bespoke corpus, or to utilize an existing corpus which meets the needs of the study. Creating a new corpus can ensure that the researcher has greater control over the sources of data, allowing greater certainty that the sampling of the data, and its subsequent annotation, is fit for purpose. On the other hand, reusing an existing corpus creates continuity with prior scholarship, extracts further value from an asset which had considerable resources put into its creation and relieves the researcher of the time-consuming data collection process.

The Cambridge and Nottingham E-Language Corpus (CANELC) (Knight *et al.*, 2014) is a roughly 1 million-word corpus composed of data taken from five different forms of CMC: blogs, discussion boards, email, short messaging service (SMS) and Twitter. The email data is further divided into business email and personal email, though the two are not evenly represented, with business email constituting 69% of the email data. The data were collected in 2010–2011. Inspection of the corpus metadata provides a breakdown of its constituent CMC types, as shown in Table 7.1. The data are not globally representative: most contributors identify as British and are in their twenties for example (Knight *et al.*, 2014: 38). However, this study does not seek to make definitive statements about online English as a language variety, a goal that would be

Table 7.1 The composition of CANELC

Data type		Tokens	% of corpus
Blogs		3,13,650	24
Discussion boards		2,90,876	23
Email	Business	1,10,008	9
	Personal	49,658	4
SMS		1,27,475	10
Twitter		3,96,318	31
Total corpus		12,87,985	100

hampered by the composition of the corpus. For the purposes of observing forms of variation from broader norms, and providing evidence for the processes that might be behind such variation, the data are suitable. CANELC is therefore used as the primary data source for this research phase.

The goal of the CANELC project was to compile a corpus for the study of language in asynchronous communication online, and the corpus therefore contains no data from sources such as online chat rooms. The authors use a heuristic definition of synchronicity provided by Herring (2007: 13), which regards synchronous formats as those that 'require that users be logged on at the same time in order to send and receive messages'. By this definition, the five CMC forms share the attribute of asynchronicity. However, a more nuanced approach to the phenomenon, as discussed in Section 7.2, suggests that regarding synchronicity as a fixed property of a platform is misleading, and it is more useful to consider the range of degrees of synchronicity that a platform might enable. Both email and SMS can be used for the rapid exchange of brief messages which resembles a synchronous interaction. The same is true of IM, particularly mobile IM, in which the sender can be reasonably confident that the recipient will be aware of the message in a short space of time. In all these contexts, the degree of synchronicity can vary over the course of the interaction. This is relevant for the study of language in CMC, as it illustrates the potential inaccuracy of regarding emails as 'digital letters', governed by similar discourse conventions as their offline antecedents.

Blogs are perhaps the most truly asynchronous form of CMC in CANELC, but two phases of blog interaction should be distinguished: the initial post itself and the subsequent conversation in the comments section. The initial post tends to be written as a self-contained statement by the author, in a similar way to a magazine article. It engages dialogically with an imagined reader, but does not require reader contributions. This is in contrast with the initial post on a discussion board. The comments section of a blog can more closely resemble the discussion on a discussion board or forum, and have a higher level of dialogicality, and therefore temporality, than the initial blog post.

Interaction in chat rooms is typically located closer to the synchronous pole of the synchronicity continuum (and certainly regarded as a synchronous medium), though this is in part a function of the number of participants in the chat. In a chat interaction with only a handful of participants, where there is less risk of getting left behind, there may be a slower pace of message exchange and lower pressure to respond. Indeed, chat discourse has evolved specific linguistic forms to manage expectations of synchronicity.

If platform synchronicity is admitted to be an unsatisfactory variable by which to group forms of CMC, then it becomes difficult to see what the five components of the corpus have in common, or what single variety of language might be evidenced by its analysis as a whole. However, the current study seeks to go deeper than analysis of the corpus as a whole, observing points of difference between the six different subcorpora: blogs, discussion boards, business email, personal email, SMS and Twitter. For this purpose, CANELC provides a valuable source of data, with care and attention having been paid to its construction.

In order to provide evidence of CMC interaction closer to the synchronous end of the synchronicity continuum, the CANELC data are complemented by one of the few publicly available sources of data taken from chat rooms: the NPS Chat corpus (Forsyth & Martell, 2007). The corpus is composed of '475,000+ posts made by 3200+ users from five different age-oriented chat rooms at an Internet chat site' (Forsyth & Martell, 2007: 19). At 34,749 words, it is the smallest corpus being used, and significantly smaller than the largest (the tweets component of CANELC at 331,707 words). For the same reasons as those discussed above, however, this small size does not preclude drawing insights into the types of language variation that may arise in such high-speed, multi-party interaction.

7.3.3 Corpus techniques

The corpora were accessed and analyzed using the web-based platform SketchEngine, a comprehensive corpus analysis package[3] owned and operated by Lexical Computing. Access was provided by Cambridge University Press (CUP) to their proprietary corpora, held at a dedicated SketchEngine domain. The NPS Chat corpus was extracted from the data files of the Python library nltk (natural language toolkit, freely available with most distributions of the Python programming language), before being uploaded to SketchEngine as a user corpus.

7.3.4 A keyness approach

The corpus analysis is based in the first instance on the use of keyword lists. These are a means of comparing two corpora – a focal corpus and a reference corpus – to observe differences in the occurrence of items between the two. The approach utilizes the relative frequencies of items in each corpus, expressed as the number of occurrences per million (pm) tokens, to calculate a *keyness score* which indicates the prominence of terms in the focal corpus compared to the reference corpus. As discussed above, CANELC and the NPS Chat corpus were used as focal corpora, with the Cambridge International Corpus (CIC, of which CANELC is a subcorpus) used as the reference. The CIC is a large corpus (over 1.5 billion words) of general English, comprising data taken from 'newspapers, best-selling novels, non-fiction books on a wide range of topics, websites, magazines, junk mail, TV and radio programs, recordings of people's everyday conversations and many other sources'.[4] The CIC is used by CUP in the creation of English learning materials, including the Cambridge Dictionary. The CIC was felt to be a good baseline for a wide variety of English use, not confined to particular regional variations or registers.

The integral functionality of SketchEngine allows for the generation of keyword lists, comparing the focal corpus and reference corpus. The statistical method used by the software calculates a keyness score for any given item by adding a 'smoothing value' to the relative frequency of the item in each corpus, and dividing the resultant value of the focal corpus by that of the reference corpus.[5] This smoothing value is primarily intended to avoid the problems of dividing by zero, but it also has the effect of prioritizing more or less frequent words, by raising or lowering the value (Kilgarriff, 2009). This functionality is incorporated into the SketchEngine interface in the form of a slider which can be set at values of 0.1, 1, 10, 100, 1,000, 10,000, 100,000 or 1,000,000, with the lower values prioritizing rare words and vice versa. Using a low value produces a keyword list of more specialized vocabulary words, providing an indication of the semantic content of the corpus: the 'aboutness' of the texts comprising it (Bondi, 2010: 4). The low value also returns items which are specialized in the sense of non-standard typography, as these are inherently low frequency. The higher-frequency words prioritized by a higher smoothing value, on the other hand, can provide an insight into the way common function words are used differently in the focal corpus as compared to the reference corpus.

These mechanics were exploited for two different forms of keyword analysis which are discussed in the following sections.

7.4 Idiosyncratic Use of Common Language Items: Analyzing CANELC

The first keyword-based corpus analysis aimed to answer SQ5 and SQ6 using CANELC to explore how common language features are used differently in online discourse. The NPS Chat corpus was not used at this stage, as the high proportion of non-standard typography in the chat corpus meant that even a high smoothing value returned a list of non-standard terms. A keyword list was generated with a high smoothing value (10,000), producing a list of common words, which were nevertheless used with still greater frequency in CANELC. A keyness score cut-off threshold of 1 was arbitrarily chosen, resulting in a list of the top 40 keywords in CANELC. Raw and relative frequencies of each of the 40 items were obtained for each of the six subcorpora. These values were added to the keyword data, producing a datasheet as shown in Table 7.3. A data bar was added to the subcorpora relative frequency values for each keyword on the list to provide a visual indication of where each item was most commonly found.

Further corpus operations were carried out to investigate the usage of the different keywords on the list. Search queries were carried out using Corpus Query Language (CQL[6]) to show commonly co-occurring words or parts of speech; these data were frequently exported into Microsoft Excel for further processing and visualization. Concordancing was used to display the occurrences of a particular item in the corpus together with the text on either side of it in each case, in order to qualitatively explore different uses or senses of the item in question. In some cases, a sampling method was used to quantify the proportion of different senses of a particular item across the different subcorpora. In these cases, a random sample of 50 instances of the item was provided by SketchEngine's interface, which was then exported to Nvivo for qualitative coding and analysis. This method was derived from Hunston (2002: 50).

7.5 Non-Standard Typography

The second keyword-based corpus analysis aimed to answer SQ7, examining forms of non-standard typography in online discourse, utilizing both CANELC and the NPS Chat corpus. Keyword lists were generated for both corpora, using a low smoothing value (10). As this phase did not intend to explore each item on the list to the same level of detail as the first analysis, the top 200 items were used from each list. Both lists were exported to Nvivo for coding and analysis.

The rest of this chapter presents the results of these analyses. After a detailed analysis of both high-frequency and low-frequency items, a summary of the findings is presented, focusing on the different forms of CMC being studied, contextualizing the keyword analysis findings with observations regarding the typical interactional dynamics of the different platforms. This discussion is then extended to a form of CMC not present in the data or, therefore, the analysis: IM. As a dominant and growing form of CMC, the absence of IM data was regrettable, and to incorporate it into the discussion of SQ6, technological parallels are drawn between IM and mobile IM on the one hand, and other forms of CMC represented in the data. Based on this comparison, likely manifestations of the phenomena identified in the empirical analysis are discussed.

7.6 Keywords in CANELC

Table 7.2 shows the top 40 keywords in the CANELC corpus, together with their raw and relative (per million tokens) frequencies in CANELC and the CIC. The second column of Table 7.2 shows the keywords coded for grammatical word class. A brief overview of this list is given here, with some preliminary remarks, before a more detailed analysis in the following sections. As noted in previous CANELC studies, the majority of the keywords are function words, carrying grammatical rather than propositional meaning (Knight, 2015: 46). There are no nouns in the list,

Table 7.2 The top 40 keywords in CANELC, in reference to the CIC

		CANELC			CIC		
	Class	**Word**	**Freq**	**Freq/mil**	**Freq_ref**	**Freq_ref/mil**	**Score**
1	pronoun	I	20,779	16,182.7	11,764,776	6,162.1	1.6
2	pronoun	you	13,204	10,283.3	6,556,857	3,434.3	1.5
3	determiner	my	4,388	3,417.4	2,209,871	1,157.5	1.2
4	glyph	x	2,678	2,085.6	123,962	64.9	1.2
5	pronoun	me	3,718	2,895.6	1,695,348	888	1.2
6	pronoun	it	11,008	8,573	11,196,673	5,864.5	1.2
7	pronoun	i	2,099	1,634.7	319,378	167.3	1.1
8	negation morpheme	n't	5,008	3,900.2	4,191,101	2,195.2	1.1
9	pronoun	u	1,749	1,362.1	47,391	24.8	1.1
10	verb	do	4,405	3,430.6	3,535,680	1,851.9	1.1
11	determiner	your	3,182	2,478.1	1,958,119	1,025.6	1.1
12	conjunction	so	3,597	2,801.3	2,644,048	1,384.9	1.1
13	adverb	just	3,005	2,340.3	2,099,576	1,099.7	1.1
14	verb	get	2,646	2,060.7	1,679,876	879.9	1.1
15	conjunction	if	3,176	2,473.5	2,462,151	1,289.6	1.1
16	interjection	Hi	1,197	932.2	34,505	18.1	1.1
17	verb	am	1,563	1,217.3	591,507	309.8	1.1
18	adjective	good	2,006	1,562.3	1,247,445	653.4	1.1
19	pronoun	we	4,004	3,118.3	3,997,273	2,093.7	1.1
20	glyph	X	1,141	888.6	77,181	40.4	1.1
21	determiner	this	4,980	3,878.4	5,424,203	2,841.1	1.1
22	verb	know	2,073	1,614.5	1,445,245	757	1.1
23	verb	have	6,735	5,245.2	7,883,974	4,129.4	1.1
24	conjunction	but	4,632	3,607.4	5,030,480	2,634.8	1.1
25	verb	think	1,926	1,500	1,349,933	707.1	1.1
26	interjection	Thanks	992	772.6	69,692	36.5	1.1
27	verb/adverb	like	2,520	1,962.6	2,235,216	1,170.7	1.1
28	adverb	too	1,603	1,248.4	1,004,103	525.9	1.1
29	preposition	up	3,180	2,476.6	3,233,204	1,693.5	1.1
30	determiner	all	3,301	2,570.8	3,485,485	1,825.6	1.1
31	adverb	really	1,370	1,067	844,199	442.2	1.1
32	verb	see	1,615	1,257.8	1,228,848	643.6	1.1
33	verb	can	3,204	2,495.3	3,490,488	1,828.2	1.1
34	wh-	what	2,457	1,913.5	2,453,864	1,285.3	1.1
35	adverb	now	1,914	1,490.6	1,697,056	888.9	1.1
36	preposition	out	2,867	2,232.8	3,092,113	1,619.6	1.1

(Continued)

Table 7.2 (*Continued*)

		CANELC			CIC		
	Class	Word	Freq	Freq/mil	Freq_ref	Freq_ref/mil	Score
37	verb	got	1,258	979.7	837,898	438.9	1.1
38	verb	need	1,283	999.2	886,886	464.5	1.1
39	negation morpheme	n,Äôt	882	686.9	322,034	168.7	1.1
40	conjunction	then	1,712	1,333.3	1,514,379	793.2	1.1

and while verbs are the largest group, they are very high-frequency verbs such as 'think' and 'know', or 'pro-verbs' (Leech, 2000: 694) such as 'do' and 'get', which are used in conversational interaction to refer to a wide variety of processes.

While verbs are the most common word type, the type with the highest keyness values are pronouns, which are clustered at the top of the table in the most prominent positions. Six of the eight pronouns are personal pronouns, with 'I' and 'you' sitting in the top two spots. The prominence of these pronouns has previously been noted as a characteristic of spoken language (Biber *et al.*, 1999: 1043; Knight *et al.*, 2014: 46; Leech, 2000: 694), which in turn has been used to argue that language online is more closely akin to spoken than written language in nature. Certainly, they are typical of the kind of conversational interaction which has historically been associated with speech. Using personal pronouns creates personal deixis, a linguistic function that serves to 'point' to people relevant to the interaction, and to establish the roles and positions of the speaker ('I'), the addressee ('you') and others ('they') (Rühlemann & Donnell, 2014: 337). Personal deixis is also created through the use of possessive adjectives, such as 'my' and 'your'. For this reason, these words, initially coded as determiners, are more usefully grouped with the pronouns, creating a category of 'deictic markers' that accounts for eight of the first 11 items on the keyword list.

In the adverbs group, 'just' and 'now' suggest time-oriented functions. 'Too' and 'really' share an intensifying function, while 'too' also functions to create inclusion. 'Really' has been observed to be especially prevalent among younger English users, in comparison with the near-synonymous 'very' (Ito & Tagliamonte, 2003: 276). 'Very' does appear on the CANELC keyword list, but much lower down in 92nd place. This may be an indication of a more youth-oriented vernacular online.

Following the inclusion of 'my' and 'your' in the deictic markers group, 'good' is the sole remaining adjective in the top 40 keywords. This is a very high-frequency word with a clear evaluative meaning, as well as a potential back-channel function.

There are three items on the list classed as conjunctions: 'if', 'so' and 'but'. 'So' and 'but' are coordinating conjunctions, used to build paratactic grammatical structures by connecting clauses of equal status.

Increased use of parataxis is a characteristic of the kind of spontaneous language use typical of speech (Leech, 2000: 700). 'If' introduces a dependent clause, creating hypotactic (hierarchical) clause relations. In general, this is more typical of written language, but 'if' might be considered a special case, given the universality of conditional constructions. In these contexts, 'if' is frequently partnered with 'then', which also appears on the keyword list, but with a rather lower relative frequency (1333.3 pm, compared to the 2473.5 pm of 'if'). In most cases, the 'then' can be omitted from conditional constructions without creating ambiguity, which may explain this disparity.

The 'other' group contains word classes with only one or two instances. It includes the interjections 'Hi' and 'Thanks', the prepositions 'up' and 'out', the wh- question word 'what' and the letter 'x', a glyph representing a kiss, in both lower and upper case. Finally, the other category includes the negational particle 'n't', in two typographic variants. The inclusion of this item on the list is a consequence of the mechanics of the corpus treating, for example, the word 'can't' as two tokens: 'ca' and 'n't'. 'N't' can therefore appear as part of many different negative auxiliary verb forms: can't, couldn't, don't, didn't, won't, wouldn't, shan't, shouldn't, haven't and hadn't. While this ubiquity could be seen as skewing the data and overrepresenting the particle, its presence on the list speaks to the use of contracted forms in CMC, something which, again, is typically associated with spoken language (Leech, 2000: 698–699).

Each of these word class groupings will be explored in greater detail in the following sections, exploring their usage across the six subcorpora of CANELC. It should be noted that each item list is limited to the specific word form shown and excludes variants such as tenses of verbs, contracted forms or variants of capitalization. This has various implications for the analysis, which will be discussed as they arise. Table 7.3 shows the breakdown of the keywords across the subcorpora.

7.6.1 Deictic markers: Pronouns and possessives

While the CANELC data as a whole demonstrate elevated personal pronoun use as compared to the CIC, there is considerable variation among the six subcorpora, showing that this 'conversationalness' is not standard across all forms of CMC.

First- and second-person pronouns, with which the speaker refers to the self and the addressed other, have the highest keyness values (Table 7.2). First-person deixis takes different forms depending on the role of the self as subject or object – 'I' or 'me', respectively – while second-person deixis is achieved only through the form 'you'. The first personal subject pronoun 'I' has a relative frequency of >14,000 pm in all subcorpora, more than twice as common as in the CIC (6162.1 pm). It is most pervasive in personal email (24,628.46 pm), with discussion boards also considerably higher than the other four at 19,905.39 pm. However,

Table 7.3 Top 40 keywords for CANELC in reference to the CIC, showing distributions across subcorpora

		Blogs		Discussion boards		Business email		Personal email		SMS		Tweets	
	word	Freq	Freq/mil	Freq	Freq/mil	Freq	Freq/mil	Freq	Freq/mil	Freq	Freq/mil	Freq	Freq/mil
1 pronoun	I	4476	14270.68	5790	19905.39	1689	15353.43	1223	24628.46	1871	14677.39	5730	14458.09
2 pronoun	you	1811	5773.95	3406	11709.46	1705	15498.87	1002	20178.02	1843	14457.74	3437	8672.33
3 determiner	my	997	3178.70	1268	4359.25	115	1045.38	226	4551.13	603	4730.34	1179	2974.88
4 glyph	x	23	73.33	51	175.33	23	209.08	113	2275.56	2036	15971.76	432	1090.03
5 pronoun	me	639	2037.30	791	2719.37	387	3517.93	264	5316.36	703	5514.81	934	2356.69
6 pronoun	it	2729	8700.78	2946	10128.03	837	7608.54	504	10149.42	1098	8613.45	2894	7302.22
7 pronoun	i	12	38.26	709	2437.46	75	681.77	215	4329.61	875	6864.09	213	537.45
8 negation morphem	n't	694	2212.66	1654	5686.27	200	1818.05	252	5074.71	646	5067.66	1652	4168.37
9 pronoun	u	3	9.56	12	41.25	5	45.45	50	1006.89	1500	11767.01	179	451.66
10 verb	do	804	2563.37	1348	4634.28	336	3054.32	280	5638.57	546	4283.19	1091	2752.84
11 determiner	your	566	1804.56	1067	3668.23	304	2763.44	138	2779.01	346	2714.26	761	1920.18
12 conjunction	so	766	2442.21	902	3100.98	362	3290.67	271	5457.33	578	4534.22	718	1811.68
13 adverb	just	661	2107.44	827	2843.14	187	1699.88	142	2859.56	454	3561.48	734	1852.05
14 verb	get	452	1441.10	788	2709.06	237	2154.39	149	3000.52	425	3333.99	595	1501.32
15 conjunction	if	575	1833.25	940	3231.62	385	3499.75	244	4913.61	518	4063.54	514	1296.94
16 interjection	Hi	6	19.13	186	639.45	707	6426.81	75	1510.33	201	1576.78	22	55.51
17 verb	am	206	656.78	494	1698.32	126	1145.37	142	2859.56	257	2016.08	338	852.85
18 adjective	good	323	1029.81	462	1588.31	127	1154.46	100	2013.77	428	3357.52	566	1428.15
19 pronoun	we	883	2815.24	657	2258.69	947	8608.46	267	5376.78	412	3232.01	838	2114.46
20 glyph	X	19	60.58	5	17.19	21	190.90	13	261.79	986	7734.85	97	244.75
21 determiner	this	1347	4294.60	1122	3857.31	919	8353.94	234	4712.23	333	2612.28	1025	2586.31
22 verb	know	330	1052.13	368	1265.14	303	2754.35	152	3060.94	370	2902.53	550	1387.77
23 verb	have	1407	4485.89	1915	6583.56	994	9035.71	396	7974.55	729	5718.77	1294	3265.05
24 conjunction	but	1205	3841.86	1359	4672.09	363	3299.76	226	4551.13	490	3843.89	989	2495.47
25 verb	think	339	1080.82	533	1832.40	210	1908.95	143	2879.70	198	1553.25	503	1269.18
26 interjection	Thanks	28	89.27	129	443.49	391	3554.29	61	1228.40	122	957.05	261	658.56
27 verb/adverb	like	651	2075.56	619	2128.05	208	1890.77	118	2376.25	306	2400.47	618	1559.35
28 adverb	too	310	988.36	374	1285.77	71	645.41	76	1530.47	214	1678.76	558	1407.96
29 preposition	up	785	2502.79	782	2688.43	216	1963.49	176	3544.24	531	4165.52	690	1741.03
30 determiner	all	866	2761.04	878	3018.47	262	2381.64	202	4067.82	375	2941.75	718	1811.68
31 adverb	really	330	1052.13	392	1347.65	72	654.50	79	1590.88	169	1325.75	328	827.62
32 verb	see	331	1055.32	354	1217.01	184	1672.61	103	2074.19	230	1804.28	413	1042.09
33 verb	can	701	2234.98	849	2918.77	613	5572.32	186	3745.62	331	2596.59	524	1322.17
34 wh-	what	612	1951.22	804	2764.06	172	1563.52	114	2295.70	227	1780.74	528	1332.26
35 adverb	now	366	1166.91	480	1650.19	182	1654.43	66	1329.09	348	2729.95	472	1190.96
36 preposition	out	731	2330.62	777	2671.24	147	1336.27	109	2195.01	361	2831.93	742	1872.23
37 verb	got	240	765.18	251	862.91	37	336.34	65	1308.95	323	2533.83	342	862.94
38 verb	need	176	561.14	266	914.48	304	2763.44	63	1268.68	247	1937.63	227	572.77
39 negation morphem	n,Äôt	555	1769.49	141	484.74	87	790.85	34	684.68	33	258.87	32	80.74
40 conjunction	then	355	1131.83	503	1729.26	183	1663.52	109	2195.01	320	2510.30	242	610.62

The data bar in each cell shows the relative strength of each item across the subcorpora. This is applied to each row separately, and it does not allow for comparison between items.

if we include the orthographic variant ‘i’, SMS joins this first-person-focused group, with a relative frequency of 21,541.48 pm for ‘I’ and ‘i’ combined.

‘I’ (including ‘i’) is used in different ways in these three subcorpora. Table 7.4 shows the 10 most frequent items following the word ‘I’ in discussion boards, personal email and SMS, combining full and contracted forms. While ‘am’/‘’m’ and ‘have’/‘’ve’ remain stable at the top of the list, ‘will’/‘’ll’ and ‘would’/‘’d’ show variability, with ‘will’ appearing in second place in SMS, falling to third in personal email, before dropping down to seventh place in the discussion boards list. ‘Would’ mirrors this trend almost exactly, coming in at third place in discussion boards, before falling to fourth in personal email and down to eighth in SMS. ‘Was’ also shows variation, being most common in discussion boards (948.86 pm), then more common in SMS (651.20 pm) than in personal email (463.17 pm).

These results suggest that the ‘I’ in discussion boards is describing hypotheticals or bestowing advice (would) based on personal experience (have/was), while the ‘I’ in SMS is describing intentions for future acts (will). The ‘I’ in personal email is closer to that in SMS, but there is greater consideration of hypothetical situations or contingencies (would). ‘I’ in discussion boards is more past-present oriented, while ‘I’ in personal email and SMS is more present-future oriented.

Referring to the self as object, using the form ‘me’, is most common in personal email and SMS (fifth place in Table 7.2).

The second-person pronoun ‘you’ is strongest in personal email (20,178.02 pm), and comparatively weak in blogs (5773.95) and tweets (8672.33). While both these latter two scores are substantially higher than

Table 7.4 Ten most common words following 'I' in discussion boards, personal email and SMS

Discussion boards			**Personal email**			**SMS**		
Item	**Frequency**	**Rel freq**	**Item**	**Frequency**	**Rel freq**	**Item**	**Frequency**	**Rel freq**
am/m	784	2,695.31	am/m	213	4,289.34	am/m	531	4,165.52
have/ve	621	2,134.93	have/ve	141	2,839.42	will/ll	290	2,274.96
would/d	357	1,227.33	will/ll	105	2,114.46	have/ve	203	1,592.47
was	276	948.86	would/d	60	1,208.26	can	85	666.8
think	200	687.58	think	46	926.34	was	83	651.11
don't	181	622.26	don't	36	724.96	think	58	454.99
will/ll	168	577.57	can	35	704.82	know	51	400.08
had/d	145	498.49	was	23	463.17	would/d	44	345.17
can	133	457.24	hope	22	443.03	need	44	345.17
do	81	278.47	can't	21	422.89	don't	43	337.32

Note: Relative frequencies are per million tokens.

the relative frequency of 'you' in the CIC (3434.3), they are nevertheless indicative of a lower degree of personal addressivity in these forms of CMC. The connection between blogs and Twitter is apparent in the use of the term 'micro-blogging' to describe the communicative practice of tweeting (Zappavigna, 2011), and while Twitter is often regarded as forming part of a wider online 'conversation' (Goutte *et al.*, 2018), the findings here suggest that the interaction might not be as reciprocal as this would suggest. Likewise, Honeycutt and Herring (2009: 1) note that Twitter was not primarily designed for interpersonal interaction.

Use of the second-person subject pronoun in SMS increases dramatically when the abbreviated form 'u' is taken into account. The SMS data account for 1500 of the 1749 occurrences of 'u' in CANELC, and combining them with the full form 'you' brings the relative frequency up to 26,224.75 pm (combining the two forms in the other subcorpora makes little difference to the relative frequencies, and so is not reported). This demonstrates the degree to which SMS interactions are interpersonal in nature, and underlines the incongruity in regarding SMS as an asynchronous form of communication.

The CANELC data as a whole show greater use of first-person pronouns than of second-person pronouns, although this difference is less pronounced than in the reference corpus. This is shown in Figure 7.1. The same pattern is true, to a varying degree, of all the subcorpora with the notable exception of SMS, in which second-person pronouns dominate. The greatest difference is in blogs, in which you/u occurs with only 40% of the frequency of I/i. This is unsurprising, as blogs are addressed only to an imagined reader and adhere strongly to the perspective of the author. Discussion board interaction revolves around a given topic rather than either speaker or addressee: Table 7.3 shows that 'it' is used particularly

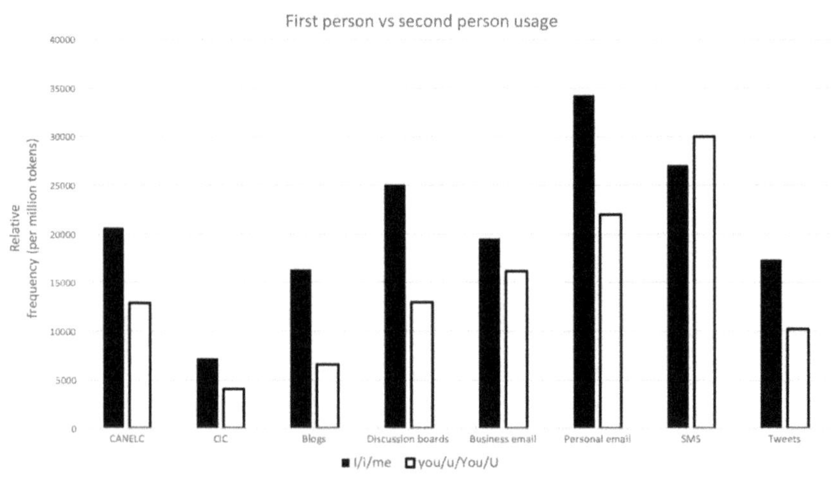

Figure 7.1 Comparing first- and second-person pronoun use

strongly in discussion boards, along with personal email. It is possible that the greater difference between first- and second-person pronouns is indicative of the distinction between interactive and broadcast formats.

The dominant use of second person over first person in SMS, together with the elevated use of the first-person object 'me', is indicative of a strong addressee-oriented function in this form of CMC. It may be that people are more likely to be motivated to send SMS messages by a desire to establish something in regard to the addressee, perhaps to make an enquiry or arrangement. However, given that the elevated use of 'me' in personal email is not reflected by a drop in the use of 'I', it may be that the SMS data are evidence of the use of syntactic forms which omit first-person pronouns.

Use of the possessive determiners 'my' and 'your' is consistent with the other forms of deixis discussed. 'My' is more prominent in discussion boards, personal email and SMS, while 'your' is particularly prominent in discussion boards, reflecting the advice-giving nature of interaction in these spaces, and is as relatively frequent in business email as in personal email and SMS. The lower use of 'my' and 'I' in business email is paralleled in a particularly high relative frequency of 'we' in this context. This suggests a style of language use in business contexts that foregrounds collective membership and responsibility.

Finally, in the group of deictic markers, the proximal demonstrative pronoun 'this' has a high relative frequency of 8353.94 pm in business email. To investigate this anomaly in relation to personal email, a random sample of 50 occurrences of 'this' in business email was taken and coded for the function fulfilled by the word 'this'. This procedure was then repeated with a similar sample from the personal email data. Codes were generated inductively, resulting in the following five categories:

(1) Temporal deixis: this accounted for occurrences of 'this week', 'this year', 'this morning', etc.
(2) Endophoric reference to a specific stretch within the same email message. For example: 'Me and the folks are not actually saying [*sic*] in Sheffield, we are just going up on the day for the ceremony so I would have no where to stay and no way of getting home in the morning. As well as this…'.
(3) Exophoric reference to the topic under discussion, or broader reason for the email exchange. This was applied in cases where 'this' was used to refer to something not explicitly stated in the same message.
(4) Exophoric reference to a link or attachment. This was coded when the word referred directly to an external object, rather than to an external object which had already been specified in preceding text, which was counted as function 3.
(5) Reference to the email itself.

Figure 7.2 shows the distribution of the five categories in personal and business email. Endophora, pointing to a specific stretch of text within the same message, accounts for the majority of uses in both forms of email. However, there is considerable variation among the other functions. Personal email is much more reliant on temporal deixis than is business email, presumably because the author is more concerned with plans and activities, and uses 'this' to locate them in time in relation to the moment of writing. Additionally, references to the message itself, such as 'I have an ulterior motive to this email' and 'please let me know as this email is just to gauge interest' are limited to personal email. Possibly statements of this nature might seem superfluous in business email, in which conciseness is often valued.

Exophoric references to the wider conversation or topic are more characteristic of business email. The following is a good example: 'Hi [Name], Do you have already some decision how should we deal with this situation?'. This usage suggests a rapid message exchange in which the author can be confident that the recipient, who had presumably sent a message pertaining to 'this situation' shortly before, would still have the information regarding it in mind, to the extent that it did not need restating. Such a degree of shared information between interlocutors is usually associated with spoken or conversational language: Leech (2000: 695) notes that 'Shared context means that generally there is no need to specify in detail the reference of linguistic expressions'. This casts doubt on the classification of email as a written-like, asynchronous mode of communication, demonstrating that it can facilitate conversational interaction.

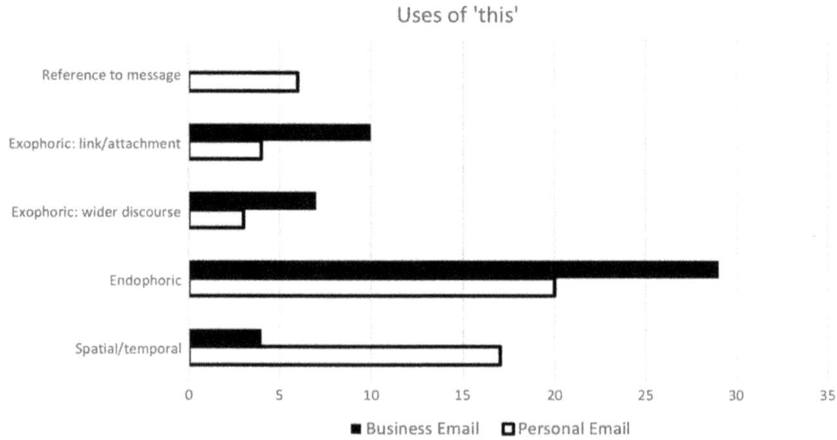

Figure 7.2 Uses of 'this' in business email and personal email

7.6.2 Verbs

The verbs that appear in the list of keywords are all high-frequency items which serve multiple functions, including non-verb functions in some cases. This multiplicity of function is particularly true of 'do', 'get' and 'have', which can be regarded as 'pro-verbs'. These can be used to refer to a wide range of processes, and their use is regarded as typical of conversational interaction (Leech, 2000: 694). Furthermore, 'do' and 'have' perform auxiliary, as well as lexical, verb functions. The flexibility of this group of verbs can be seen in their lengthy dictionary entries: the online Cambridge Dictionary[7] lists 59 different verb meanings of 'do', 'get' and 'have' combined. By contrast, 'think', 'know', 'see' and 'need' together have only 21 meanings. Both 'do' and 'get' appear most frequently in personal email, SMS and discussion boards, suggesting a 'shared context' element of these forms of CMC, as discussed above. 'Have' is strongest in business email, reflecting the formality of using the full form of the word, rather than the contracted ''ve'.

'Think', 'know' and 'see', all verbs of perception and cognition, are strongest in personal email. 'Need' has the highest relative frequency in business email, as does the modal verb 'can'. The two are related, in that the interrogative form of 'can' can be used to make requests for needed objects or services. The declarative form of 'can', on the other hand, expresses ability, constructing a professional image of competence. These two communicative functions might be considered central to business discourse. 'Can' is also typically associated with a more direct, potentially less polite register than 'could'.

Most of the verbs on the list appear in their base forms, and their high level of frequency is, at least in part, due to the wide range of structures in which base forms, or finite forms that are identical to the base form, are used. This is notably not so in the case of 'am', which appears in 17th place on the list with a relative frequency of 1217.3 pm. 'Am' is limited to first-person singular use, although the widespread auxiliary function of the verb 'to be' expands the range of its application. As discussed above, 'am' does not include the contracted form ''m', and as such it might be expected that it occurs in more formal, written-like contexts, as contraction is generally regarded as typical of informal and conversation language. However, the opposite is the case. 'Am' occurs most frequently in personal email and SMS, and to a lesser extent discussions boards. It is particularly weak in blogs and tweets, and only 40% as frequent in business email as in personal email.

In order to observe this use of 'am' in personal email and SMS, a random sample of 50 concordance lines was taken from both subcorpora, and each instance coded for the function of 'am'. In both cases, the majority of occurrences were in simple declarative statements, in which it was unclear why the writer chose the full, rather than contracted form. However, the SMS data also contained 10 instances of short answers: 'Yes, I am'. In this structure the 'am' cannot be contracted, but it also requires the same sort of conversational interaction with shared context discussed above, and would not be possible in truly asynchronous interaction. There were also nine instances in each sample of structures with subject ellipsis: 'Out of town starting Friday eve, but am up for stuff tonight', 'Also am gonna be around for a week in mid-July'. Subject ellipsis is a documented feature of conversational interaction, although it's difficult to say whether 'am' is used in place of 'I'm' in natural speech, since 'I'm' is frequently pronounced more like 'am' or 'ahm' in any case. It's possible that L2 users might find this form of subject ellipsis more difficult to understand in writing than other forms of subject ellipsis in which the ellipted element is more explicit, such as those given by Leech (2000: 694): 'Doesn't matter'; 'You want a double?'. Establishing this empirically is beyond the scope of this book, however.

'Like' is a versatile word with many different uses, some of which do not easily correspond to traditional grammatical word classes. CANELC contains 2520 instances of 'like', coded in four different ways by the automated tagging software (which is not 100% accurate). These are IN (preposition/subordinating conjunction), VV (verb, base form), VVP (verb, singular, present, non-third person) and JJ (adjective). Table 7.5 shows the distribution of these classifications across the six subcorpora.

For the most part, non-verb uses of 'like' predominate. The exception to this is in business email, in which there is a more frequent occurrence of the base form of the verb. Closer inspection of this shows that all but five instances of this usage are accounted for by the construction 'would like', used as a more indirect, and therefore polite, alternative to 'want'. This is a more formal aspect of business email. Closer inspection of concordance line samples suggests that the higher usage of 'like' in personal email and SMS is at least partly due to structures which reformulate and

Table 7.5 Classification and distribution of 'like' across subcorpora

	IN		VV		VVP		JJ	
	Freq	**Rel freq**	**Freq**	**Rel freq**	**Freq**	**Rel freq**	**Freq**	**Rel freq**
CANELC	1804	1400.64	351	272.52	308	239.13	57	44.26
Blogs	522	1664.28	50	159.41	63	200.86	16	51.01
DBs	456	1567.68	74	254.4	65	223.46	24	82.51
Business email	82	745.4	98	890.84	28	254.53	0	0
Personal email	67	1349.23	39	785.37	10	201.38	2	40.28
SMS	237	1859.19	28	219.65	36	282.41	5	39.22
Twitter	440	1110.22	62	156.44	106	267.46	10	25.23

evaluate information given in previous utterances: 'Sounds like a plan!', 'You're right, it does seem like they're exploiting you'.

7.6.3 Conjunctions

'So' and 'if' appear close together in the keyword list, in 12th and 15th place, respectively. Both are strongest in personal email and SMS. They are used to structure propositions based on causality and conditionality, and their use in personal email and SMS is consistent with other findings demonstrating the functionality of these platforms for discussing contingencies and making arrangements. 'Then' also falls into this category, often appearing together with 'if' in canonical conditional structures. It too is strongest in personal email (2195.01 pm) and SMS (2510.30 pm), but much weaker than 'so' and 'if', perhaps due to its tendency to be ellipted. 'But', which signals contradiction between propositions, is strongest in discussion boards (4672.09 pm), though almost as strong in personal email (4551,13 pm). This is consistent with the deliberative nature of discourse on discussion boards, in which interlocutors co-construct meaning through the sharing and comparing of information, and the identification of dissonance and inconsistency (Gunawardena *et al.*, 1997: 414).

7.6.4 Adverbs

'Just' is the most prominent adverb in the keyword list, appearing in 13th place with a relative frequency of 2340.3 pm. It is strongest in the SMS subcorpus by some margin: personal email is next, but at 2013.77 pm it is only 60% as relatively frequent in personal email as in SMS (3357.52 pm). Knight *et al.* (2013) identify 'just' as the most common (in CANELC) of a set of 'hedging' words, used to mitigate potential threats to face in interaction. They note that the need to do this is more strongly associated with formal, high-stakes interaction and regard the strong presence of 'just' in the SMS data as notably contrary to this theoretical assumption. However, they also note that 'just' has a number of different functions, not all of which are 'hedging' in nature, and call for a more qualitative approach to investigate this.

In response to this, it was decided to probe the different functions of 'just' in CANELC and compare their use across the subcorpora. To this end, a random sample of 50 concordance lines was taken from CANELC as a whole and from each subcorpus. Each use of 'just' was coded according to its function in the message. Where this was not immediately clear from the concordance line, the wider co-text was consulted in the corpus, although three occurrences proved unclear even then, and were coded as such.

The following four adverbial functions or meanings of 'just' were found in the data:

(1) 'Merely'. This is a down-toning function that disambiguates between potential interpretations of a previously invoked proposition, focusing on one which is in some way less complex than the alternatives. Perhaps the most concise and idiomatic manifestation of this is the phrase 'just kidding'. The speaker implies that the recipient may have been assuming literal truth to a previous utterance which would have had significant ramifications for the recipient's conception of the speaker; but no, a simpler alternative is true: it was 'merely' meant in jest. Other examples in the data include 'Just ask for local anaesthetic cream' (=you may have been assuming it would be complicated or difficult to get treatment) and 'I think people should just let the urban foxes get on with it' (=rather than some sort of active intervention, which may have been implied or inferred).
(2) 'A moment ago' (or perhaps 'immediately prior to the present moment'). This sense of 'just' functions to anchor the subsequent proposition to the moment of the utterance: 'I just finished my tea' (=I finished my tea immediately before writing this). It adds a sense of temporal awareness to the message. It is most unproblematically used with the past tense, as above, or present or past perfect tense: 'I have just finished my tea'. However, the data also contain uses of 'just', clearly with this meaning, but using the present continuous tense, or present tense copula verb: 'Just having food now', 'Im [sic] just at [Name]'s having a bacon buttie'. This suggests that this sense of 'just' functions not primarily to position the action *before* the message, but to emphasize the high degree of temporal proximity between the action and the message, to bring the speaker's immediate context to the forefront of the message. This reduces the physical and temporal separation of the participants, creating a sense of intimacy between sender and recipient.
(3) 'By a small margin'. This adds a sense that the subsequent proposition is close to the boundary of an alternative outcome: 'I arrived just after 12'.
(4) 'Precisely': 'Just what the doctor ordered!'.

Both Senses 1 and 2 can provide a hedging function. Sense 1 can be used to emphasize a lack of complexity in what is being asked of the recipient, or of the message itself, thereby downplaying the cognitive demands being placed on the recipient: 'If your guys could just upload a test file…', 'Just let me know you have confirmation', 'Just wanted to ask if this is a draft…'. Sense 2 can be used in a more specific sense, implying that something has occurred immediately prior to the message, thereby minimizing expectations of what can have been done in response to it: 'Just got your message…'. The sense of intimacy created by its use can augment the interpersonal aspect of the message. Neither sense is used exclusively for hedging, however; indeed, the intensifying function of 'just' noted by Knight *et al.* ('Just do it') is accomplished by the complexity reduction of Sense 1 (=doing it is less complex than thinking about it, planning it, weighing up the pros and cons, etc.).

Figure 7.3 shows the distribution of the four senses of 'just' in CANELC as a whole and across the six subcorpora. Sense 1 predominates generally, but this is especially so in the two email data sets. SMS and tweets show a contrary distribution, with Sense 2 marginally outweighing Sense 1. SMS is often regarded as being used for intimate interaction, and it appears that this sense of 'just' is a key mechanism in creating this intimacy. Use of 'now' performs a similar function, and like 'just', this is strongest in SMS (see Table 7.3).

Twitter is not normally regarded as being an intimate mode of discourse however, and a closer inspection of the concordance lines taken from the tweets subcorpus suggests that this sense of 'just' is used in connection with the stimulus which then prompts the user to tweet: 'I just went into YT to have a listen…', 'We've just seen an advert for bleach…', 'Just woken up'.

A final observation with regard to Figure 7.3 is that the majority of occurrences of Sense 3 are in blogs and discussion boards. This sense of 'just' provides a dramatic element to the text: '…along the corridors of Westminster, just in time to add another jab of pain to…' which adds color to longer textual forms such as these. However, given the very small numbers involved here, it is not possible to be confident of this association.

'Too' has two main functions, either expressing inclusion ('me too') or excessiveness ('too big'). These two functions map dependably on to phraseological patterns: the former occurs in a clause-final position, while the latter precedes an adjective or adverb. This allows for the two

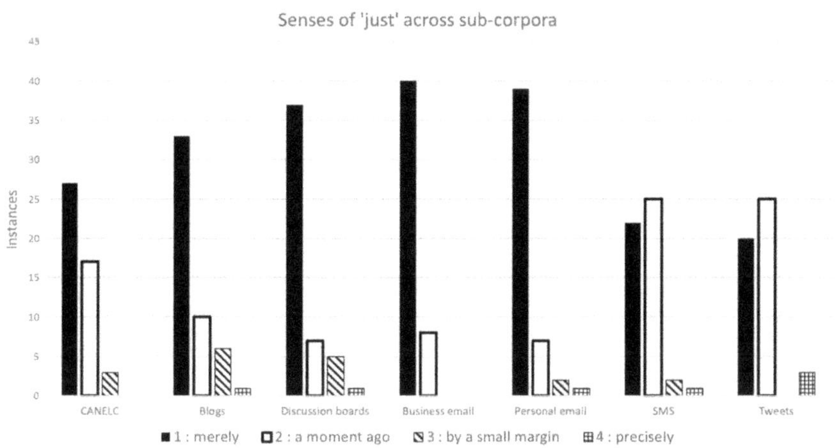

Figure 7.3 Distributions of the four senses of 'just' in samples of 50 concordance lines in CANELC and across the subcorpora

senses to be explored quantitatively. To investigate the uses of 'too' in CANELC and its subcorpora, a CQL query was run for [word='too'] []. This returned every instance of 'too' in the corpus, with the subsequent item also included in the node. A breakdown of the part-of-speech tags of the nodes was then inspected for manifestations of the two functions described above. Manual inspection showed that 'too + JJ' (adjective – 'too big'), 'too + RB' (adverb – 'too much') and 'too + VVN' (past participle verb, used in these cases as an adjective – 'too excited') all reliably returned instances of the inclusion sense of too. There were a larger number of items that accounted for the excessiveness sense, as a number of tags in the corpus can indicate clause-finality. The tag SENT covers sentence-final punctuation such as full stops and exclamation and question marks, while ':' and ',' also indicate clause finality. SYM refers to a number of different typographical symbols, including '@',[8] square brackets, 'x' used as a sign-off and multiples of question or exclamation marks ('!!!', '?!?'). There were 74 instances of this tag, and manual inspection showed 100% of them created clause finality in some way, and corresponded to the inclusion function of 'too'. Finally, prepositions, conjunctions, base-form verbs (most of which took the form of 'please') and proper nouns were all found to signal the inclusion function. A summary of these forms can be seen in Table 7.6. There were a number of other word forms on the list, but these did not reliably associate with one sense or other, and accounted for very few occurrences, so disregarding them was considered both necessary and justifiable.

The instances of these patterns were aggregated to provide a total frequency of each sense of too in CANELC and in each subcorpus. Figure 7.4 shows the proportions of each.

In the corpus as a whole the two senses are fairly evenly represented, with a small majority (53%–47%) in favor of the inclusion sense 'me too'. This varies across the subcorpora however, with the reverse being true

Table 7.6 Phraseological patterns associated with senses of 'too'

Inclusion: 'me too'		**Excessiveness: 'too big'**	
node tag	**gloss**	**node tag**	**gloss**
RB SENT	sentence-final punctuation	RB JJ	adjective
RB :	colon	RB RB	adverb
RB ,	comma	RB VVN	past participle verb
RB SYM	symbol		
RB IN	preposition		
RB CC	conjunction		
RB VV	base-form verb		
RB NP	proper noun		

Note: In each case the initial 'RB' refers to the word 'too'.

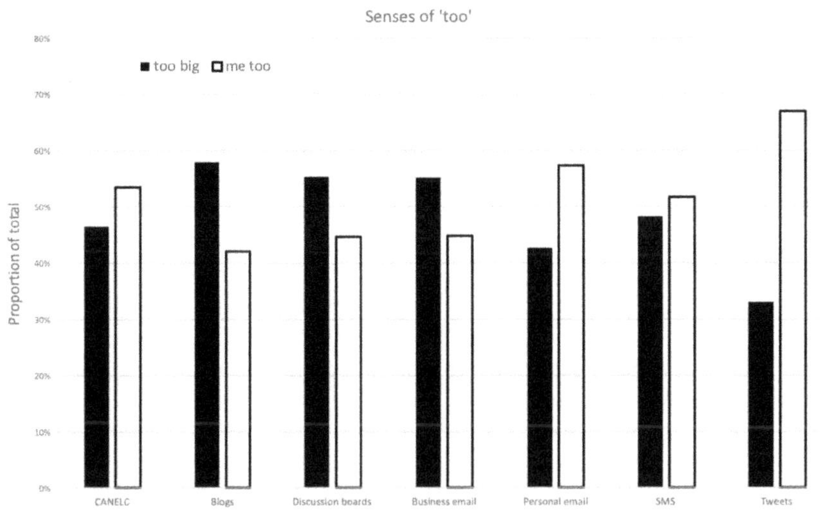

Figure 7.4 Proportions of the two senses of 'too'

of blogs, discussion boards and business email. The excessiveness sense is strongest in blogs, then discussion boards and business email, though these latter two show the lowest overall use of 'too' (see Table 7.3). It is intrinsically evaluative in nature, and negatively so: even something that is 'too good' is being evaluated negatively in some way, and it's negative ('not too bad') merely mitigates a negative evaluation, without reversing it. These findings suggest an inherent evaluative function to discourse in these forms of CMC.

The inclusion function is very strong in tweets, and this may be evidence of what has been called 'ambient affiliation' in Twitter discourse (Zappavigna, 2011), a process by which users employ various strategies to indicate their allegiance to different points of view. This too is an evaluative function, but works interpersonally: rather than explicitly evaluating some*thing*, the user indicates their support for or agreement with some*one*. However, the inclusive 'too' can be used to refer not to another person, but to another object in the same class. This distinction is less easy to detect through the kind of phraseological analysis used above: 'I like apples too' could mean 'as well as you' or 'as well as oranges'. Disambiguation is provided by context, or by word-stress in the case of speech (compare '*I* like apples, too' and 'I like *apples*, too'). Consequently, distinguishing between the two is not attempted here, but it would be interesting to explore how the intonational aspect of this is approached in text-based interaction.

The intensifying adverb 'really' is notably weak in business email and tweets, in relation to the other subcorpora. As noted above, 'really' is regarded as more spoken-like then the near-synonymous 'very', and consequently its presence in the keyword list might suggest that the language in CANELC as a whole is closer to the spoken than written end of a spoken–written spectrum. Its particularly low relative frequency in business email (654.5 pm) might be seen as corroborating this, if business email is assumed to be a more formal context than the other forms of CMC in the corpus. To test these hypotheses, the relative frequencies of both 'really' and 'very' were compared across the corpus (Figure 7.5).

The results show that 'very' is more frequent than 'really' in CANELC, in spite of the higher keyness score of the latter in comparison with the CIC. The margin between the two is smallest in blogs, discussion boards and business email, but the relative frequency of both is notably lower in business email. It's possible that the use of intensifiers is considered extraneous to the conciseness of workplace communication. The higher rate of 'really' in personal email and SMS is consistent with the assumption that these are more 'chatty' forms of CMC, while the opposite of this in tweets might be explained by the need for brevity in this character-limited medium: 'very' saves on two valuable characters over 'really'.

The presence of 'up' and 'out' on the keyword list is indicative of their frequent use in the construction phrasal verbs, which are characteristic of spoken-like language. 'All' is particularly strong in personal email, with a relative frequency of 4067.82 (202 occurrences). This is, to an extent, accounted for by the formulaic interpersonal expression 'Hope all is good/well' (20 occurrences), and by collectively addressing respondents: 'you all/we all/us all' (25 occurrences). This collective address is a reminder of the potential for one-to-many interaction in email. It is not as common in business email, in which there are only 10 occurrences

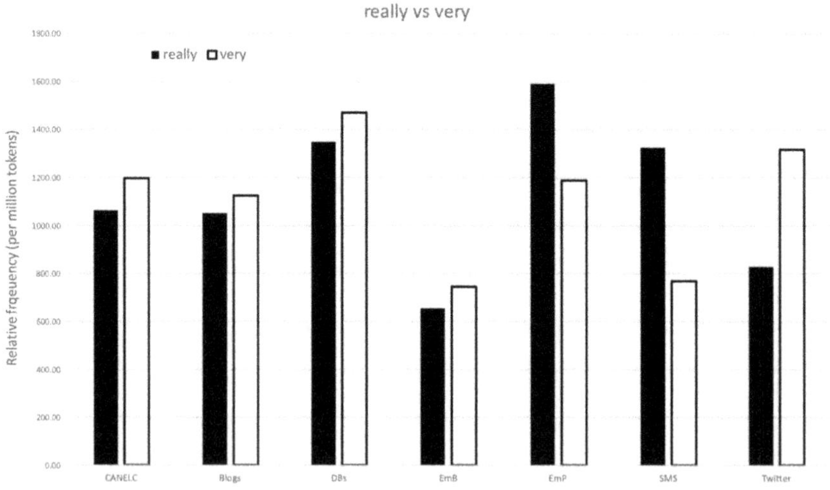

Figure 7.5 Relative frequency of 'really' and 'very'

of 'you/we/us all' in a data set more than twice as large as the personal email subcorpus. It seems that the sense of inclusiveness and familiarity which such collective addressivity creates is less likely to be appropriate in a business environment, in which professional relationships require the maintenance of a degree of distance.

7.6.5 Others

Other items on the keyword list include the opening/closing interjections 'Hi' and 'Thanks'. Particularly strong in business email, these are suggestive of an informal register which is not dependent on traditional structural elements of written communication. The symbolic use of x or X to represent a kiss is almost entirely limited to the SMS data and almost always in a message-final position, demonstrating the ubiquity of this as an informal, intimate sign-off (Knight *et al.*, 2014: 51). Finally, the sole remaining adjective 'good' is strongest in SMS (3357.52 pm). Closer inspection reveals that 124 of 428 occurrences of 'good' in SMS are part of idiomatic 'well-wishing' structures, such as 'Have a good one!' (31 occurrences) or 'Hope you had a good birthday'.

Finally, the contracted negation morpheme 'n't' demonstrates the widespread use of contracted forms in CMC, with the exceptions of blogs and business emails. It is particularly weak in the latter, having a lower relative frequency than in the reference corpus. Clearly, this is an aspect of informal language use that is not tolerated in electronic workplace communication.

7.7 Typographic Variation

The prominent presence of 'i' and 'u' in Table 7.2 suggests that non-standard typographic forms are common in CMC. They also represent two quite different processes of formation: while 'i' is a consequence of a tendency to ignore orthographic conventions of capitalization, 'u' involves the substitution of a single letter for a whole word, based on their identical phonology. 'i' is strongest in SMS, but is also strong in personal email, and with a significant presence in discussion boards. 'u', on the other hand, is almost entirely limited to SMS, where it has a relative frequency of 11,767.01 pm. Crystal (2008: 40) points out that this kind of ludic use of language is nothing new, but it was taken up with particular enthusiasm with the advent of SMS text messaging.

In order to investigate typographic variation in CMC more widely, another keyword list was generated, comparing CANELC and the CIC. The frequency threshold was set to 10, so that less frequent items would be prioritized. As discussed in Chapter 3, this returns items which are very specific to the corpus, rather than more general items which are used more often in the corpus than in the reference corpus. The top 200 items in the keyword list were then coded for the processes they represented.

Of the 200 items in the list, 64 were classified as typographically non-standard in one or more ways. Most cases involved several different processes.

To supplement the CANELC data and to provide evidence of typographical variation in highly synchronous online discourse, the same procedure described above was carried out using the NPS Chat corpus. In the resulting keyword list, 133 of the 200 items were classified as typographically non-standard in some way, suggesting a higher prevalence of this kind of linguistic behavior in chat room interaction. Table 7.7 shows the result of the coding, showing the form of variation, the number of instances in each of the two keyword lists and some examples.

Spoken forms are the most common category, and although these are classified as 'non-standard', they exist on a continuum of standardization. 'Yeah', 'hey' and 'wow' are widespread in their usage, while 'hiya' and 'howdy' are more restricted and perhaps indexical of certain regional identities.

Disregard for capitalization is common, although this is in part connected to the widespread use of initialisms. Given that standard (offline) practice is to use capital letters in the creation of initialisms,[9] online initialisms such as 'lmao' and 'brb' were classified as non-standard uses of capitalization. In these initialisms, lower case use is almost universal, but some variation and uncertainty still exist, as the forms 'Lol', 'LoL' and 'LOL' are found in addition to 'lol'. Some capitalization effects may be a consequence of technological factors, as the assistive language technologies built in to some platforms automatically engage upper case after a full stop and space. This is particularly true in the case of mobile platforms and is discussed further in a moment. Embracing a complete

Table 7.7 Forms of non-standard typography in CANELC

	NPS Chat	CANELC	Total	Examples
Spoken form	37	10	47	Howdy, hiya, nope, yeah
Capitalization	29	13	42	i, im, christmas, london
Initialism	27	8	35	lol, lmao, brb, asl
Back clipping	19	14	33	fab, prob, pic, hav, tho
Omitted punctuation	16	9	25	im, dont, thats, cant
Paralinguistic	13	8	21	haha, hehe, awww, hmmm
Phonetic representation	18	2	20	yer, da, gurls, prolly
Contraction	12	2	14	wanna, outta, sup
Lengthening	12	2	14	heyyy, hiii, ohhh
Phonetic representation	4	4	8	u, r, ur, cya
Vowel omission	1	5	6	pls, ppl, gd, yr
Spelling	5	1	6	hun, gurls, nite, kool
Front clipping	1	0	1	bout

disregard for capital letters may be part of becoming an established member in some online communities.

For the most part, the items classified as initialisms are formed from each word in a set phrase: 'Laughing My Ass Off', 'Write Back', 'Thank You', 'Be Right Back', etc. and as such are highly opaque to inexperienced users. Some, such as 'lol', have passed into wider language use, and are less difficult as a consequence. Many others, however, require an in-depth knowledge of chat room culture, or indeed of a specific chat community. This is as true for first language (L1) English speakers as for L2 speakers. Yus (2011: 24) observes that 'social groups on the Net ... exhibit jargons and assumed shared information that are only available to those users who belong to the group', and that part of the function of these jargons is to 'create discursive barriers of non-comprehensibility for non-members of the group'. However, the questionnaire data showed a tendency to attribute a lack of knowledge of these sorts of terms to non-native speaker status, and assume the group division is between native speakers and themselves. This is a direct consequence of discourses of native-speakerism that current approaches to English teaching often fail to challenge (Holliday, 2005: 15).

The category of omitted punctuation is realized in every case but one by an omitted apostrophe. Apostrophes are not essential to intelligibility in the majority of cases (Crystal, 2008: 18), though it is likely that their omission will cause a degree of confusion for L2 users who cannot be so confident that 'dont' or 'cant' are not hitherto unknown words. The single case of omitted punctuation which does not involve an apostrophe involves the omission of full stops between the letters 'ps', with the meaning 'postscript'. The decision was taken to classify this as omitted punctuation, but not to do so with the many other instances of initialisms. 'PS' stands apart from the other initialisms in having a much longer history of use and consequently much more standardized conventions surrounding it. It is notable too for its redundancy in an age when messages can be easily rewritten prior to sending: the postscript message could simply be worked into the body of a text if the writer chose. Using it is therefore a deliberate reference to its historic use, and its manipulation to fit typographic conventions of CMC is more marked than other initialisms which have emerged from the new patterns of discourse enabled by the technologies.

Typographical representation of paralinguistic vocal gestures is common, with various forms of laughter ('haha', 'hehe', 'hahaha') accounting for most occurrences. There are also instances of the common[10] 'thinking' sound 'hmmm'; sounds indicating a reaction to something cute or lovable: 'ahhh', 'awww'; and something which might either function as a vocal shrug, or as a generic question tag: 'huh'. These paralinguistic features are interesting because they continue to be used in spite of alternative forms of expression which have emerged for the very purpose of representing them, such as emoticons and initialisms. 'Haha' continues to be used alongside laughing-face emoticons and 'lol'.

Items were classed as phonetic representation when they were judged to be representing deliberately non-standard pronunciations. These include 'gurls', 'sup', 'da' (for 'the') and 'lil'. Many of these are opaque, although often not confined to online usage. Many are indexical of established subcultures: 'da' has been documented as an appropriation from African-American Vernacular English which is used to construct identity in reference to black American culture (Bucholtz, 1999: 456). This form of typographic manipulation has a long history, and was labelled 'eye-dialect' in 1925:

> The term 'eye dialect' was first coined in 1925 by George P. Krapp in The English Language in America (McArthur, 1998). The term was used to describe the phenomenon of unconventional spelling used to reproduce colloquial usage. When one encounters such spellings 'the convention violated is one of the eyes, and not of the ear'. Furthermore, eye dialect would be used by writers 'not to indicate a genuine difference in pronunciation, but the spelling is a friendly nudge to the reader, a knowing look which establishes a sympathetic sense of superiority between the author and reader as contrasted with the humble speaker of dialect'. While the phrase 'the humble speaker of dialect' may smack of prescriptivism to the modern reader, this passage is important, as it finally gives a term for a device that has been used in literature for centuries. Krapp was referring to spellings like enuff for 'enough', wimmin for 'women', animulz for 'animals' and numerous other examples in which the standard spelling of the word belies in some way its pronunciation.
>
> (Brett, 2009: 49)

Krapp's examples, though almost a century old, are still entirely relevant: *enuff* is exactly paralleled in the keyword list data in the form 'laffs', while 'cuz' (for cousin) and 'lez' (for lesbian) both show the same phonetic z-s substitution as *animulz*. Krapp's analysis shows that these forms are likely to be used, not by members of the communities whose speech is being represented, but by others indexing such communities for aesthetic effect.

A number of different techniques are present that contract or truncate words in some way. Back clipping removes tail-end components of words, and can be further analyzed into forms which omit syllables from words ('fab', 'prob', 'pic'), and forms which omit non-essential letters without affecting the hypothetical pronunciation ('tho', 'hav'). Front clipping removes initial word elements and is only present in the keyword lists in the form 'bout'. Vowel omission is a common way to shorten words that allows their meaning to be recovered more reliably than the removal of consonants (Crystal, 2008: 26–27). Examples in the keyword lists are 'ppl', 'pls', 'yr' and 'gd'. This is the only category in the data which occurs more often in CANELC than in the NPS Chat corpus. It may be that this stylization was popularized in SMS messaging, where the character limit made such space-saving measures necessary, but was not taken up to such an extent in chat contexts, where other forms of language play were prioritized.

Contractions, particularly written representations of contracted spoken forms, are often easily accessible for L1 speakers, who may be able to deduce the standard form from the transcribed spoken form, especially if they share membership of a speech community that uses the form. 'Wanna' and 'outta' are reasonably transparent, and in any case have passed into the wider language to an extent, particularly through pop culture ('Wannabe', 'Straight Outta Compton'). Contractions become more difficult when combined with other forms of typographical manipulation, as discussed below.

In addition to shortening words, lengthening is used to represent intonation and prosody. Often, the exact meaning will depend a great deal on context: 'heyy' might be intended flirtatiously, but this would need careful interpretation. In some instances, typographic difference is simply a case of alternative spelling, such as 'kool' or 'nite'.

Finally, the category of phonetic substitution contains forms in which a single letter (or indeed number, though there are no examples on the keyword lists) stands in for a syllable. The numbers 2 and 4 are often used in this way, in place of homophonic words, and in the data, the letters 'u', 'r' and 'c' appear with this function. It is not contraction or truncation, but complete substitution: it is entirely coincidental that the words 'you' and 'are' contain the letters which can be used to represent them, and this is not the case for 'see'. This is an ancient form of word play sometimes called a *rebus* (Crystal, 2008: 39–41). How accessible such forms are for L2 speakers will depend on how clearly delineated the parts of the 'puzzle' are: the form in the keyword list data 'cya' is not obvious at all, as the 'c' must be processed quite differently (as letter name, rather than phoneme), than the 'ya'.

This ludic use of typography was embraced by early users of SMS messaging as a means of maximizing message brevity that was both effective and fun. As noted above, such forms had existed for a long time as word games or puzzles. SMS presented an opportunity to use them for practical communication. Technological developments have since removed the practical need for such abbreviated forms. Predictive text 'solved' the problem of character-by-character input using multiple button presses. The seamless chaining together of multiple messages removed the pressure of the impending character limit, though this remained dependent on the details of the mobile phone tariff. The move to full QWERTY keyboards in personal digital assistants (PDAs) and ultimately smartphones removed still further the obstacle of inputting text on a numeric keypad (though typing on mobile devices must still be done using only two thumbs).

Nevertheless, typographic forms popularized through SMS remained, and indeed have spread to other forms of CMC in which they aren't 'necessary'. This can be seen by the presence of 'u' in the email data in CANELC (see Table 7.3). It may be that the use of forms such as these has become indexical of the intimacy and playfulness of a text message.

7.7.1 Combinations

Many items in the keyword lists show several different forms of mutation, and these are often some of the most opaque, due to being several steps removed from the standard versions. 'ima' is one of the more difficult items, showing processes of capitalization, contraction, omitted punctuation, phonetic representation and probably others, from the original form of 'I'm going to', via 'im gonna'. It is easy to see how intimidating such language use would appear to unprepared L2 speakers.

A very common usage which combines techniques is the form 'ur', either representing 'you are', 'you're' or 'your'. In the first case, it can be explained as a rebus, as described above: 'u' for 'you', 'r' for 'are'. However, in the case of the possessive 'your' the formation process is less clear. The first three letters are substituted for the 'u', but the vowel sound of 'your' is not the same as in 'you', and the 'r' in final position has, at least in standard British English, no intrinsic phonetic realization of its own. Even in rhotic varieties such as standard American English, the resulting implied phonetic sequence of /juɹ/ is not consistent with the pronunciation of the word (commonly /jɔɹ/, /jəɹ/ or /jʊəɹ/[11]). 'Ur' therefore seeks to work by using the 'r' to tell the reader to replace the 'u' with 'you', not phonetically, but typographically. This shows that these processes of typographic deformation and mutation can sometimes be applied loosely, relying on the reader's familiarity with the language to fill in the gaps. This is clearly more difficult for readers less familiar with the language.

However, it should be mentioned that these and other orthographic phenomena are not limited to English. All languages (or at least all languages with a written form) can and do play with their scripts in this way (Crystal, 2008: 123). Learners should be encouraged to explore how language is manipulated online in their L1 and how this compares with English.

Omitted punctuation, like capitalization, seems to be a standard characteristic of chat room interaction. It is consistent with an approach to written language that is unconcerned with norms, and seeks to replicate the informality of speech. Just as punctuation and capitalization are not apparent in spoken language, so they are disregarded in chat.

7.7.2 Summary: Conversationalness online

The analysis presented in this chapter demonstrates varying degrees of the dimensions of conversation discussed in Section 7.2. Despite being regarded by traditional classifications as asynchronous, all forms of CMC in CANELC except blogs demonstrated at least some characteristics of conversation. While some formats of CMC appear to be most purely conversational in nature, others show fundamental characteristics of conversation while differing in the application and manifestation of these characteristics.

Personal email and SMS messaging are the most conversational forms. Both show widespread use of personal deixis and ellipsis of non-essential parts of speech, indicative of a shared context between interlocutors (Section 7.2.4). They are present-future focused, and show signs of being used to make plans and arrangements, discussing potentialities and contingencies with conditional constructions. SMS in particular demonstrates a tendency to create intimacy, compensating for the lack of spatial co-presence by foregrounding the sender's physical context using frequent constructions with 'just'. Both SMS and personal email show signs of a strong sense of shared context between interlocutors, with a strong presence of pro-verbs such as 'do' and 'get', rather than more specific lexical verbs. They also show signs of interactivity: short messages with unelaborated responses to a question in a previous message: 'Yes I am'.

Business email shares many aspects of conversationalness with personal email and SMS, while also showing characteristics of language often regarded as more 'written-like'. Rapid, interactive message exchange depending on shared context is evidenced by the use of 'this' to refer to an ongoing subject of discussion. The informal opening and closing pair 'Hi' and 'Thanks', far more common than the traditional formulaic items used in written correspondence, demonstrate that displaying formality in this way is unnecessary. However, the conversation going on in business email tends toward concision and efficiency with language. Use of 'just' in its hedging capacity acts to play down the demands on the recipient's time expected by the sender, while a scarcity of the intensifiers 'really' and 'very' is suggestive of their perceived extraneousness. There is a mixture of levels of formality in the use of modal verbs: 'can' is used to make requests more often than 'could', but 'would like' is preferred to 'want'.

It seems that politeness in business email communication is a function of displaying respect for the time of one's interlocutor. The above characteristics function to communicate minimally and efficiently, mindful of the position of the message in relation to the recipient's other cognitive demands, in implicit observance of Leech's (1983: 132) Tact Maxim: 'minimize cost to other'.

A further characteristic of business email is the use of 'we' over 'I', creating a sense of collective agency and responsibility. It is also a form of politeness, downplaying the prominence of the individual sender.

Discussion board interaction is concerned with opinions and advice. It is strongly first-person oriented and topic focused, with 'I' and 'it' featuring prominently. Second-person deixis is less frequent, but still significantly stronger than in the reference corpus, indicating a degree of conversationalness. This is consistent with Bieswanger's (2016) finding of varying levels of synchronicity at different times over the development of a discussion thread. The frequency of the form 'I was' suggests the use of personal anecdotes, while the prominence of 'I would' coupled with the strength of 'your' is indicative of advice-giving. 'But' suggests deliberation or debate, while the frequency of 'too' signifying excessiveness has an evaluative function.

Despite being regarded as a form of online conversation, the Twitter data in CANELC have more in common with blogs than with SMS, email or even discussion boards. Personal pronoun use is comparatively low, and while this can, to an extent, be explained by the use of Twitter's @ addressivity function, this is better considered in comparison with proper noun use, rather than pronoun use. Indeed, the CANELC data support the characterization of Twitter as a 'microblogging' service: a broadcast medium in miniature, rather than a truly conversational platform. The strongest effects in the Twitter keyword data are seen with regard to the use of 'just' to indicate the 'trigger' that stimulates the tweet, as well as the use of inclusive 'too' to create ambient affiliation.

Non-standard typography is most commonly found in SMS messages and chat rooms. The overwhelming non-standardness of the language used in chat rooms is indicative of the highly phatic nature of communication in these spaces. Ludic language use seems to be a primary motivation for participation, and the development of opaque codes based on abbreviation seems to be a prime driver of the establishment of group identity. On the other hand, typographic representation of phonetic variation is used to index different aspects of individual identity. A general tendency to omit capitalization and punctuation in chat room discourse might suggest that this form of CMC is the most conversational of all, at least in the sense of spoken. Capital letters and apostrophes are written conventions with no equivalents in speech, and abandoning them might be seen as emulating speech in the written mode. However, it might be more accurate to characterize chat as an intensely ludic *form* of conversation, in which the co-construction of propositional meaning is relatively unimportant. The potential ambiguity introduced by omitting orthographic elements designed to provide clarification between forms and structure information is thus tolerated, and even welcomed as a source of language play.

7.8 Filling in the Gaps: Instant Messaging

CANELC does not contain any data taken from IM platforms, and no stand-alone corpus comparable to NPS Chat could be located. Consequently, this analysis has been unable to attest directly to the language used in IM. Nevertheless, extrapolating from the CANELC analysis, and utilizing existing knowledge regarding the characteristics of IM interaction, it is possible to make some predictions about the kinds of language learners can expect to encounter in IM.

The conversational nature of IM has been documented for some time. It has been described as a hybrid medium, 'incorporating, as it does, elements of spoken and written discourse' (Lewis & Fabos, 2005: 484). Its popularity was greatly enhanced by the development of IM apps for smartphones, such as current market leader WhatsApp.[12] Mobility greatly expanded the range of opportunity for IM interactions, but it also led to a blending of IM interaction with SMS. Indeed, WhatsApp's early growth was greatest in regions where prohibitively high SMS tariffs charged by mobile phone networks made the internet-based messaging app an attractive alternative (Church & Oliveira, 2013: 352). Although mobile instant messaging (MIM) provides greater multimodal capabilities, and there is no upper character limit, in purely text-based interactions MIM and SMS are often indistinguishable. Apple's Messages app integrates the two, functioning as MIM by default but allowing users to send a message as SMS when there is no internet connection.[13] While WhatsApp provides IM capabilities, user accounts are dependent on an associated phone number, and contacting others requires knowledge of their phone number. This technological hybridity provides reasonable grounds for assuming that MIM discourse will have certain features in common with SMS, and it is quite different from the anonymity of online chat.

WhatsApp subsequently introduced web-based and desktop apps, which allow users access to their accounts (still dependent on the associated mobile phone) on a computer terminal. It would be instructive to undertake research comparing interactions using the mobile and desktop apps, and between the desktop app and older, static IM platforms.

The internet-based architecture of IM and MIM enables certain interactive features not possible in SMS. While SMS sends packets of data from one device to another, IM establishes a direct connection between the devices, which can be used to provide feedback. This provides functionalities like the 'message received' and 'message read' notifications, along with a dynamic indicator that shows when the interlocutor is entering text. The latter creates a degree of 'turn monitor' (Jenks, 2014: 79), allowing interlocutors to have some sense of the other's turn production, even if its content remains unseen until it is sent.

These features suggest that MIM should be more conducive to conversational interaction than SMS, and it may be assumed that much of the intimacy and conversationalness of SMS is likely to be found in MIM. The lack of constraint on the size of the message implies that certain typographic features typical of SMS, such as abbreviations by means of vowel omission and forms such as 'u' and 'cya', might not be reproduced, as there is no need for such brevity. However, the presence of 'u' in personal email in the CANELC data suggests that such forms have a tendency to transfer between platforms, so they might indeed be found in MIM discourse.

A further point to make regarding MIM in relation to other forms of CMC is that the inexorable spread of smartphone usage has had the effect of collapsing differences between media. In the past there was a clear distinction between phone- and keypad-based SMS, and terminal- and keyboard-based IM. Even on the same hardware, the display size of a computer allowed for significant interface differences between IM and email. Now, mobile devices account for an increasing proportion of internet use.[14] SMS and IM apps are largely indistinguishable, and while email apps tend to present message threads in the form of stacked 'cards' rather than the alternating speech bubbles of SMS and IM, text entry is often done in a very similar way. All platforms now rely on the same pair of thumbs, with other fingers largely forgotten. It seems reasonable to assume that these converging characteristics have resulted, and will continue to result, in the transfer of linguistic forms between media.

While analysis of MIM discourse is needed to provide an up-to-date account of language use in this most up-to-date medium, the forms of language variation found in the CANELC and NPS Chat analyses demonstrate the kinds of factors that might shape the language used in IM.

7.9 Relating Speech, Writing and CMC

The analysis presented in this chapter has illustrated a number of points in connection with the discussions earlier in the chapter regarding the relationship between online and offline language use. Firstly, while CANELC was compiled as a repository of examples of a posited 'e-language', substantial variation between the subcorpora casts doubt on the validity of this unifying description. Secondly, while CMC platforms were chosen for inclusion in the corpus based on their classification as 'asynchronous' forms of communication, the analysis found many examples of interactivity more typically associated with synchronous communication. Similarly, attempts to classify the CANELC data as more like 'spoken' or 'written' language were inconclusive. Many features commonly associated with 'spoken' language were observed, but many other observed phenomena were uniquely visual in nature, especially with regard to non-standard typography, and explaining them in terms of speech was of limited effectiveness.

The earlier discussions demonstrated that attempts to locate CMC along a 'spoken–written continuum' stem from a misleading conflation of speech and conversation. They also set out a number of essential characteristics of conversation: synchronicity, interactivity, contextual embedding. These derive from a togetherness-in-time, and ultimately in space, although this latter aspect is lost in telephone conversation, with little detriment to the interaction. Section 7.2 also showed that the spoken–written distinction has much in common with the synchronous/asynchronous dichotomy: the features of spoken (i.e. conversational) discourse are largely due to its synchronicity. Kalman and Rafaeli (2007: 4) argue that synchronicity should not be thought of as a technological characteristic, but a dynamic feature of an interaction, determined as much by the interlocutors' preferences and choices as by the technical architecture of the medium. They argue that it should be measured in terms of the time between messages, or 'response latency'.

It is therefore proposed that the concept of a 'spoken–written continuum' be reinterpreted as a response latency dimension, at whose zero point is located truly synchronous interaction. This is best typified by face-to-face interaction (i.e. conversation; i.e. 'spoken language'), but it is also true of telephone conversation. In both these cases, interlocutors have access to each other's turn construction, and this is what sets them apart from what are commonly termed 'synchronous' CMC environments, which are more accurately described as 'quasi-synchronous', as turn construction occurs before transmission. CMC systems do exist (such as VAX) which allow interlocutors to see what others are typing, however, and these can be considered equivalent to face-to-face interaction. The difference between face-to-face conversation, telephone conversation and truly synchronous CMC is one of perceptual channel: audio-visual, audio only and visual only. This provides a second dimension for classification. A third dimension may be postulated as interpersonal distance, allowing for variation in the tenor of the discourse. Further dimensions might be proposed, potentially drawing on Herring's (2007) classificatory facets, such as participation structure (dyadic vs group interaction), though specifying a detailed and comprehensive model accounting for all forms of communication is beyond the scope of this book. Figure 7.6 visualizes this framework, with some sample values indicated.

As noted above, response latency is a dynamic, emergent characteristic of any given interaction, based on the expectations, choices and communicative needs of the interlocutors. It is not an inherent feature of any given medium, and consequently the positions indicated in Figure 7.6 refer to individual (fictitious/imagined) instances of communication. The minimal, but non-zero, response latency of the instance of visual communication indicated in Position 3 is perhaps most typical of a conversation via an IM platform such as WhatsApp, but it could equally be conducted via email if the interlocutors chose to appropriate the technological

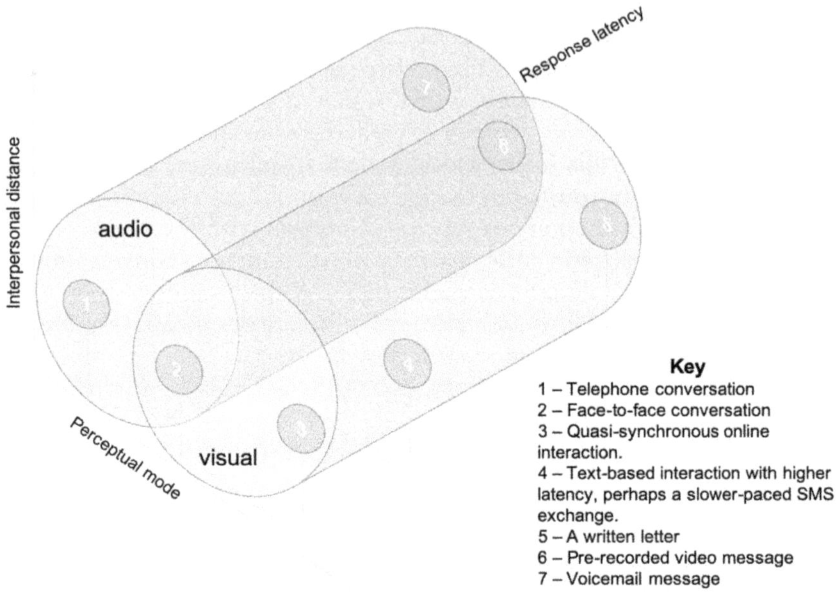

Figure 7.6 Response latency model, showing the relationship between different communication types, whether spoken, written or computer mediated. Numbered positions are intended as approximate exemplars of (fictional) instances of communication

affordances in this way. The closer an interaction approaches the zero point on the response latency scale, the more 'conversation-like' it becomes, demonstrating the features of 'spoken language'. Whether in the audio or visual mode, or both, participants will utilize whatever resources they have at their disposal to facilitate the interaction in all its aspects: interpersonal, transactional and evaluative.

This proposed model interacts with the activity theory framework elaborated in previous chapters. The position of any given interaction in the matrix illustrated in Figure 7.6 provides values for the components of the activity system of the communicative task at hand. In particular, it will determine certain rules of the interaction, with regard to the need to structure information unambiguously and explicitly specify extra-contextual referents (rather than indicating contextualized referents deictically). It will also contribute to the resources (or tools) available to the subject for meaning-making, both in terms of the perceptual mode and the response latency, which can itself be manipulated to create meaning. These, in turn, interact with the social dimensions of the model in the community and division of labor components of the activity system, with interpersonal power relations giving rise to expectations of politeness levels (which again can be co-opted as an additional meaning-making resource).

By taking a critical approach to notions of 'spoken language' and 'written language', and by shifting focus away from CMC platforms and toward individual interactions, it is possible to move past questions regarding the nature of digital discourse as more spoken-like or written-like. Instead, it enables us to begin to understand the degree to which text-based interaction online has expanded our communicative repertoire, broadening the range of resources at our disposal for making meaning in this hyper-connected age.

7.10 Conclusion

This chapter has presented analyses of language used in seven different forms of online interaction, and discussed possible implications for language in an eighth. The analysis has shown that much of the variation in the use of standard linguistic forms is due to the degree to which the interaction approaches a conversational nature, or what has previously been referred to as 'spoken' language. However, typographic variation is idiomatic to a text-based medium, and demonstrates the desire of many language users to play with the language they use in purely or largely phatic situations. Crystal (2008: 71) refers to this as 'the human ludic temperament'.

The contextual and cultural resources that individuals draw on to play with language in this way are multiple and complex. Popular culture, the stereotypical speech patterns of particular ethnic, social or cultural groups, even patterns of language associated with other forms of communication whose use has particular connotations: these and many more are incorporated into a densely woven text of multiple layers of indexicality. Such resources operate on various levels of sharedness: some will be understood by a wide array of people, some will be confined to particular groups or even individuals. Being a native speaker of English is of some help in decoding such texts, but it does not guarantee understanding or acceptance into the communities fostered by such language use. The first step to helping L2 speakers interact online is to emphasize that non-native speaker status does not, in itself, prohibit participation in these spaces, just as native-speaker status does not guarantee it.

Chapter 8 takes this discussion further, exploring the ways in which L2 users in formal learning situations might be supported in their use of EL2 CMC, in order to maximize both the communicative opportunities and the learning outcomes.

Notes

(1) https://aclweb.org/aclwiki/POS_Tagging_(State_of_the_art).
(2) https://www.sketchengine.eu/guide/glossary/?letter=T.
(3) https://www.sketchengine.eu.
(4) http://www.cambridge.org/elt/corpus/international_corpus.htm.
(5) https://www.sketchengine.eu/documentation/simple-maths/.

(6) https://www.sketchengine.eu/documentation/corpus-querying/.
(7) https://dictionary.cambridge.org.
(8) Occurrences of @ were limited to the tweets subcorpus, and always functioned as a proper noun, using the addressivity conventions of Twitter.
(9) http://publications.europa.eu/code/en/en-4100800en.htm.
(10) https://dictionary.cambridge.org/dictionary/english/hmm.
(11) https://dictionary.cambridge.org/dictionary/english/your.
(12) https://www.statista.com/statistics/258749/most-popular-global-mobile-messenger-apps/.
(13) https://support.apple.com/en-gb/HT207006.
(14) https://www.pewinternet.org/fact-sheet/mobile/.

8 Towards an Integration of EL2 CMC and Formal Instruction

The internet has made the world a smaller place. It has enabled communication between far distant interlocutors by video, voice, text and image. It has given rise to a new modality in which to have a conversation, something previously so wholly dependent on speech that the two terms are almost synonymous. It has collapsed physical space to such an extent that interlocutors might be in neighboring rooms or neighboring continents without any noticeable difference in the interaction. It has likewise quickened the pace of globalization, bringing people into intercultural contact in professional, as well as personal contexts. Intercultural computer-mediated communication (CMC) is not just a hobby, but an integral part of many occupations worldwide, and consequently presents many opportunities and obligations to employ the resources of a second language (L2). This is particularly so in the case of English, with its global language status.

This book has demonstrated that L2 English users in a wide variety of global contexts engage in extensive online communication using their English. Chapter 5 showed widespread EL2 CMC practices, with forms of email and instant messaging (IM) in particular being near-universal in their English language application. Chapter 6 highlighted many of the difficulties that L2 English users encounter in online communication. The benefits of EL2 CMC activities for language learning, both in the acquisition of linguistic items and the development of L2 identity, were discussed at length in Chapter 2. Chapter 5 further demonstrated a high level of interest among L2 English users in addressing online English use more directly in their language learning. Chapter 7 examined features of English used in different forms of CMC to understand how it differs from the English language more generally, with a view to understanding the learning needs of L2 English users as they interact in online spaces.

This chapter outlines a rationale and a proposal for the integration of learners' EL2 CMC activities in classroom learning. Integration is regarded as going beyond merely including online discourse as a language variety. Integration seeks to embrace the dialogism emphasized by ecological approaches to language learning (Van Lier, 2004), supporting learners in their EL2 CMC activities by equipping them with the tools to participate online, and to maximize the incidental learning outcomes of such participation. Furthermore, the proposed approach seeks to draw EL2 CMC activities directly into the classroom without diminishing their 'extramural' nature. In order to conceptualize the dialogic interaction between the chat room and the classroom, the framework of activity theory is utilized, establishing EL2 CMC and formal learning as inter-linked activity systems. An approach is then proposed that draws the two together, exploiting the effects of one upon the other. While the book does not provide space for the testing and evaluation of this approach, recommendations are made for how this might be done.

The chapter is structured as follows. Initially, the rationale for and the goals of the integration are set out. This is followed by establishing the theoretical foundation for these goals. Activity theory is utilized to conceptualize EL2 CMC and formal learning as linked activity systems, and the discussions around incidental learning first expounded in Chapter 2 are revisited. Incidental learning is recontextualized within the terms of activity theory, using the distinction between different types of motives to account for the presence of incidental learning outcomes within the activity system of EL2 CMC. Drawing on the findings of the previous chapters, and again within an activity theory framework, a basic set of learner needs is established, to be addressed by the proposed approach to integration. The principles on which the integration is based are then outlined, drawing on the notion of language awareness. Finally, the proposed model is elaborated, including a hypothetical demonstration of how the model might work, and a discussion of potential difficulties in its implementation.

8.1 Why Integrate?

The analysis presented in Chapters 4–6 provides empirical evidence of widespread EL2 CMC use among L2 English users around the world, building on previous studies which have demonstrated similar behaviors in smaller populations (Sockett, 2014; Sundqvist & Sylvén, 2016). Not only is online communication 'squarely mundane in the business of everyday life' (Squires, 2016: 1), but L2 communication, whether by necessity or design, is also a daily reality for many people. This communication has not only been facilitated by the growth of internet connectivity, but has also been a consequence of more general trends of globalization. These trends have themselves presented L2 English users with a broader array of reasons for coming into contact with other English users, whether L2 or first language (L1), utilizing a wider range of communicative resources than ever before.

The importance of contextual experiences with the target language in the development of an empowered L2 speaker is attested in the literature

(Norton, 2013), as is the capacity of L2 activity online to enable the L2 speaker to break out of cycles of disempowerment (Lam, 2000). The analysis in Chapter 5 demonstrated a belief among questionnaire respondents in the beneficial effects of EL2 CMC on their language learning, and this is attested empirically elsewhere in the literature (Sockett, 2014). Supporting learners in their online interactions in order to maximize and exploit these learning-related benefits has the potential to provide an enhanced learning experience.

This is underlined by 'big picture' approaches to the study of language learning, such as those underpinned by commitments to complexity (Beckner *et al.*, 2009) or ecology (Van Lier, 2004). These perspectives foreground the wider systems within which the classroom is entangled, as one component in a broader process of learning that dynamically interacts with many, indeed all, areas of the life of the individual. Regarding out-of-class activities as beyond the purview of the language teacher is therefore to artificially isolate the classroom from the wider system.

A further finding highlighted in Chapter 5 was the high level of interest among respondents in learning more about their EL2 CMC activities, both in terms of finding out more about the nature of language used online, and the incorporation of EL2 CMC-related content in English textbooks. There was only slight variation along demographic dimensions, with the lowest level of agreement with the statements 'I would be interested in learning more about the kind of English I use online' and 'I would like more content related to online English use in the English textbooks I use' coming from respondents in high-exposure contexts (i.e. English-speaking countries such as the US and the UK). Even in this demographic sub-group, however, overall agreement with the statements was around 67%–68%. The analysis of this part of the questionnaire showed that learners are aware of the role that EL2 CMC has in their language development, and are keen to explore it further.

8.2 Goals

The proposed integration of EL2 CMC and classroom learning has four primary goals, which correspond to the distinction noted in Chapter 2 between direct and indirect learning benefits of extramural English activities such as EL2 CMC.

(1) To support learners' EL2 CMC interactions to help them to develop as empowered participants in these discourse domains.
(2) To enhance motivation in formal learning.
(3) To maximize the incidental learning outcomes of EL2 CMC interactions.
(4) To maintain the extramural nature of EL2 CMC activities.

8.3 Linked Activity Systems: The Case of Almon

To understand the requirements of an approach to teaching English that achieves these goals, EL2 CMC and the language classroom are conceptualized as components of a wider system of language learning. Activity theory is used to position the two as linked activity systems, each of whose outcomes affect the components of the other, in a dynamic, dialogic cycle. Supporting and enhancing this cycle is the basis of Goals 1 and 2.

The cyclical reinforcement between EL2 CMC and formal learning can be observed in operation in the oft-cited case of Almon, a teenager who had moved to the US from Hong Kong some years before the commencement of a study undertaken by Eva Lam (2000). Although Lam's seminal paper is now over 20 years old, it is a cornerstone of the field, and the case of Almon is used and reanalyzed here in anticipation that it might be familiar to readers. Applying the theoretical framework developed throughout this book to such an established case is intended to ground it firmly in the field.

As discussed in Chapter 2, Almon found adjusting to his new home difficult, and he struggled in his efforts to learn English at school. It was only after he became involved with an English-speaking online community of Japanese pop music fans that he was able to establish himself as an empowered participant with a right to use English.

At school, Almon might best be described as disengaged. The structures of his schooling treated him as an outsider: '[m]ost of his classes at school were ESL, bilingual, or remedial courses, which stigmatized him as a low-achieving student' (Lam, 2000: 466). In his remedial composition class, it was made clear to him that he must strive to adopt a language provided to him by more authoritative sources: 'the teacher put a great deal of emphasis on imparting the correct linguistic code... through the use of grammar charts and corrections'. It was clear to him that he must learn 'proper' English to integrate into American society, but around him he could see many Chinese immigrants who never achieved this, and as a consequence he had little hope that he would be able to do so. In an interview with Lam, Almon says:

> The Chinese are prospering quite okay here. The problem is mainly with discrimination. The Chinese have more problems with English, and so it's more difficult for them to find jobs. Even those who have been here for a long time don't speak like the native-born Americans... English is my biggest problem... It's like this place isn't my world, I don't belong here. I guess it's going to be very hard for me to develop my career here. And I have a feeling that my English won't be that good even in 10 years.
>
> (Lam, 2000: 467)

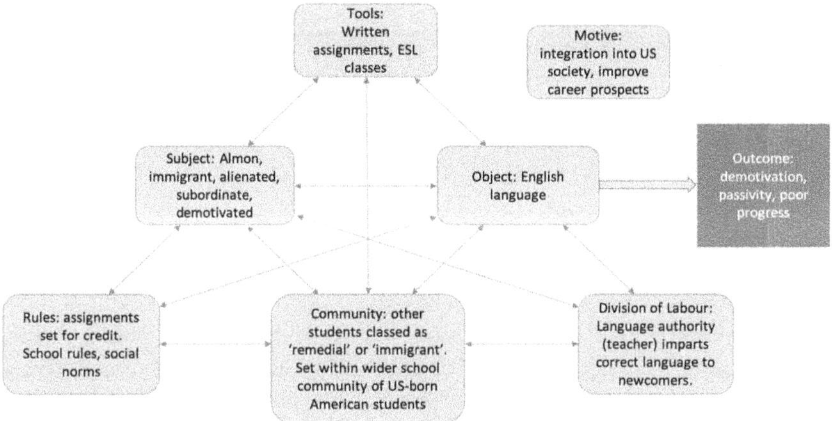

Figure 8.1 Almon's unsuccessful classroom learning activity system

Almon's school experience is represented as an activity system in Figure 8.1. The object of the system is the English language, and the attendant motive is social integration and laying the foundation for a future career. However, Almon as the subject of the activity is disempowered and alienated as a recent immigrant, and this is exacerbated by the social stratum of the activity system. The subject is regarded by the institutional structures as a subordinate member of the community (in need of 'remedial' support), and the division of labor is set up in such a way that the subject is a passive recipient of an externally imposed 'correct linguistic code'. This hierarchical structure is a clear contradiction to the motive of integration in an egalitarian society (Lam, 2000: 476). The rules of the activity required him to complete written assignments on topics in which he had little interest (Lam, 2000: 468).

The unintentional outcome of this activity system is not social integration and a bright future, but further disempowerment, alienation and disengagement on the part of the subject. This creates a negative feedback loop, the 'Catch-22' noted by Norton (2013: 79) in relation to Eva. However, Almon was able to break this cycle through his EL2 CMC.

The brief description of Almon's early forays into the CMC and web content creation suggest that the primary motive was simply an interest in web technologies and a desire to try out for himself what he had learned: 'After attending an introductory class on e-mail and browsing for information on the Web... he continued to look up different Web sites for tutorials on how to make personal home pages and conduct online chat' (Lam, 2000: 467). This analysis would suggest a close alignment between object and motive, with the desired outcome simply being a web page that matched his intentions. If we look beyond the web page and incorporate Almon's IM activities on the platform ICQ, we might also suggest a further motive of finding a community in which he could participate as an equal member, rather than the subordinate subject position imposed on him in the offline world. There is no indication that Almon involved himself in these online communities in order to practice or learn English. This was neither the object nor the motive of the activity (see Figure 8.2).

As subject of the activity, Almon was able to free himself from a number of the imposed aspects of his social identity in the offline world: his immigrant status and his alienation from his surroundings. The community relationships and division of labor within his EL2 CMC activity are very different to the school activity system. Almon was able to establish himself as 'a knowledgeable and helpful member of the international J-pop community' (Lam, 2000: 470–47). The outcome of his EL2 CMC activity is a thriving and dynamic addition to J-pop culture online, in the form of Almon's web page. However, a further outcome reflexively alters the nature of the activity's subject, that is, Almon. As a result of Almon's successful EL2 CMC activities, he is more confident and self-assured having found his voice as a 'legitimate speaker' of English. As he put it: 'Yeah, maybe the Internet has changed me' (Lam, 2000: 468). To differentiate this type of reflexive outcome from other external outcomes of the activity, the term 'subject-outcome' is proposed.

This subject-outcome of the EL2 CMC activity system fundamentally alters a component of the school learning activity system: the subject is no longer alienated and disengaged, but empowered and motivated, taking proactive steps to further his formal learning: 'He could now write more fluently in school and was planning to take a public speaking class to improve his oral delivery skills' (Lam, 2000: 467). The completion of the cycle is not directly discussed by Lam, but it seems likely that Almon's development as an independent English user enabled him to then transfer his school English learning to his online English use. Once he was able to engage more proactively with his schooling, he could use it to develop the linguistic tools available to him in his EL2 CMC activity system (Figure 8.3).

It is this transformative, cyclical effect of Almon's EL2 CMC activity on his formal learning activity, which then further enables his EL2 CMC activity, that the current approach to integration seeks to support and exploit.

This is not to suggest that all learning environments are like Almon's, or that all formal language learning activities are inherently alienating and demotivating. However, the analysis presented in Chapter 5 highlighted a widespread concern among questionnaire respondents that the language they learned in class was not the 'real' language used by other English users, especially in uncontrolled language spaces such as those found online. Additionally, there was a frequently voiced feeling that native speakers of English were an authority to which respondents felt

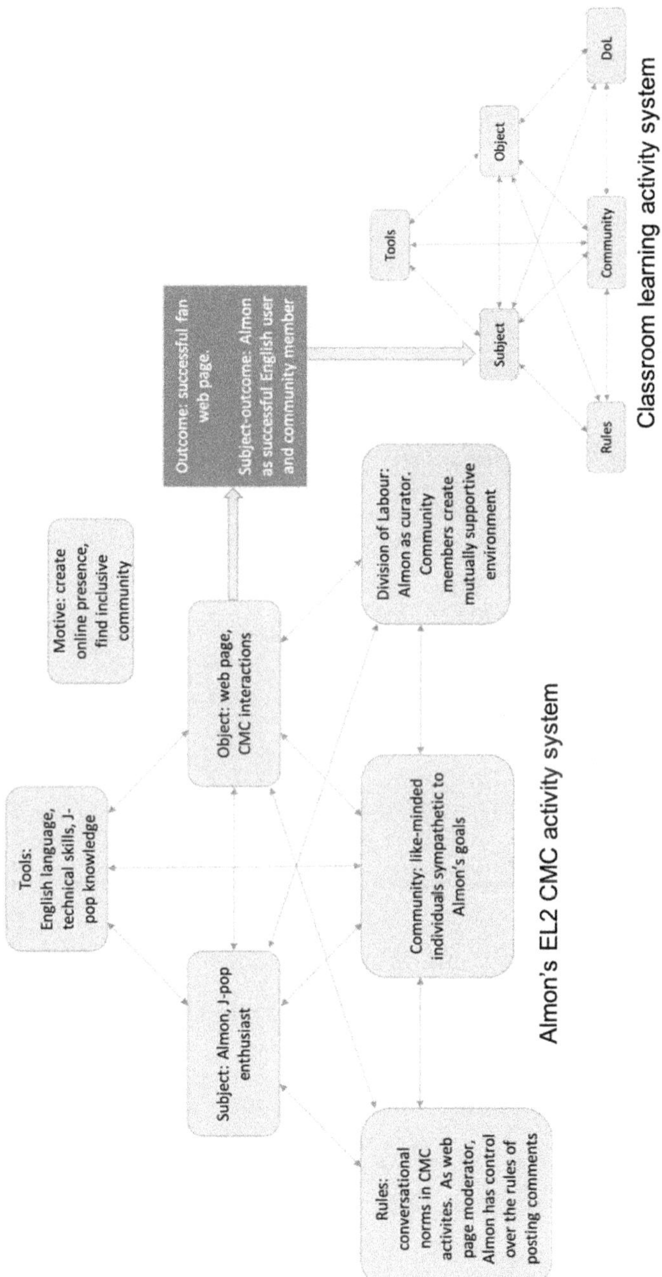

Figure 8.2 Almon's EL2 CMC activity system, linking to his classroom learning system

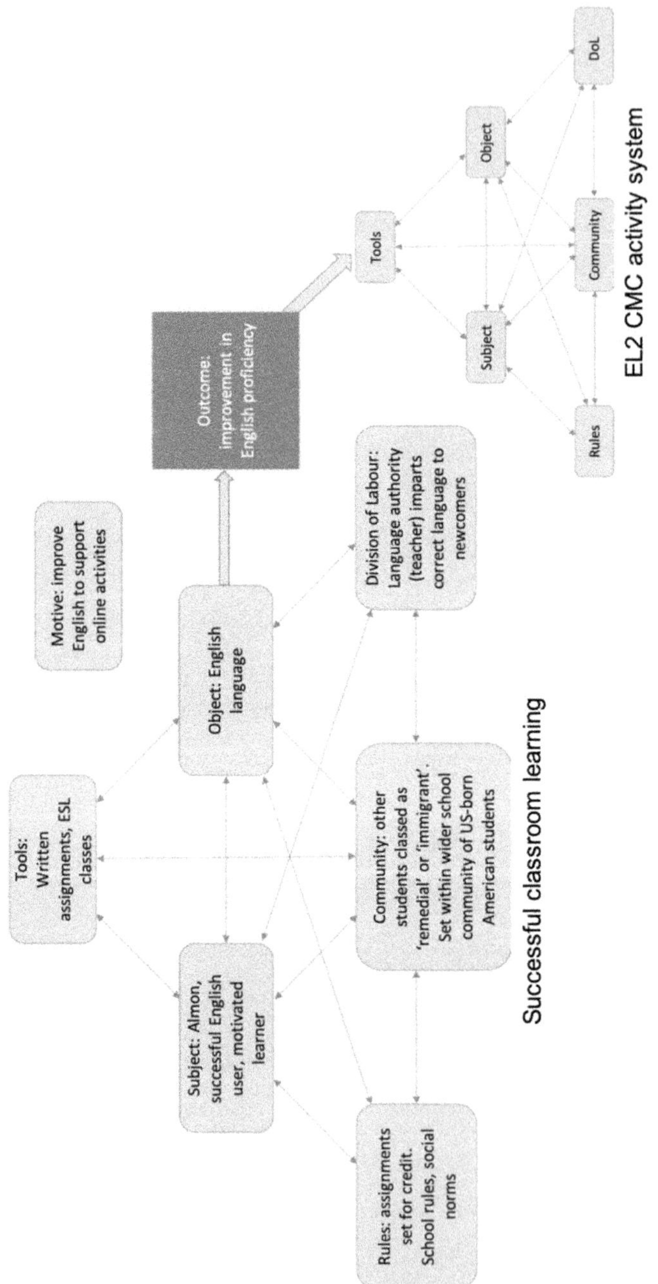

Figure 8.3 Almon's successful classroom learning developing the tools of his EL2 CMC system

subordinate. This latter was an element of Almon's offline context, but questionnaire respondents report it in relation to EL2 CMC, so clearly the act of simply going online does not automatically remove these obstacles. Supporting learners to help them derive empowering outcomes from their EL2 CMC is the first goal of the integration.

8.4 Incidental Learning and Multiple Motives

While the first two goals of the proposed approach to integrating EL2 CMC and formal learning seek to empower learners in order to enhance their classroom learning, the third goal is related to what were discussed as the 'direct' benefits of EL2 CMC for language learning, that is, the acquisition of linguistic items through incidental learning. The insistence on viewing such learning as incidental or informal stems from the observation that the kind of activities under discussion are entered into for reasons quite independent from language learning, and so any learning outcomes are a 'byproduct' of the activity. In terms of activity theory, the primary sense-forming motive(s) of the activity is not learning related. However, unintentional, or incidental learning, caused by learners noticing salient language, may take place, and the positive affect results in a motive-stimulus for the activity.

Chapter 2 (Section 2.2.1) discussed the conclusion drawn in the literature (Ellis, 1995: 89; Schmidt, 1990: 149) that for incidental learning to take place there must be 'noticing' on the part of the language user. This noticing is defined as a state of focal awareness, in which the language user distinguishes a particular linguistic item or phenomenon from a background of co-text (Schmidt, 1990: 132).

Sockett uses the verb 'notice', in a different sense, in his notion of the continuum of awareness of the learning benefits of what he calls the online informal learning of English (OILE, of which the current term EL2 CMC is here conceived as a subset). In a keynote speech at the 2018 Informal Second Language Learning Conference at the University of Oxford, UK, he observed that this continuum stretches from 'Shut up I'm watching TV!' to varying degrees of 'I've noticed this is helping my English'. The L2 user notices the effect that his or her noticing has had on his or her language proficiency, or, in other words, he or she becomes aware of the incidental learning outcomes of his or her EL2 CMC activity. Where this realization elicits a positive affective response, it acts as a motive-stimulus for the continuation or repetition of the activity, without altering the nature of the activity itself.

The potential multiplicity of activity motives was discussed briefly in Section 2.4.2, citing Leontiev's distinction between sense-forming motives and motives-stimuli. However, the precise mechanics of the co-existence of motives, as well as a clear definition of the difference between the two types, has been a source of debate and controversy among subsequent scholars of activity theory. Kaptelinin and Nardi (2006: 144) note that, while Leontiev (1978: 169) explicitly allows for the co-existence of multiple motives, he does not develop this aspect of his work, and instead tends to refer to objects and motives of activities as unitary. In particular, Kaptelinin and Nardi (2006: 145) focus on Leontiev's hierarchy of motives, which Leontiev proposes as a means of resolving conflict between motives: more important motives take precedence over less important ones, and sense-forming motives are always more important than motives-stimuli. Instead, they propose a model in which the object of an activity is separated from the activity's motives more explicitly than is the case in Leontiev's work. This allows the object to be 'jointly defined by the whole set of motives the individual strives to attain in her activity' (Kaptelinin & Nardi, 2006: 149).

Kaptelinin and Nardi (2006: 148) are keen to retain Leontiev's sense-forming motives/motives-stimuli distinction, criticizing approaches that ignore it. However, they do not go on to discuss the intrinsic difference between motive types, beyond the initial observation that 'sense-forming motives… give the activity its meaning, and motives-stimuli… provide additional motivation but do not change the meaning of an activity' (Kaptelinin & Nardi, 2006: 145). This, and the affective nature of motives-stimuli proposed by Leontiev (1978: 169), neatly describe the pleasure derived from noticing unintended learning benefits, as noted above.

Similarly, in using the differentiation between motive types to analyze motives for out-of-class L2 literacy practices, Inaba (2019) tends to classify motives as one type or the other in accordance with the weight given to them by her interviewees. When an interviewee mentions of her L2 literacy practices that 'I do them for fun and they double as study, which is good', Inaba (2019: 102) classifies 'for fun' as the sense-forming motive, and language learning as a motive-stimulus. Inaba (2019: 93) notes that learning outcomes can form either type of motive, and indeed were treated as sense-forming by the majority of participants, who 'viewed non-class-related literacy activities as learning activities'. She also observes that while the two types are present in theory, there is a great deal of overlap between the two and it is not always possible to distinguish them (Inaba, 2019: 102). Furthermore, it is unclear from the sources hitherto discussed what the relationships would be between multiple sense-forming motives.

As mentioned briefly in Chapter 2 (Section 2.4), activities are realized by goal-directed actions. McCafferty *et al.* (2001: 292) show that acquisition of a language item is more likely when that item is the goal of an action within some wider activity. This is perhaps the manifestation within activity theory of the concept of noticing: the moment of 'focal awareness' (Schmidt, 1990: 132) that is necessary for language acquisition to take place. Actions are necessarily conscious, and the findings of McCafferty *et al.* echo and support the conclusions of Schmidt that awareness in the form of noticing is a prerequisite for the conversion of input to intake (see Chapter 2 for further discussion).

It might be proposed that the difference between sense-forming motives and motives-stimuli is one of intention. This is perhaps to risk introducing tautological terminology, as intention and motive are not so different in meaning. However, we might argue that we intend for the sense-forming motive to direct the activity, while we do not intend to indulge motives-stimuli. Kaptelinin and Nardi (2006: 145) illustrate the difference between the two using the example of buying a car: 'a person may buy a car not only as a means of transportation [sense-forming motive] but also because of its prestigious brand name [motive-stimulus]'. We *intend* to buy a car, that is the sense-forming motive, but motives-stimuli may see us being drawn toward high-end makes or models, without it necessarily being our *intention* to buy a luxury car. Of course, we might indeed intend to buy a luxury car, but then that is the sense-forming motive and the activity is different.

This linking of intention with motive type presents a potential resolution to a point made by Lamb and Arisandy (2019) in relation to the use of intentionality by Toffoli and Sockett (2015: 7) to define the scope of OILE as concerned with activities 'driven by the intention to communicate, with language learning being only a by-product of this communication'. Lamb and Arisandy (2019: 4) contend that it cannot be assumed that L2 users have no intention at all to exploit the learning benefits of such interactions: 'a young person might choose to watch an English language TV series on Netflix mainly for entertainment, but also knowing they make [*sic*] pick up some new language along the way, and use L1 subtitles (or not) to promote that process'. The use of Leontiev's motive types allows for the motive-stimulus of learning to exist alongside the sense-forming motive of watching Netflix, with intention given to the latter, but with awareness of the former.

The role of intention in the discussions around incidental learning is mentioned in Chapter 2. Rieder (2003) analyzes incidental vocabulary acquisition as unintentional, achieved by both implicit learning processes (which are both unintentional and unaware) and explicit learning processes (which are intentional, but still lack awareness). By this analysis, the intention to learn results in learning which is non-incidental. This is outside the scope of the current enquiry: activities whose primary sense-forming motive is to derive learning outcomes are explicitly not the focus of this book. However, if the motive-stimulus of noticing that EL2 CMC is improving language proficiency can be used to generate a secondary sense-forming motive, an intention to enter into EL2 CMC activities with learning outcomes in mind (but not dominant), then these learning outcomes will be enhanced. The second goal of integration thus becomes to foster an *intention to notice*.

8.5 A Macro-Functional Needs Analysis

The empirical research presented in Chapters 4–7 provided an insight into the needs of L2 English users in their online interactions. Communicative activities undertaken online using L2 English were the focus of Chapter 4, where these activities were categorized, following the Common European Framework of Reference (CEFR) for languages, under three 'macro-functions': evaluative, transactional and interpersonal. These can be represented as three separate activity systems. As discussed in Section 4.5, each of the three represents the prioritization of certain types of meaning over others, based on the primary sense-forming motive. Each of the three activities results in a subject-outcome, which changes and develops the subject of the activity, and of all other activities that share the same subject. The three activity systems will each be discussed in turn, drawing on the findings from previous chapters to diagnose likely learner needs in each case. A summary of the three activities' motives and outcomes is presented in Table 8.1.

8.5.1 Evaluative activities

Evaluative language activities have as a primary sense-forming motive the intention 'to assign value to objects of interest, to position social actors with respect to those objects, to calibrate alignment between stancetakers, and to invoke presupposed systems of social value'

Table 8.1 Summary of motives and outcomes of macro-functional activities

		Outcomes	
Macro-function	**Motive**	**Successful**	**Unsuccessful**
Evaluative	Attribute value to something, and to align with others in its regard.	Acknowledgement of opinion (including disagreement).	Dismissal or ridiculing of opinion.
		Subject-outcome: subject as authoritative, with right to speak and evaluate.	Subject-outcome: subject as subordinate, powerless.
Transactional	Accurately convey information.	Demonstration by others of correct understanding. Concrete consequences (e.g. meeting in the right place at the right time).	Unintended consequences, misunderstanding. Consequences may be adverse (e.g. missing important appointment).
		Subject-outcome: subject as able to effect real-world change through language.	Subject-outcome: subject as ineffective language user.
Interpersonal	Initiate and maintain relationships, presentation of self.	Interlocutors respond to subject as intended. Establishment of connection between subject and interlocutor(s).	Interlocutors fail to 'get' the subject's intentions. Interlocutors remain affectively distant.
		Subject-outcome: subject able to connect with others using language.	Subject-outcome: subject struggles to foster relationships with others.

(Du Bois, 2007: 139). The subject engages in the activity with the intention of expressing an opinion or position with regard to some stance-object (Du Bois, 2007: 143), and of expressing agreement or disagreement with other members of the activity's community. The assertiveness inherent in these motives has the potential to come into conflict with the rules of the activity which underpin smooth conversational interaction. The extent of this danger is affected by the other components of the activity system. In a community comprised of acquainted interlocutors, it is likely that assertions of opinion that contravene norms of politeness may be given the benefit of the doubt, while unacquainted interlocutors may be more likely to react negatively. Similarly, in a communicative context with an asymmetric division of labor such as a blog post, the primary participant (such as the author of the original blog post) may have more authority derived from the activity structure.

A fully realized successful outcome of an evaluative language activity would involve the acknowledgement of the subject's stated stance by other community members. This does not have to be in the form of agreement, but an opinion that is summarily dismissed or ridiculed by others, or which causes others to disengage with the activity due to a failure to negotiate politeness-related rules might be said to be an unsuccessful outcome. A further outcome is the development of the authority of the subject and an implicit self-awareness of their right to evaluate.

Some evaluative language activities may not lead to direct acknowledgement by others, such as writing a comment on a YouTube video, to which no one replies and which gains no 'likes'. In such cases, the activity may be considered successful in principle by the fact of its existence in the ongoing discourse and by a lack of negative feedback. However, it will lack the effectiveness in developing the authority of the subject that results from the engagement with the subject's stance by others.

Subjects in evaluative language activities require linguistic tools that enable them to assert their opinions while negotiating the rules of the activity, particularly those regarding politeness. This is a form of what Leech (1983: 83) regards as negative politeness: 'minimizing the impoliteness of impolite illocutions'. The lean-medium nature of CMC entails 'a hyper-reliance on purely textual attributes' (Yus, 2011: 269) for achieving this delicate balance.

8.5.2 Transactional activities

Transactional language activities have as a primary sense-forming motive the accurate conveyance of information. A successful outcome will involve some form of demonstration by others in the activity's community of the intended comprehension of the information. Transactional language activities may have concrete, real-world outcomes which have the potential to expose shortcomings in the accuracy of information conveyed, and which may have adverse consequences for the subject. However, in successful transactional language activities, the consequent subject-outcome will be an increased awareness of the power of the subject to effect real-world change by using their L2.

Information accuracy is likely to be more easily achieved (though not automatically so) in activity systems whose rules do not require instant responses from the subject, allowing more time for message composition and editing to check accuracy. Activities undertaken in a work-related community may have more severe professional consequences than those undertaken with friends. Activities in a commercial setting depend upon information accuracy to ensure financial transactions and purchases are not erroneous.

Accurately conveying intended meaning was a commonly voiced concern in the comments elicited by the questionnaire. Subjects in transactional language activities require linguistic tools which enable them to ensure comprehension of key information, and to provide alternative explication if necessary.

8.5.3 Interpersonal activities

Interpersonal language activities have as a primary sense-forming motive the initiation and maintenance of relationships with other users. This is largely done by provoking affective or physical responses in others, manifest in their subsequent actions, or verbal responses. A key part of this is the construction and projection of identity. Subjects in interpersonal language activities require linguistic tools that enable them to engage in what has been described as 'hyperpersonal' interaction (Walther, 2007). This term refers to the exploitation of the technical affordances of CMC platforms in conjunction with stylized linguistic techniques to heighten the sense of personal identity being projected through the textual medium. Successful outcomes from interpersonal activities will be responses from interlocutors that are in line with the subject's intentions. If we tell a joke, a successful outcome involves the laughter of others. If successful, the subsequent subject-outcome of interpersonal activities is the realization by the subject of their power to provoke such responses.

Different socio-technical configurations (STCs) of CMC present different affordances and barriers to the communication of interpersonal meaning, altering the composition of the tools component of the interpersonal activity system. STCs with low synchronicity allow for more careful message preparation prior to sending, therefore perhaps more deliberate self-presentation. High synchronicity contexts require more rapid, and therefore less well-prepared, responses, but the possibility for back-and-forth 'banter' enabled by such a dynamic has the potential for a high degree of interpersonal content. This is particularly true in contexts with a high tolerance for non-standard language, in which orthographic creativity can be used to expand the levels of meaning enabled by the text-based medium. It should be noted that interpersonal meanings are just as necessary in formal contexts as in informal ones. Explicit adherence to politeness conventions will be a significant element of this. Table 8.1 presents a summary of the motives and outcomes of the three macro-functional activities.

8.5.4 Macro-functional requirements and examples of their linguistic realizations

Synthesis of the above analysis of the motives and outcomes of the three macro-functional activities provides the following set of requirements that EL2 CMC users should be able to employ in a text-based medium. As discussed previously, the three activities represent the prioritization of one of the three macro-functions, and while they are separated for purposes of analysis, the three functions are co-present in all communicative activities. Therefore, the requirements listed below are similarly applicable in varying degrees to all interactions.

- Express stance within the rules of the activity, including interacting with expectations of politeness. This does not necessarily mean always being polite, but they should be able to exercise control over the degree of adherence to, or contravention of, politeness norms.
- Ensure informational accuracy and deploy strategies to check understanding.
- Project personality and identity in a reduced-cues environment. Interact with the rules of the activity, including politeness, in order to provoke intended affective or physical responses in others.

The corpus analysis presented in Chapter 7 demonstrated a number of examples of these requirements being met in online discourse. In many cases, the techniques were not unique to CMC interaction, but the keyword analysis method showed that they were characteristic of CMC being more relatively frequent in the CMC corpora than in the general English reference corpus.

Chapter 7 presents some examples of evaluative language in use, although as evaluation is often spread over extended phraseological constructions (Hunston, 2011), the word-based approach taken was not suitable to examine this in more detail. However, the appearance of 'too' on the keyword list was shown to be used evaluatively in two different senses: firstly, used as a mark of excessiveness ('too big'), and also as a marker of ambient affiliation (Zappavigna, 2011), aligning the subject with other stance-takers. This latter function is as much interpersonal as evaluative.

Chapter 7 also demonstrated the use of framing devices to assert stance indirectly, either qualified as an objective opinion using 'I think', or, in the case of advice, phrased in a conditional structure using 'would', to indicate what the subject's preference would be ('I would do x'), rather than using more direct structures that create obligation ('You should do x').

Evidence of ensuring informational accuracy is scant in the Chapter 7 analysis, in part because many such techniques occur across several utterances. This is discussed by Lee (2002: 279), who presents a detailed list of strategies used in CMC to check comprehension and self-correct. This is an area of language use which learners would benefit from having presented to them through the use of authentic CMC data, as discussed further below.

Most of the interpersonal linguistic techniques evident in the Chapter 7 analysis are indicative of an informal register. This is largely due to the intrinsic informality of CMC in comparison with the texts comprising the reference corpus, causing informal forms such as the contracted negation particle 'n't' to appear at the top of the keyword list. This should not be taken to imply a conflation of interpersonal and informal, however: the choice of language creating a formal register carries interpersonal meaning just as much as an informal one. Consequently, caution must be used in claiming any linguistic form identified by quantitative means is inherently interpersonal in nature. Understanding interpersonal meaning in utterances requires a discourse or conversation analysis approach, taking context into account.

Nevertheless, there were some signs of interpersonal meaning in action in the Chapter 7 analysis. Use of the letter x to represent kisses as a message closer clearly functions interpersonally to create an unspoken sense of affection and intimacy. It was noted that the use of 'just' functions interpersonally in two different ways: in one sense it evokes the physical context of the subject, creating intimacy through providing a snapshot of the subject's life: 'I'm just having my tea'; in another sense, it functions as part of Leech's Tact Maxim, minimizing the imposition on the recipient by downplaying the complexity of what is often a request: 'could you just have a quick look at this…?'. While neither of these is unique to CMC, their strategic use is more important in text-based communication, when paralinguistic forms of expression are unavailable.

Forms of CMC with a high tolerance of non-standard linguistic forms (chat rooms, short messaging service [SMS], personal IM) provide rich resources for displaying interpersonal meaning, and constructing and projecting identity through non-standard orthography. Chapter 7 provided numerous examples, including indexing particular sociocultural groups using 'eye-dialect', lengthening by character repetition to suggest intonation or prosody and the use of opaque initialisms to index group membership.

The above discussion provides some examples of the sort of linguistic phenomena that the current approach to the integration of EL2 CMC and formal learning proposes to focus on. More tightly focused research into this, utilizing corpus analysis or conversation analysis, would provide a more comprehensive picture. However, the emphasis of the current approach is on utilizing language data encountered and experienced by learners in EL2 CMC to provide input for learning, rather than identifying a set of linguistic items to teach. The approach outlined below for addressing EL2 CMC in the language classroom proposes the use of learner-generated data as input for reflective learning, following the principles of a language awareness approach to language teaching. This is discussed further in the next sections.

8.6 A Language Awareness Approach

The approach to integration aims to address the fundamental contradiction of the linked activity system comprising EL2 CMC and classroom learning. This contradiction was identified as that between the exchange value and use value of the language being learned. To many English learners/users who responded to the questionnaire, the contradiction was manifest as a perceived disjunct between language learned in the classroom (described by one respondent as 'textbookish') and the 'real' language encountered online. It would be overly simple and inaccurate to propose a one-to-one mapping between these two dichotomous pairings, leading to an unfair devaluation of the real-world benefits of classroom learning. The contradiction is present within language itself, of all types and in all contexts: it is a manifestation of what Bakhtin (1981: 270–272) describes as the tension between the centripetal forces that seek to posit a unified language and the centrifugal forces of heteroglossia. Even the most obscure vernaculars encountered online have an exchange value aspect: Yus (2011: 152) observes that online communities often develop deliberately opaque linguistic markers, mastery of which constitutes a form of social capital that is 'worth' continued group membership.

Nevertheless, the approach to integration seeks to minimize the perception of an 'authenticity gap' (Henry, 2013) between classroom and chat room, supporting learners as they navigate the mutability and evanescence of online language.

The concern with language as dynamic and evolving is central to a language awareness approach to language learning and teaching (Svalberg, 2007). Building on much of the research into L2 acquisition discussed in Chapter 2 (Section 2.2.1) with regard to noticing and incidental learning, a language awareness approach promotes 'explicit knowledge about language, and conscious perception and sensitivity in language learning, language teaching and language use' (Svalberg, 2007: 288). Svalberg (2007: 290) cites Borg (1994: 62) in outlining five principles of a language awareness approach to language teaching. These are set out below for the purposes of reference and discussion:

(1) It involves an ongoing investigation of language as a dynamic phenomenon rather than awareness of a fixed body of established facts.
(2) It involves learners in talking analytically about language, often to each other.
(3) It considers essential the involvement of learners in exploration and discovery.
(4) It aims to develop not only the learners' knowledge about and understanding of language but also their learning skills, thus promoting learner independence.
(5) The aim is to involve learners on both a cognitive and an affective level.

The first of these speaks directly to the experience of questionnaire respondents with language online, and argues against the conventional teaching of words or phrases 'typical' of online language. This approach proposes using authentic texts taken from CMC interactions to provide input for the investigation of contemporaneous language use. This proposed use of authentic texts presents a number of issues, which are dealt with later.

The second point, paraphrased by Svalberg (2007: 291) as the 'talk-about' element, requires metalinguistic discussion on the part of learners. Assuming such discussion is conducted in the L2, the complexity of the metalanguage expected from learners must be proportional to their language level. However, there is no reason that lower-level learners cannot talk about, and reflect on, language use.

In relation to the third principle, the approach taken here proposes to involve learners by utilizing their own EL2 CMC activities. A key priority is maintaining the extramural nature of these activities, and seeking to avoid co-opting them as new forms of homework. While it is true that this approach will encourage learners to look for ways to expand their online activities, this will be done in such a way as to emphasize communicative activities undertaken for their own sake, rather than as explicit English practice. It might be suggested, for example, that learners avoid online groups with names such as 'Let's Chat In English!', in favor of less learner-oriented CMC interactions.

The fourth principle is treated in the current approach not as developing learner independence, but independence as a user of English. The emphasis on incidental learning, combined with a heightened propensity for noticing developed through an attention to language awareness, results in an approach that seeks to empower learners (in the classroom) to interact as autonomous users online, and to attend to new and notable language as it is encountered.

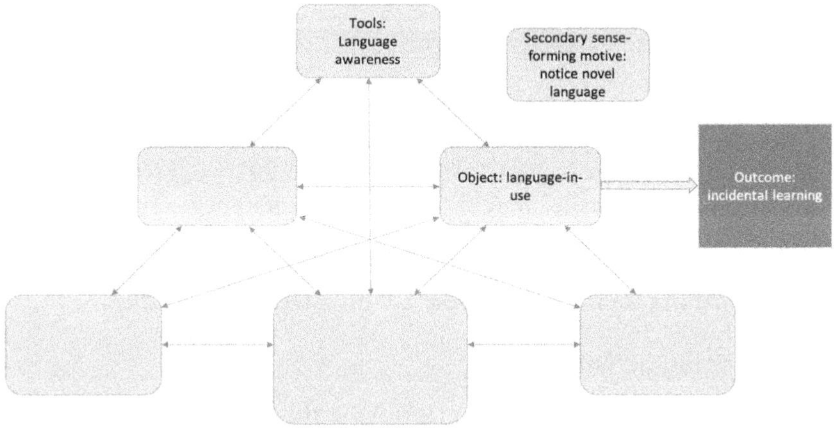

Figure 8.4 Additional elements in the EL2 CMC activity system, fostered through a language awareness approach

The fifth principle is at the heart of the current approach. Utilizing learners' existing EL2 CMC activities aims to, as it were, take the learning to them, to begin with their interests and needs and activities and to enable them to get the most out of such interactions.

The principles of language awareness are utilized in the proposed classroom methodology to foster a secondary sense-forming motive in L2 English users' EL2 CMC activities: to look out for, and notice, new or interesting language points in their ongoing discourse. This is represented in Figure 8.4, which shows additional elements in the EL2 CMC activity. The tools available to the subject now include a heightened language awareness, which is utilized in the subject's engagement with the interaction to produce incidental learning outcomes, in addition to other outcomes already produced by the EL2 CMC activity.

8.6.1 Consciousness-raising tasks

Svalberg aligns a language awareness approach with the notion of consciousness-raising (CR) tasks (Ellis, 1997: 160). These are classroom tasks with the aim of developing explicit linguistic and metalinguistic knowledge, but do not expect production of target forms by learners. Ellis (1997) defines a CR task as 'a pedagogic activity where the learners are provided with L2 data in some form and required to perform some operation on or with it, the purpose of which is to arrive at an explicit understanding of some linguistic property or properties of the target language'. Good examples in a CMC context might be presenting learners with a tweet or other electronic utterance containing both the forms 'u' and 'you', and asking learners to discuss why the author has used both, and what the meanings or effects of each are, or presenting learners with a discussion board post giving advice in the form 'If I were you I would...', and asking them to contrast the effect with that of 'You should...'.

Ellis proposes a number of variables in the creation of CR tasks. In the first instance, he differentiates between inductive (data driven) and deductive (theory driven) tasks. Svalberg (2007: 292) suggests the inductive type is most consistent with a language awareness approach. The other variables discussed by Ellis refer to options for the nature of the data presented to learners, and the kinds of operations that are required to be carried out on the data. These are discussed further below.

8.6.2 Bridging activities

Addressing many of the same priorities as this book, Thorne and Reinhardt (2008) approach the problem of integrating online literacy activities in classroom language learning with the concept of 'bridging activities'. Similar to the goals of the current proposal, the authors describe these activities as having a 'focus on developing learner awareness of vernacular digital language conventions and analyzing these conventions to bridge in-class activity with the wider world of mediated language use' (Thorne & Reinhardt, 2008: 562). A bridging activities approach 'involves incorporating and seriously analyzing student-selected texts within the advanced foreign language curriculum' (Thorne & Reinhardt, 2008: 562). This process of analyzing L2 data in order to develop awareness of linguistic phenomena is a clear parallel with Ellis's CR activities. However, the bridging aspect comes in the use of texts encountered by learners in their own target language activities, and selected by them for investigation in the classroom. Furthermore, the emphasis on 'vernacular digital language conventions' demonstrates a prioritization of the 'use value' of the language, preparing learners for the inherent variability of language outside the classroom, and especially online. This might be termed a 'show and tell' approach to the selection and presentation of L2 data, and its effectiveness has been demonstrated in empirical research (Sundqvist & Sylvén, 2016: 93).

Thorne and Reinhardt focus exclusively on advanced-level language learners, and explore the possibilities for these bridging activities of this group's advanced linguistic and metalinguistic knowledge. The expectations of learners are correspondingly high. However, the emphasis on advanced learners is due to a gap identified in the literature, rather than an assertion that their approach would be too complex for lower-level learners. They do not discuss issues of level, beyond noting that CMC 'is now a high-frequency context for language use at any proficiency level' (Thorne & Reinhardt, 2008: 560). This observation has only become more salient in the decade since Thorne and Reinhardt's paper was published: this book has demonstrated extensive EL2 CMC use among learners of all levels. It therefore seems viable and desirable to extend the benefits of their approach to learners who are not yet of advanced proficiency, but active online nevertheless. The complexity of analysis advocated by Thorne and Reinhardt may be beyond lower-level learners, but there is no reason that adapted bridging activities utilizing user-generated texts cannot help lower-level learners 'to see how such texts may differ from the standard Englishes promoted in the curriculum and assessed in institutional/national exams' (Lamb & Arisandy, 2019: 18).

8.7 Proposed Classroom Methodology: Show and Tell

Guided by the principles of a language awareness approach, and drawing on elements of both CR tasks and bridging activities, I would like to propose a 'show and tell' model for the integration of EL2 CMC and classroom learning. The term is taken from the commonly used format in US elementary schools, in which students bring an object of interest from the outside world into class, where they discuss its material and cultural significance with their classmates and teacher. The term is used as a memorable designation for the approach as a whole, but will also refer to a particular type of activity within it.

The show and tell model seeks to accomplish the four goals of integration stated earlier in this chapter. Learners will be supported in their EL2 CMC activities by an in-class focus on appropriate language use in a range of authentic online contexts (Goal 1). Motivation will be enhanced by the inclusion of tasks which bridge the gap between the classroom and the real world (Goal 2), breaking down the perceived difference between 'textbookish' and 'real' English. Incidental learning outcomes of EL2 CMC interactions will be enhanced by priming learners to notice new and/or interesting linguistic phenomena (Goal 3). Finally, the model does not construct and impose new forms of homework for learners, but encourages them to explore their existing EL2 CMC use, or to develop current interests and activities in new online contexts (Goal 4).

This approach is built on the empirical research presented in earlier chapters of this book, synthesized in the discussions above. One of the primary insights emerging, especially from the qualitative component of the research, was the dynamic, almost whimsical nature of language online, and the importance of regarding it 'in the wild'. Following this principle, and similar arguments set out above in the discussion of bridging activities, this approach is not intended to provide specific language for classroom input, even where such language would be attested in use by the corpus analysis presented in Chapter 7. While such a corpus-driven glossary of high-frequency terms found in specific CMC contexts could certainly be of value, to do this on a scale that would provide a practical resource for teachers is beyond the scope of this book. The approach presented here seeks to have students' own language use provide input for the classroom.

The show and tell model comprises four main components: discussion activities, collaborative blogging activities, show and tell activities and role-play activities. Each of these are developed in the following sections. The case of Almon is then speculatively revisited, presenting a hypothetical application of the model in his context. This is followed by discussions of potential obstacles and considerations of learner proficiency level and learning context.

8.7.1 Discussion activities

These are intended as an initial phase of the show and tell approach, and consist of two parts. The first part is designed to provide an opportunity for learners to reflect on their existing activities, and perhaps to consider explicitly the relationship of such activities with their formal learning. It is likely that there will be a high level of variation between learners in the same class, regarding the frequency and contexts of EL2 CMC use. Chapter 5 showed that leisure activities such as gaming and chat rooms are unusual for a majority of learners, but highly frequent for some. Thus, the first part of the discussion also functions to enable the teacher to gain an understanding of the breadth of experience present in the classroom, and an insight into the learners' needs.

It is entirely possible that some, or indeed all, learners in the class engage in little to no EL2 CMC, despite the findings in Chapter 5 suggesting that such practices are widespread. In order to engage such learners, and to ensure that the approach caters to all learners in a class, the second part of the discussion phase asks learners to discuss their lives and interests, and to consider what aspects of these they might be interested in exploring and extending in English language spaces online. Learners might ask one another how they might go about pursuing an interest online using English, and what the benefits might be of being able to engage with a global community. This part of the discussion might also extend to any concerns learners have about interacting online using English, or indeed their L1.

The second part of the discussion is intended as a mechanism for 'triggering learners' interests' (Inaba, 2019: 156–157) and stimulating ideas for exploring the possibilities of EL2 CMC, which they will be encouraged to follow up outside the classroom. A core principle of the approach is to minimize the imposition of new forms of homework on the learners, so the goal is to inspire learners to explore the communicative possibilities of the internet for their own interest and enjoyment.

8.7.2 Collaborative blogging

A notable finding from Chapter 5 was that writing blogs was, almost universally, an unusual STC of EL2 CMC. While in most cases the show and tell approach recommends foregrounding those STCs which

Chapter 5 showed to be extensively engaged with, the possibilities offered by blogs for the development of learners' extended writing (Armstrong & Retterer, 2008) suggest that encouraging learners to express themselves in this format can contribute to the overall goal of empowering learners as independent language users.

The show and tell approach therefore proposes using collaborative blogging to continue and extend the process of reflecting on EL2 CMC activities begun in the discussion phase, and to act as a form of scaffolding to enable learners to develop their L2 writing online in a controlled environment, before entering the global blogosphere if they wish. The approach does not advocate expecting learners to produce lengthy blog posts unless they wish to or already do, as this would likely be daunting and demotivating. Instead, it is proposed that teachers establish a communal online space, using a service such as Padlet (www.padlet.com) which allows multiple invited users to post text and images to a shared wall. The platform includes affordances for adding interactive elements such as commenting on and 'liking' posts. Teachers might recommend that learners use the space to record and reflect on their EL2 CMC activities and interesting points of language they come across, though it is not unlikely that learners will appropriate the space for purposes not foreseen by the teacher. Ground rules may be necessary!

8.7.3 Show and tell activities

These are activities based on principles from Ellis's CR tasks and Thorne and Reinhardt's bridging activities. They aim to develop the linguistic tools that learners take with them as subjects in EL2 CMC activities, as well as to develop learners' language awareness as an additional tool to enhance incidental learning. The show and tell activities further aim to center learning on learners' experiences and needs, dealing with the 'real' language encountered by learners in EL2 CMC.

Show and tell activities are a form of CR task, in which the L2 data analyzed by learners are provided by the learners themselves, as in a bridging activity. Learners will be asked to record, by means of screenshot images or interaction logs, a short episode of EL2 CMC in which they were involved and which presented them with some form of difficulty or point of interest. They are asked to provide the teacher with these data prior to class, so that the teacher can prepare, but the focus of the activities should be on inductive, exploratory activities, rather than the top-down teaching of isolated phrases or structures taken from the data. Working in pairs or small groups, learners explain to their peers what they found notable about the data they have brought, and subsequent discussion will seek to decode the text. Learners may wish to ask for help from their teacher and classmates in understanding a particular moment of discourse, or conversely, they may wish to demonstrate to others how they successfully interpreted and negotiated such a moment. In analyzing challenging language encountered online, learners should be encouraged to explore the source of the difficulty, and to question whether native English speakers would find such language easier to understand, or whether the nature of the problem is due to some aspect of group membership online.

This approach sidesteps a number of debates around the use of authentic materials in class. Arguments regarding which texts and variants of English should be selected as authentic in relation to a specific group of learners are rendered largely irrelevant when the language has been encountered in interaction by the learners themselves. Furthermore, observations that language produced for authentic communicative purposes is, even if exactly reproduced, rendered fundamentally inauthentic by its extrication from its original context and the loss of meaning this entails (Widdowson, 1998: 711), are mitigated by the presence of one of the interlocutors party to its original formulation.

8.7.4 Role-play activities

Although the emphasis of the approach is on utilizing authentic communicative interactions for their learning benefits, the final element of the approach uses a role-play structure in order to prepare learners for EL2 CMC in a more controlled and structured way than the show and tell tasks. Show and tell tasks fulfil the key role of enabling learners to learn from authentic interactions, but they may be rather unstructured and haphazard in nature. Role-play activities are therefore proposed to enable controlled practice of key interactional requirements in EL2 CMC. The goal of the role-play activities is not to produce specific lexicogrammatical items, but to encourage learners to reflect on their decision-making processes as they compose messages in online interactions.

Scenarios to be presented to learners in the role-play activities would represent different STCs of CMC, varying along dimensions of synchronicity, participation structure, participant characteristics, topic, purpose, etc. Learners would be provided with tasks to perform within the STC's parameters. Ideally, the role play would take place using relevant technologies, in order to approximate as closely as possible the affordances and constraints of the STC. Learners would be encouraged to be creative with their language use, but to interact appropriately in the text-based medium, demonstrating sensitivity of register and developing awareness of the requirements of the situation. These role plays could be more or less closely linked to the texts collected by the learners and provided to the teacher in advance, and the teacher can encourage learners to look out for real-world examples of the role-play scenarios in their extramural EL2 CMC.

Table 8.2 demonstrates which of the goals of integration the four activity types aim to address.

Table 8.2 Activity types in the show and tell model and the goals they aim to address

Activity type	Goal(s) addressed
Discussion	2: This aims to enhance motivation by centering activities on learners' interests.
Collaborative blogging	1: This aims to support learners' EL2 CMC interactions by providing a digital space for them to share and reflect on their activities.
	2: This aims to enhance motivation by enabling learners to share their activities, thereby seeing a range of possible forms of interaction online.
Show and tell	1: This aims to support learners' EL2 CMC interactions by providing real-world data and leading learners to analyze language use.
	4: This aims to maintain the extramural nature of EL2 CMC activities by asking learners to utilize existing activities, not presenting them with new forms of homework.
	3: This aims to maximize incidental learning outcomes by demonstrating forms of language for learners to look out for.
Role play	1: This aims to support learners' EL2 CMC interactions by allowing them to practice language in a controlled environment.
	3: This aims to maximize incidental learning outcomes by modelling forms of language that learners are then encouraged to look out for online.

8.7.5 Potential obstacles to implementation

There are a number of contextual, methodological and ethical considerations that would need to be addressed in the implementation of the show and tell model. Teachers need to be sensitive to the needs of their particular context when planning the activities.

8.7.5.1 Ethical concerns

The collection of CMC data by learners for use in the classroom may be ethically sensitive. While it is increasingly easy to collect such data using screenshot functionalities on mobile phones and computers, increased sensitivity to the use of personal data may present ethical conflicts with these practices. Publicly visible interactions such as Twitter conversations or interactions on YouTube comment threads are the least problematic, but it may still be necessary to encourage learners to redact user names. Learners should be asked only to collect and utilize data from private conversations after asking permission of all other parties. This may add a degree of awkwardness to conversations that learners are not comfortable with, leading to a lack of participation. Asking permission in this way could usefully be addressed in role-play activities in the initial stages of implementation of the model.

8.7.5.2 Antisocial behaviour and cultural sensitivity

Many online spaces are infamous for enabling aggressive, antisocial and abusive behavior. It is probable that an integrated approach such as the show and tell model would have to deal directly with this possibility, preparing learners to disengage from interactions with offensive interlocutors, and ensuring learners are familiar with mechanisms for reporting bad behavior. EL2 CMC activities engaged with independently are the responsibility of the L2 English user alone, but where the teacher has actively encouraged behaviors that did not previously exist, they bear some responsibility for the learner's well-being.

The same is true of the potential for interacting with content which may be sensitive in some cultural contexts. Teachers will need to use their discretion and familiarize themselves with any relevant conventions or legislation.

8.7.5.3 Participation

While the show and tell model seeks to avoid the imposition of extra homework, it may require forms of participation that learners find unfamiliar. Learners may not engage with the tasks for a number of potential reasons. They may not want to use conversations with online friends as class material, or they may be reluctant to ask for interlocutors' permission to use their data. There were examples in the comments analyzed in Chapter 6 of questionnaire respondents who did not participate in EL2 CMC, and regarded such activities as rather puerile. Communication apprehension may hold learners back from going online, especially where it shades into general shyness. As discussed in a moment in a hypothetical extension of the case of Almon, it may be that some people compartmentalize their online identity from their offline identity and don't wish to mix the two.

The show and tell model is dependent on learner participation, especially the show and tell activities which have no structure without the learner-derived data. Teachers may have to approach implementation slowly and sensitively, perhaps waiting to introduce show and tell activities until a degree of trust has been established between classmates. The collaborative blogging component is a good way to foster this. Learners can begin with descriptive, journal-like entries discussing their online activities without necessarily providing links and revealing online alter-egos. More interactive content will hopefully be forthcoming when it is clear that everyone is in the same situation.

8.7.5.4 Curriculum and level

Many English teachers work within tightly controlled curricula with little room to deviate from institutional requirements. They may also have been trained within a specific paradigm and with a specific skill set. In these cases, implementation of the show and tell model may be unrealistic, although it may be possible to introduce elements of it, perhaps in a more general form of discussing and encouraging learners' EL2 CMC activities. It may be necessary to run workshops training teachers in the principles and goals of the model.

The show and tell model was developed with intermediate-level learners in mind, and can easily be made more complex for higher-level learners. In the case of lower-level learners, at CEFR levels A1 or A2, implementation should be adjusted to learner needs and abilities, perhaps following a basic discussion of social media, etc. If there is evidence of EL2 CMC in the class and an appetite for something like the show and tell model, there is no reason not to try it. It might be better to focus on the controlled activities like role play and collaborative blogging at first, however.

8.8 Almon Revisited

The case of Almon, explored in the case study by Lam (2000), was discussed in some detail earlier in the chapter. In this section, the case is revisited, in order to consider how the show and tell model might have facilitated his (in any case successful) English language development.

8.8.1 Discussion activities

Almon's response to the discussion phase of the model would have depended on whether or not he had yet begun to engage in his online activity. If he had yet to do so, the discussion would have encouraged him to talk about his interest in Japanese pop music and to consider the online communities that might exist in connection with it. In his initial, demotivated and alienated subject position, Almon may have felt that this particular interest further separated him from his American peers, but Lam (2000: 466) notes that most of his classes were remedial or English as a second language (ESL) specific, so it's possible that they may have had a more multicultural composition and J-pop may not have been so conspicuous.

If, on the other hand, Almon had already begun the work of constructing his web page and online identity, he could have shared his experiences with his classmates, discussing the people he encountered and interacted with online and the kinds of language he found himself using. This would have helped him reflect on his online language use and that of others, as well as enabling him to have the value of his EL2 CMC recognized in his formal learning space.

8.8.2 Collaborative blogging

Following the commencement of these online activities, Almon could have posted content on a class-restricted online space set up by the teacher, introducing his classmates to his web page. It is possible that Almon would want to maintain separation between his online life and his school life, and might be reluctant for his classmates to visit his website and intrude on his online identity. This is indeed a potential difficulty of the approach. However, provided this is handled sensitively, and there is mutuality of sharing among classmates, this should prove surmountable.

8.8.3 Show and tell activities

Again, providing he was willing to allow his classmates access to his online life, Almon would have a wealth of examples of CMC interaction to analyze in class. For example, Lam (2000: 472–473) quotes a particular stretch of dialogue in which Almon replies to an acquaintance: 'Yes, I'm 100% agreeing what you're saying'. He could use this stretch to demonstrate his use of hyperbole in fostering agreement and alignment with interlocutors.

8.8.4 Role-play activities

Almon's teacher could have utilized the knowledge of Almon's EL2 CMC activities to construct role-play activities relevant to his needs, for example welcoming a new visitor or subscriber to his web site. The knowledge could even be used to construct more fantastical role plays to practice language in different CMC contexts, such as playing the role of a J-pop studio executive writing an email to a new pop group to offer them a recording contract. Almon surely would find this engaging and stimulating, but his teacher would not have been aware of this interest of his without an approach that engaged Almon's out-of-class language activities.

8.8.5 Summary

Almon was able to exploit the cycle of development between EL2 CMC and classroom learning independently of such an approach as the one described in the preceding sections. However, engaging with his EL2 CMC activities in this way would surely have made his school learning more relevant to his life and learning needs, and helped him out of his demotivated state more quickly. The show and tell model would have allowed him to construct his classroom learning around his own interests, to utilize his extramural activities to motivate his school work and to capitalize on the development of his English language identity taking place online. While there are presumably many learners like Almon, others may require the assistance of an approach to language instruction that provides a degree of scaffolding to enable them to exploit the communicative and developmental potential of the internet, and to kick-start the cycle of empowerment and development illustrated in Figures 8.2 and 8.3.

8.9 Conclusion

This chapter has discussed the potential for integrating EL2 CMC activities more closely in formal classroom learning. Continuing discussions begun in previous chapters, and drawing on insights from the analysis presented in Chapters 4–7, a rationale for such an approach was presented. The benefits of aligning classroom learning with learners' extramural communicative activities were cited from the literature, and findings from the questionnaire analysis showing a high level of interest among English learners for such an integration were invoked in support of the proposal.

The goals of the integration were structured in such a way as to not only maintain the intrinsically extramural nature of EL2 CMC activities, but to capitalize on them to reinforce and enhance the developmental cycle between chat room and classroom. This was conceptualized as linked activity systems, with the outcome of the EL2 CMC system effecting change in the subject of the formal learning system, whose outcome in turn developed the tools of the EL2 CMC system. Furthermore, incidental learning outcomes were present in the theoretical model as motives. In the first instance, learning outcomes were present as motives-stimuli that provided affective feedback to the subject when increased language proficiency was noticed by the subject. However, it was proposed that prompting the language user to be more aware of these benefits, and to approach them strategically, would recast them as a secondary sense-forming motive to the activity, thereby enhancing the outcomes. It was proposed that this shift could be effected through a language awareness approach, priming L2 users to notice salient language in their EL2 CMC activities (see Figure 8.4).

This language awareness approach was argued also to be consistent with the other goals of integration, due to its emphasis on language as a dynamic and evanescent phenomenon, rather than as a fixed body of knowledge. It was proposed that this would help bridge the gap noted by questionnaire respondents between English in the classroom and textbook, and English used in authentic communication.

Addressing the goals of integration, the model outlined in the latter sections of the chapter proposes activities that seek:

- to encourage learners to expand their repertoire of online activities;
- to prepare learners for interactions in online spaces;
- to develop their awareness of language required and used in CMC interactions;
- to capitalize on learners' interests and activities to enhance motivation in the classroom.

The scope of the book did not extend to implementing and assessing the effectiveness of this model: this would provide fertile ground for further research. This is discussed in more detail in the concluding chapter.

9 Conclusion

This book has demonstrated the scale of second language (L2) English computer-mediated communication (CMC) (EL2 CMC) activities by users of English as an L2 all over the world and provides insights into the kinds of concerns and difficulties they have when participating in English language interactions online. It reveals a widespread interest in learning more about online language use and shows key elements of language use that are commonly found in online discourse. Building on these findings, the book proposes an approach to teaching that brings interactions in the 'digital wilds' into the classroom without taming them, helping learners to participate confidently in online interactions, and maximizing their learning benefits.

This concluding chapter revisits the research questions stated in Chapter 1, discussing how they have been answered in the course of the book. The contributions to knowledge made by the research are then set out, followed by a critical reflection on the research methodology, discussing any limitations imposed on the conclusions by elements of the study design. Finally, a number of suggestions are made for future research, building on the foundation laid by this book.

9.1 Research Questions Revisited

Revisiting the research questions posed in Chapter 1 provides an overview of the outcomes of the analysis and exploration undertaken in the course of the book.

9.1.1 RQ1: How widespread are L2 English CMC activities?

The first research question aimed to provide empirical evidence of the scale of L2 English communicative activities online among a broad range of English learners. This was addressed in Chapter 5 from the perspective of socially and technically described contexts of use. All the socio-technical configurations (STCs) surveyed were used highly frequently by at least some respondents, but email and instant messaging (IM) were used most frequently, with personal contexts more common than professional. Individual IM was used with high levels of frequency in all demographic groups, including the lowest language proficiency level. Personal email was similarly widespread, being used highly frequently in all demographic groups except external countries. There was evidence of a shift toward IM in younger L2 English users, including for professional purposes. This corroborates findings elsewhere in the literature (Taipale, 2016: 88), and it was suggested in Chapter 7 that the increasing shift to mobile devices may be leading to a flattening of the differences between platforms and the contexts in which they are used.

Perhaps unsurprisingly, STCs with no public-facing component – IM and email – were the most commonly engaged with, though group IM, with its potential for complex, overlapping discourse dynamics, tended to drop into lower frequency categories in many demographic groups. Consumer activities were dependably occasional, while more social activities such as social media, comment threads and blogs, which were rated occasional overall, nevertheless leaned toward habitual usage. Leisure activities, games, chat rooms and forums, as well as professional networking were regarded as rather niche – unusual overall but with substantial minorities in higher frequency categories. Work-related IM and social media were almost perfectly evenly split between the four response categories.

9.1.2 RQ2: What challenges do L2 English users face in online interactions?

This was addressed quantitatively in Chapter 4, and in two parts in Chapter 6, both quantitatively and qualitatively. The notion of 'challenges' was first explored at the level of activity, asking questionnaire respondents about their level of comfort when engaging in a number of different activities online using English. There was a generally high level of comfort reported with all of the activities listed, but those activities with a substantial evaluative component provoked the highest levels of discomfort. These same activities also received the lowest levels of 'I don't do this' responses and this combination of widespread engagement with evaluative activities and their perceived difficulty makes a strong case for exploring these kinds of interactions further, both in research and in language teaching. The activity theory analysis, supported by evidence from the problems component of the questionnaire, suggested potential conflict between the assertiveness inherent in the motives of evaluative activities, and their socially derived rules of cooperation and politeness. This is equally true of face-to-face interaction as of CMC, but in the latter L2 users are dependent on text to navigate this treacherous terrain.

In the second instances, challenges were explored qualitatively, asking questionnaire respondents to comment on particular difficulties they had experienced online. Themes arising from the comments were analyzed with regard to the components of activity theory. Prominent themes revealed a frustration among respondents with the nature of the English they encountered online. Respondents felt that they were confronted online with a dynamic, colloquial form of the language that was distinct from the language they learned in formal instruction contexts. There was a perception that native speakers had access to this opaque vernacular and that non-native-speaker status precluded participation. Many respondents reported feelings of communication apprehension, fearing to be judged for their use of English, especially by native speakers.

Further themes highlighted the difficulties of fast-paced, multi-party online conversation, keeping up with rapid, interwoven discussion threads. This was often mentioned in connection and conflict with the use of language support resources such as online translation tools and dictionaries. The multitasking inherent in switching between CMC applications and language support resources added a level of cognitive load that was difficult to sustain, especially in highly synchronous interaction.

9.1.3 RQ3: How does the English language used in CMC differ from the language more generally? What kinds of language knowledge are important for learners in this regard?

In answering the third research question, the book explored in more detail the language used online, analyzing two corpora of online discourse representing seven different STCs of CMC. The analysis examined idiomatic use of standard linguistic forms, as well as non-standard typographic forms. The use of language was shown to respond to the degree to which online discourse in any given STC approaches a conversational nature. It was shown that a simple distinction between synchronous and asynchronous technologies was not a good indicator of this conversationality. The analysis provided evidence of a wide array of techniques used to express nuanced meaning and identity through written text, providing online English users with resources.

9.1.4 RQ4: How can L2 English CMC activities be supported and integrated in formal language learning?

Drawing on the findings of the empirical analyses presented in Chapters 4–7, Chapter 8 approached the fourth research question by constructing EL2 CMC and classroom learning as interlinked activity systems, with the outcomes of each affecting the components of the other. This was both a rationale for integration, and a means of analyzing the mutual effects. Responding to concerns raised by questionnaire respondents regarding a perceived disjuncture between the English of the classroom and the 'real' one encountered online, Chapter 8 outlined a model comprising classroom activities that seek to maintain contact between the two, drawing learners' EL2 CMC activities directly into the classroom. By supporting EL2 CMC interactions, the proposed 'show and tell' model aims to produce three forms of enhancement for the learner: enhanced participation online, enhanced motivation for classroom learning and enhanced incidental learning from EL2 CMC activities.

9.2 Contributions

This research was prompted by a number of observations over a decade of English language teaching. Observing L2 English users engaging in online discourse; frustrations with certain students whose English development was due more to playing video games than to doing their homework; L2 English colleagues participating more or less successfully in WhatsApp groups; a friend who declined AirBnB enquiries for his home from L2 English tourists who sounded 'unfriendly'. These encounters suggested a network of internet-facilitated forms of exposure to, and interaction using, English, that were not necessarily anticipated by language teaching practices. How did such interactions affect the language learning process for those individuals? Did they feel more confident as a result of their online activities? More motivated to learn? Did they feel part of a global anglophone community? How widespread were these practices? And how could language teaching adapt to them?

Many of these questions could be addressed through small-scale ethnographic research, and indeed have been in the sources discussed in previous chapters. However, a dearth of evidence attesting to the scale of these activities prompted the decision to focus on the latter questions for this book. It was felt that effecting change in established teaching practices required proof that the significance of online English use was not limited to a minority of 'Almons', but was a ubiquitous characteristic of contemporary life.

This proof is the first main contribution of the book. The short answer to RQ1 is that EL2 CMC is engaged with to at least some degree by learners of all ages and levels all over the world. It is particularly notable in this regard that many lower-level learners have reason to use their English online, suggesting that the sort of 'bridging activities' proposed by Thorne and Reinhardt (2008) should not necessarily be confined to learners of advanced level only, though they must be adjusted accordingly.

The second contribution of the book is an understanding of the needs of L2 English users as they engage in interactions online. While this is on an admittedly broad scale, the analyses of the problems encountered by L2 English users online and the nature of the language in two corpora of online discourse demonstrate the ways in which L2 English users need to be able to manipulate language in order to compensate for the leanness of the medium and express themselves in a text-based medium.

Finally, the book contributes a proposal for an approach to English teaching that supports these activities and maximizes their positive effects on language learning. It is not intended to be the last word on the matter, but as a contribution to an ongoing process of aligning language teaching with the needs of hyper-connected learners.

From an academic perspective, these contributions add to the growing body of knowledge with regard to out-of-class English use and informal learning, providing an empirical foundation on which to base further research that can assume a widespread applicability. The representation of L2 English CMC and formal language learning as interlinked activity systems provides a further example of this kind of interactivity systems analysis proposed and developed by Russell and Yañez (2003: 340), Lantolf and Thorne (2006: 249) and Yamagata-Lynch (2010: 102) among others.

From a language pedagogy perspective, the contributions of the book provide a rationale and justification for the closer integration of extramural activities in the classroom, and a proposal for how this might be done. From the perspective of Cambridge University Press, the book demonstrates the importance of EL2 CMC activities for language learning and provides a profiling of learner age, level and location with regard to their likely EL2 CMC habits.

These two perspectives should not be considered as entirely distinct, however. Not only do complexity-driven approaches emphasize the interrelatedness of theory and practice, but the combination of technical and practical knowledge that characterizes applied linguistics (Ellis, 1997: 7) incorporates elements of both.

9.3 Limitations

The design of the research resulted in a number of limitations which restrict the applicability of the findings. The intention to distribute the questionnaire to a large number of respondents with a broad range of unknown first languages (L1s) meant that it was necessary to gather data in the respondents' L2. Every effort was made to keep the text of the questionnaire items simple and comprehensible, but there was some evidence of misunderstanding on the part of some respondents. There were a total of 59 comments that mentioned some phonological aspect of language suggesting that the authors were not referring to text-based CMC at that time. All but two of these are in the question asking respondents about 'real-time chat', and in hindsight, the wording of the question leaves the mode of the chat ambiguous. This may therefore represent an exception, but the possibility of misunderstanding in less detectable ways remains. However, the large number of respondents should ensure that problems of comprehension were absorbed.

A further point to mention with regard to the questionnaire is the degree of self-selection of respondents. The target population was L2 English users active online, so the recruitment method of placing a banner on the Cambridge Dictionary website was not intrinsically problematic. However, there may have been a further aspect of self-selection, in that it may have been particularly proactive, independent learners who both visit the Cambridge Dictionary, and indeed are inclined to complete questionnaires; 10,000 is a large sample, but still a only fraction of the many hundreds of millions of L2 English users and learners in the world. True representativeness cannot therefore be assumed. However, an underlying principle of the research is that it only sets out to inform a process of needs analysis that in any case should be completed by individual teachers with their students.

A final limitation is in the corpus analysis, in which no data were taken from IM. Chapter 7 discussed the empirical findings and extended them to IM given its relations to the other media present in the corpora, but without data it isn't possible to make conclusive statements about IM.

9.4 Future Research Directions

The analysis presented here is wide ranging and touches on many possible areas of fruitful research. In particular, following the broad scale of the book, more in-depth work utilizing ethnographic approaches would help to observe in detail some of the phenomena suggested by the data. A particularly interesting example would be a recreation of Norton's (2013) study, in which she followed the experiences of immigrant women in Canada as they learned English in their new homes. The case of Eva was discussed in Chapter 2: she was trapped in a vicious circle, unable to gain access to social interaction in order to develop her English, due to her poor English. Norton's study took place in the 1990s before the widespread uptake and use of CMC. The findings of this study pose the intriguing question: what if Eva had had a smartphone? Would she have been able to break out of her cycle of disempowerment more easily? Ethnographic work in this mold could study how the use of EL2 CMC changes the relationships between learners, learning and language.

A particular phenomenon that stands out from the book findings is related to learners in countries categorized as 'institutional' as learning contexts. These countries showed a wider array of CMC engagement, including more highly frequent STCs than any other demographic group, including work-related STCs used with such a degree of frequency nowhere else. Institutional countries also showed disproportionately high levels of comfort in all activities surveyed. These anomalies might be caused by a disproportionately large number of upper-intermediate learners in this group, but in fact institutional countries report the lowest average proficiency levels. Understanding these findings better would be a fascinating source of future research. The language level data is self-reported, so the findings might be indicative of a tendency to underestimate ability in these contexts. It may also highlight the intrinsic difference in the balance of user and learner identities within individuals in these contexts compared with others.

Another pressing matter for further investigation highlighted by the book is the implementation and assessment of the show and tell model, along with other approaches seeking to fulfil the same objectives. Any form of assessment should take into account the four aims of the approach, stated in Chapter 8. Assessment measures should incorporate participation online, motivation in class and some indicator of incidental learning outcomes, though this would potentially be challenging.

Further exploration of the purposes of learners' EL2 CMC interactions and commonly occurring difficulties encountered would help to specify potential areas of support. Research into forms of language and discourse commonly encountered in online spaces would provide materials creators with content relevant to the communicative needs of learners in online spaces. Investigating the link between EL2 CMC and learner motivation would develop our understanding of the role of online extramural English in helping learners take ownership of their L2 and establish themselves as legitimate users.

9.5 Closing Remarks

Globalization and hyper-connectivity have brought new opportunities and obligations to use L2 English, in a wide range of contexts and for a wide range of purposes. This increased exposure has the potential to engender a demotivating 'authenticity gap' in the language classroom if it is ignored (Henry, 2013). However, it likewise has the potential to provide a rich source of motivation and L2 identity development to be embraced and exploited by evolving teaching practices (Lamb & Arisandy, 2019: 17). This book has provided an insight into the contexts and purposes of EL2 CMC. It has demonstrated a wide range of EL2 CMC practices, along with strong qualitative evidence of Henry's authenticity gap. The approach to teaching proposed and discussed in Chapter 8 represents an attempt to minimize the disruptiveness of this gap, and instead capitalize on the benefits of real-world language exposure.

A priority in undertaking this research and writing this book was to acknowledge and embrace the dynamism and pace of change of technological development. Terminology related to the internet often has a tendency to be out of date almost as soon as it is coined, and individual CMC platforms come and go: even the mighty Facebook is falling out of favor with the younger generation.[1] This book sought to avoid making statements with regard to discrete bodies of knowledge to be taught to language learners, and instead focus on approaches that teach an awareness of change. In order to remain relevant to the lives and needs of English learners, we need to recognize their varied experiences with the language in today's hyper-connected world.

Note

(1) https://www.pewinternet.org/2018/05/31/teens-social-media-technology-2018/.

References

Ahmed, W., Bath, P.A., Sbaffi, L. and Demartini, G. (2019) Novel insights into views towards H1N1 during the 2009 pandemic: A thematic analysis of Twitter data. *Health Information and Libraries Journal* 36 (1), 60–72. https://doi.org/10.1111/hir.12247

Anderson, J.F., Beard, F.K. and Walther, J.B. (2010) Turn-Taking and the local management of conversation in a highly simultaneous computer-mediated communication system. *Language@Internet* 7, 1–28. Retrieved from http://www.languageatinternet.org/articles/2010/2804. Accessed February 15 2022.

Arminen, I., Licoppe, C. and Spagnolli, A. (2016) Respecifying mediated interaction. *Research on Language and Social Interaction* 49 (4), 290–309. https://doi.org/10.1080/08351813.2016.1234614

Armstrong, K. and Retterer, O. (2008) Blogging as L2 writing : A case study. *AACE Journal* 16 (3), 233–251.

Bakhtin, M.M. (1981) *The Dialogic Imagination* (M. Holquist, ed.). Austin, TX: University of Texas Press.

Baron, N.S. (1998) Letters by phone or speech by other means: The linguistics of email. *Language & Communication* 18, 133–170.

Baron, N.S. (2008) *Always On: Language in an Online and Mobile World.* New York: Oxford University Press. https://doi.org/10.1017/S0272263114000254

Baron, N.S. (2010) Discourse structures in instant messaging : The case of utterance breaks. *Language @ Internet* 7, 1–25. See http://www.languageatinternet.org/articles/2010/2651/Baron.pdf. Accessed February 15 2022.

Barton, D. and Lee, C. (2013) *Language Online: Investigating Digital Texts and Practices.* Abingdon: Routledge.

Becker, A.L. (1991) Language and languaging. *Language and Communication* 11 (1–2), 33–35. https://doi.org/10.1016/0271-5309(91)90013-l

Becker, J.A.H. and Stamp, G.H. (2005) Impression management in chat rooms: A grounded theory model. *Communication Studies* 56 (3), 243–260. https://doi.org/10.1080/10510970500181264

Beckner, C., Ellis, N.C., Blythe, R., Holland, J., Bybee, J., Ke, J., Christiansen, M.H., Croft, W. and Schoenemann, T. (2009) Language is a complex adaptive system: Position paper. *Language Learning* 59 (1), 1–26.

Benson, P. (2011) Language learning and teaching beyond the classroom: An introduction to the field. In P. Benson and H. Reinders (eds) *Beyond the Language Classroom* (pp. 7–16). Basingstoke: Palgrave MacMillan. https://doi.org/10.1057/9780230306790

Berger, P.L. and Luckmann, T. (1966) *The Social Construction of Reality.* London: Penguin.

Biber, D. (1988) *Variation Across Speech and Writing.* Cambridge: Cambridge University Press.

Biber, D., Johansson, S., Leech, G.N., Conrad, S. and Finegan, E. (1999) *Longman Grammar of Spoken and Written English*. Harlow: Pearson. https://doi.org/10.1353/lan.2001.0127

Bieswanger, M. (2016) Electronically mediated Englishes: Synchronicity revisited. In L. Squires (ed.) *English in Computer-Mediated Communication* (pp. 281–300). Berlin: De Gruyter.

Bondi, M. (2010) Perspectives on keywords and keyness. In M. Bondi and M. Scott (eds) *Keyness in Texts* (pp. 1–18). Amsterdam: John Benjamins.

Borg, S. (1994) Language awareness as methodology: Implications for teachers and teacher training. *Language Awareness* 3 (2), 61–71. https://doi.org/10.1080/09658416.1994.9959844

Bourdieu, P. (1977) The economics of linguistic exchanges. *Social Science Information* 16 (6), 645–668. https://doi.org/10.1177/053901847701600601

boyd, d. (2007) Why youth (heart) social network sites: The role of networked publics in teenage social life. *MacArthur Foundation Series on Digital Learning – Youth, Identity, and Digital Media* 7641 (41), 1–26. https://doi.org/10.1162/dmal.9780262524834.119

Brandl, K. (2020) *Communicative Language Teaching in Action: Putting Principles to Work*. San Diego, CA: Cognella, Incorporated.

Braun, V. and Clarke, V. (2006) Using thematic analysis in psychology. *Qualitative Research in Psychology* 3 (2), 77–101.

Brett, D. (2009) Eye dialect: Translating the untranslatable. In *Annali della Facoltà di Lingue e Letterature Straniere di Sassari* (Vol. 6, pp. 49–62). Sassari: University of Sassari.

Brown, P. and Levinson, S.C. (1987) *Politeness: Some Universals in Language Usage*. New York: Cambridge University Press.

Bucholtz, M. (1999) You da man: Narrating the racial other in the production of white masculinity. *Journal of Sociolinguistics* 3 (4), 443–460. https://doi.org/10.1111/1467-9481.00090

Bucholtz, M. and Hall, K. (2005) Identity and interaction: A sociocultural linguistic approach. *Discourse Studies* 7 (4–5), 585–614.

Cameron, L. and Larsen-Freeman, D. (2007) Complex systems and applied linguistics. *International Journal of Applied Linguistics* 17 (2), 226–240. https://doi.org/10.1111/j.1473-4192.2007.00148.x

Canale, M. (1983) From communicative competence to communicative language pedagogy. In J.C. Richards and R.W. Schmidt (eds) *Language and Communication* (pp. 2–27). London: Longman.

Carter, R. and McCarthy, M. (2006) *Cambridge Grammar of English: A Comprehensive Guide*. Cambridge: Cambridge University Press.

Carter, R. and McCarthy, M. (2015) Spoken grammar: Where are we and where are we going? *Applied Linguistics* 1–21. https://doi.org/10.1093/applin/amu080

Chen, H. (2013) Identity practices of multilingual writers in social networking spaces. *Language Learning & Technology* 17 (2), 143–170.

Church, K. and de Oliveira, R. (2013) What's up with WhatsApp ? Comparing mobile instant messaging behaviors with traditional SMS. *Fifteenth International Conference on Human-Computer Interaction with Mobile Devices and Services* 352–361.

Cole, J. and Vanderplank, R. (2016) Comparing autonomous and class-based learners in Brazil: Evidence for the present-day advantages of informal, out-of-class learning. *System* 61, 31–42. https://doi.org/10.1016/j.system.2016.07.007

Cook, V. (2002) Background to the L2 user. In V. Cook (ed.) *Portraits of the L2 User* (pp. 1–28). Clevedon: Multilingual Matters.

Cook, V. (2011) The nature of the L2 user. In L. Wei (ed.) *The Routledge Applied Linguistics Reader* (pp. 77–89). London: Routledge.

Council of Europe (2001) *The Common European Framework of Reference for Languages: Learning, Teaching, Assessment.* Cambridge: Cambridge University Press. https://doi.org/10.1093/elt/cci105

Council of Europe (2018) *Common European Framework of Reference for Languages: Companion Volume with New Descriptors.* Cambridge: Cambridge University Press. https://doi.org/10.1017/CHOL9780521221283

Council of the European Union (2012) Council recommendation of 20 December 2012 on the validation of non-formal and informal learning – 2012/C 398/01. *Official Journal of the European Unon* C 398, 1–5. See https://eur-lex.europa.eu/legal-content/EN/TXT/?uri=uriserv:OJ.C_.2012.398.01.0001.01.ENG. Accessed February 15 2022.

Crystal, D. (2001) *Language and the Internet* (2nd edn). Cambridge: Cambridge University Press. https://doi.org/10.1093/elt/XXV.2.140

Crystal, D. (2006) *Language and the Internet.* Cambridge: Cambridge University Press.

Crystal, D. (2008) *Txtng: The Gr8 Db8.* Oxford: Oxford University Press.

Daft, R.L. and Lengel, R.H. (1984) Information richness: A new approach to managerial behavior and organization design. *Research in Organizational Behaviour* 6, 191–233. https://doi.org/N00014-83-C-0025

Davis, F.D. (1989) Perceived usefulness, perceived ease of use, and user acceptance of information technology. *MIS Quarterly* 13 (3), 319. https://doi.org/10.2307/249008

Dennis, A.R., Fuller, R.M. and Valacich, J.S. (2008) Media, tasks, and communication processes: A theory of media synchronicity. *MIS Quarterly* 32 (3), 575–600. https://doi.org/10.2307/25148857

Dörnyei, Z. (2005) *The Psychology of the Language Learner: Individual Differences in Second Language Acquisition.* Mahwah, NJ: Taylor & Francis.

Dörnyei, Z. (2009) The L2 motivational self system. In Z. Dörnyei and E. Ushioda (eds) *Motivation, Language Identity and the L2 Self* (pp. 9–42). Bristol: Multilingual Matters.

Dörnyei, Z. and Taguchi, T. (2010) *Questionnaires in Second Language Research* (2nd edn). London: Routledge.

Dressman, M. and Sadler, R.W. (2020) *The Handbook of Informal Language Learning.* Hoboken, NJ: Wiley.

Du Bois, J.W. (2007) The stance triangle. In J. Englebretson (ed.) *Stancetaking in Discourse: Subjectivity, Evaluation, Interaction* (pp. 139–182). Amsterdam: John Benjamins.

van Ek, J.A. and Trim, J.L.M. (1998) *Threshold 1990* (revised). Cambridge: Cambridge University Press.

Ellis, R. (1995) Interpretation tasks for grammar teaching. *TESOL Quarterly* 29 (1), 87–105. https://doi.org/10.2307/3587806

Ellis, R. (1997) *SLA Research and Language Teaching.* Oxford: Oxford University Press.

Engeström, Y. (1987) *Learning by Expanding: An Activity-Theoretical Approach to Developmental Research* (1st edn). Helsinki: Orienta-Konsultit.

Engeström, Y. (1993) Developmental studies of work as a test bench of activity theory: The case of primary care medical practice. In S. Chaiklin and J. Lave (eds) *Understanding Practice: Perspectives on Activity and Context* (pp. 64–103). Cambridge: Cambridge University Press.

Engeström, Y. (1999a) Activity theory and individual and social transformation. In Y. Engeström, R. Miettinen and R.L. Punamäki (eds) *Perspectives on Activity Theory* (pp. 19–38). Cambridge: Cambridge University Press.

Engeström, Y. (1999b) Innovative learning in work teams: Analyzing cycles of knowledge creation in practice. In Y. Engeström, R. Miettinen and R.L. Punamäki (eds) *Perspectives on Activity Theory* (pp. 377–404). Cambridge: Cambridge University Press.

Engeström, Y. (2001) Expansive learning at work: Toward an activity theoretical reconceptualization. *Journal of Education and Work* 14 (1), 133–156. https://doi.org/10.1080/13639080020028747

Engeström, Y. (2015) *Learning by Expanding: An Activity-Theoretical Approach to Developmental Research* (2nd edn). New York: Cambridge University Press.

Firth, A. and Wagner, J. (1997) On discourse, communication, and (some) fundamental concepts in SLA research. *The Modern Language Journal* 81 (3), 285–300.

Forsyth, E.N. and Martell, C.H. (2007) Lexical and discourse analysis of online chat dialog. *ICSC 2007 International Conference on Semantic Computing* 19–26. https://doi.org/10.1109/ICOSC.2007.4338328

Friedlander, B., Jacobs, A., Davis, B. and Wetstone, H. (1972) Time-sampling analysis of infants' natural language environments in the home. *Child Development* 43 (3), 730–740.

Friemel, T.N. (2016) The digital divide has grown old: Determinants of a digital divide among seniors. *New Media & Society* 1–19. https://doi.org/10.1177/14614448145 38648

Garcia, A.C. and Jacobs, J.B. (1999) The eyes of the beholder: Understanding the turn-taking system in quasi-synchronous computer-mediated communication. *Research on Language and Social Interaction* 32 (4), 337–367. https://doi.org/10.1207/S15327973rls3204

García, O. and Li, W. (2014) *Translanguaging: Language, Bilingualism and Education.* Basingstoke: Palgrave MacMillan.

Gardner, R.C. and Lambert, W.E. (1972) *Attitudes and Motivation in Second Language Learning*. Rowley, MA: Newbury House.

Gass, S.M. (1997) *Input, Interaction, and the Second Language Learner.* Mahwah, NJ: Lawrence Erlbaum.

Gass, S.M. (2003) Input and interaction. In C.J. Doughty and M.H. Long (eds) *The Handbook of Second Language Acquisition* (pp. 224–255). Malden, MA: Blackwell.

Gilmore, A. (2007) Authentic materials and authenticity in foreign language learning. *Language Teaching* 40 (2), 97–118. https://doi.org/10.1017/s0261444807004144

Godwin-Jones, R. (2019) Riding the digital wilds: Learner autonomy and informal language learning. *Language Learning and Technology* 23 (1), 8–25. https://doi.org/10.125/44667

Goffman, E. (1959) *The Presentation of Self In Everyday Life.* New York: Anchor Books. https://doi.org/10.2307/258197

Goffman, E. (1981) *Forms of Talk.* Philadelphia, PA: University of Pennsylvania Press.

Goutte, C., Wang, Y., Liao, F., Zanussi, Z., Larkin, S. and Grinberg, Y. (2018) Eurogames16: Evaluating change detection in online conversation. *LREC 2018 – 11th International Conference on Language Resources and Evaluation*, 1755–1761.

Grice, H.P. (1975) Logic and conversation. In P. Cole and J.L. Morgan (eds) *Syntax and Semantics 3: Speech Acts* (pp. 41–58). New York: Academic Press.

Gunawardena, C.N., Lowe, C.A. and Anderson, T. (1997) Analysis of a global online debate and the development of an interaction analysis model for examining social construction of knowledge in computer conferencing. *Journal of Educational Computing Research* 17 (4), 397–431. https://doi.org/10.2190/7mqv-x9uj-c7q3-nrag

Halliday, M.A.K. (1973) *Explorations in the Functions of Language.* London: Arnold.

Hanna, B. and de Nooy, J. (2003) A funny thing happened on the way to the forum: Electronic discussion and foreign language learning. *Language Learning & Technology* 7 (1), 71–85. See http://llt.msu.edu/vol7num1/hanna/default.html. Accessed February 15 2022.

Hauk, N., Hüffmeier, J. and Krumm, S. (2018) Ready to be a silver surfer? A meta-analysis on the relationship between chronological age and technology acceptance. *Computers in Human Behavior* 84, 304–319. https://doi.org/10.1016/j.chb.2018.01.020

Helsper, E.J. and Eynon, R. (2010) Digital natives: Where is the evidence? *British Educational Research Journal* 36 (3), 503–520. https://doi.org/10.1080/01411920902989227

Henry, A. (2013) Digital games and ELT: Bridging the authenticity gap. In E. Ushioda (ed.) *International Perspectives on Motivation: Language Learning and Professional Challenges* (pp. 133–155). Houndsmill: Palgrave MacMillan. https://doi.org/10.1057/9781137000873_8

Henry, A., Korp, H., Sundqvist, P. and Thorsen, C. (2017) Motivational strategies and the reframing of English: Activity design and challenges for teachers in contexts of extensive extramural encounters. *TESOL Quarterly* (July). https://doi.org/10.1002/tesq.394

Herring, S.C. (1999) Interactional coherence in CMC. *Journal of Computer-Mediated Communication* 4 (4). https://doi.org/10.1111/j.1083

Herring, S.C. (2001) Computer-mediated discourse. In D. Schiffrin, D. Tannen and H.E. Hamilton (eds) *Handbook of Discourse Analysis* (pp. 612–634). Malden, MA: Blackwell.

Herring, S.C. (2007) A faceted classification scheme for computer-mediated discourse. *Language @ Internet* 2007 (1), 1–37. See http://www.languageatinternet.org/articles/2007/761/. Accessed February 15 2022.

Herring, S.C. and Androutsopoulos, J. (2015) Computer-mediated discourse 2.0. In D. Tannen, H.E. Hamilton and D. Schiffrin (eds) *The Handbook of Discourse Analysis* (2nd edn, pp. 127–151). Chichester: Wiley.

Holliday, A. (2005) *The Struggle to Teach English as an International Language*. Oxford: Oxford University Press.

Holliday, A. (2015) Qualitative research and analysis. In B. Paltridge and A. Phakiti (eds) *Research Methods in Applied Linguistics: A Practical Resource* (pp. 49–62). London: Bloomsbury.

Honeycutt, C. and Herring, S.C. (2009) Beyond microblogging: Conversation and collaboration via twitter. *Proceedings of the 42nd Annual Hawaii International Conference on System Sciences HICSS*, 1–10. https://doi.org/10.1109/HICSS.2009.89

Horrigan, J.B. (2007) A typology of information and communication technology users. See http://www.pewinternet.org/2007/05/06/a-typology-of-information-and-communication-technology-users/. Accessed February 15 2022.

Hunston, S. (2002) *Corpora in Applied Linguistics*. Cambridge: Cambridge University Press.

Hunston, S. (2011) *Corpus Approaches to Evaluation: Phraseology and Evaluative Language*. Abingdon: Routledge.

Hunston, S. and Francis, G. (2000) *Pattern Grammar: A Corpus-Driven Approach to the Lexical Grammar of English*. Amsterdam: John Benjamins.

Hymes, D. (1972) On communicative competence. In J.B. Pride and J. Holmes (eds) *Sociolinguistics: Selected Readings* (pp. 269–293). Harmondsworth: Penguin. https://doi.org/10.1007/s11606-007-0364-4

Ikkala, T. and Lampinen, A. (2014) Defining the price of hospitality: Networked hospitality exchange via Airbnb. *CSCW 2014 Proceedings* (February 2014), 173–176. https://doi.org/10.1145/2556420.2556506

Inaba, M. (2019) *Second Language Literacy Practices and Language Learning Outside the Classroom*. Bristol: Multilingual Matters.

Irvine, J.T. (1979) Formality and informality in communicative events. *American Anthropologist* 81 (4), 773–790. https://doi.org/10.1525/aa.1979.81.4.02a00020

Ito, R. and Tagliamonte, S. (2003) Well weird, right dodgy, very strange, really cool: Layering and recycling in English intensifiers. *Language in Society* 32 (2), 257–279. https://doi.org/10.1017/S0047404503322055

Jarvis, H. and Achilleos, M. (2013) From computer-assisted language learning (CALL) to mobile-assisted language use (MALU). *TESL-EJ* 16 (4). See http://www.tesl-ej.org/wordpress/issues/volume16/ej64/ej64a2/. Accessed February 15 2022.

Jenks, C. (2014) *Social Interaction in Second Language Chat Rooms*. Edinburgh: Edinburgh University Press.

Jones, R.H. (2004) The problem of context in computer mediated communication. In P. LeVine and R. Scollon (eds) *Discourse and Technology: Multimodal Discourse Analysis* (pp. 20–33). Washington, D.C.: Georgetown University Press.

Jordan, B. (2009) Introduction: Blurring boundaries: The 'real' and the 'virtual' in hybrid spaces. *Human Organization* 68 (2), 181–193. https://doi.org/10.17730/humo.68.2.7x4406g270801284

Jurkovič, V. (2019) Online informal learning of English through smartphones in Slovenia. *System* 80, 27–37. https://doi.org/10.1016/j.system.2018.10.007

Kachru, B. (1985) Standards, codification and sociolinguistic realism: The English language in the outer circle. In R. Quirk and H. Widdowson (eds) *English in the World* (pp. 11–30). Cambridge: Cambridge University Press.

Kalman, Y. and Rafaeli, S. (2007) Modulating synchronicity in computer mediated communication. Paper presented at the 2007 Conference of the International Communication Association, San Francisco, CA. See https://www.kalmans.com/synchasynch ICAsubmit.pdf. Accessed February 15 2022.

Kaptelinin, V. and Nardi, B.A. (2006) *Acting with Technology: Activity Theory and Interaction Design*. Cambridge, MA: MIT Press.

Katzner, K. and Miller, K. (2002) *Languages of the World* (3rd edn). London: Routledge.

Kilgarriff, A. (2009) Simple maths for keywords. In M. Mahlberg, V. González-Díaz and C. Smith (eds) *Proceedings of the Corpus Linguistics Conference, CL2009 Liverpool, UK* (p. 6). See https://www.sketchengine.eu/wp-content/uploads/2015/04/2009-Simple-maths-for-keywords.pdf. Accessed February 15 2022.

Knight, D. (2015) e-Language: Communication in the digital age. In P. Baker and T. McEnery (eds) *Corpora and Discourse Studies* (pp. 20–40). Basingstoke: Palgrave MacMillan.

Knight, D., Adolphs, S. and Carter, R. (2013) Formality in digital discourse: A study of hedging in CANELC. In J. Romero-Trillo (ed.) *Yearbook of Corpus Linguistics and Pragmatics* (pp. 131–152). London: Springer. https://doi.org/10.1007/978-94-007-6250-3_7

Knight, D., Adolphs, S. and Carter, R. (2014) CANELC: Constructing an e-language corpus. *Corpora* 9 (1), 29–56. https://doi.org/10.3366/cor.2014.0050

Kramsch, C. (2013) *The Multilingual Subject*. New York: Oxford University Press.

Krashen, S.D. (1981) *Second Language Acquisition and Second Language Learning*. Oxford: Pergamon.

Krashen, S.D. (1982) *Principles and Practice in Second Language Acquisition*. Oxford: Pergamon.

Kusyk, M. (2017) The development of complexity, Accuracy and fluency in L2 written production through informal participation in online activities. *CALICO Journal* 34 (1), 75–96. https://doi.org/10.1558/cj.29513

Kuutti, K. and Bannon, L.J. (2014) The turn to practice in HCI: Towards a research agenda. In *CHI 2014, One of a CHInd, Toronto, ON, Canada, April 26–May 1 2014* (pp. 3543–3552). New York: ACM.

Lai, C., Zhu, W. and Gong, G. (2015) Understanding the quality of out-of-class English learning. *TESOL Quarterly* 49 (2), 278–308. https://doi.org/10.1002/tesq.171

Lai, C., Hu, X. and Lyu, B. (2018) Understanding the nature of learners' out-of-class language learning experience with technology. *Computer Assisted Language Learning* 31 (1–2), 114–143. https://doi.org/10.1080/09588221.2017.1391293

Lam, W.S.E. (2000) L2 literacy and the design of the self: A case study of a teenager writing on the internet. *TESOL Quarterly* 34 (3), 457–482. https://doi.org/10.2307/3587739

Lamb, M. and Arisandy, F.E. (2019) The impact of online use of English on motivation to learn. *Computer Assisted Language Learning* 33 (1–2), 85–108. https://doi.org/10.1080/09588221.2018.1545670

Lantolf, J.P. and Thorne, S.L. (2006) *Sociocultural Theory and the Genesis of Second Language Development*. Oxford: Oxford University Press.

Larsen-Freeman, D. and Cameron, L. (2008) *Complex Systems and Applied Linguistics*. Oxford: Oxford University Press.

Latzko-Toth, G. (2010) Metaphors of synchrony: Emergence and differentiation of online chat devices. *Bulletin of Science, Technology & Society* 30 (5), 362–374. https://doi.org/10.1177/0270467610380005

Layder, D. (1997) *Modern Social Theory*. London: UCL Press.

Lee, J.S. (2017) Informal digital learning of English and second language vocabulary outcomes: Can quantity conquer quality? *British Journal of Educational Technology* 5 (2), 767–778. https://doi.org/10.1111/bjet.12599

Lee, J.S. (2019a) EFL students' views of willingness to communicate in the extramural digital context. *Computer Assisted Language Learning* 32 (7), 692–712. https://doi.org/10.1080/09588221.2018.1535509

Lee, J.S. (2019b) Quantity and diversity of informal digital learning of English. *Language Learning & Technology* 23 (1), 114–126. https://doi.org/https://doi.org/10125/44675

Lee, J.S. and Dressman, M. (2018) When IDLE hands make an English workshop: Informal digital learning of English and language proficiency. *TESOL Quarterly* 52 (2), 435–445.

Lee, L. (2002) Synchronous online exchanges: A study of modification devices on non-native discourse. *System* 30 (3), 275–288. https://doi.org/10.1016/S0346-251X(02)00015-5

Leech, G.N. (1983) *Principles of Pragmatics*. London: Longman.

Leech, G.N. (2000) Grammars of spoken English: New outcomes of corpus-oriented research. *Language Learning* 50 (4), 675–724. https://doi.org/10.1111/0023-8333.00143

Leontiev, A.N. (1978) *Activity, Consciousness, and Personality*. Engelwood Cliffs, NJ: Prentice Hall.

Lewis, C. and Fabos, B. (2005) Instant messaging, literacies, and social identities. *Reading Research Quarterly* 40 (4), 470–501. https://doi.org/10.1598/RRQ.40.4.5

Lin, H. (2015) A meta-synthesis of empirical research on the effectiveness of computer-mediated communication (CMC) in SLA. *Language Learning & Technology* 19 (192), 85–117. See https://www.lltjournal.org/item/10125-44419/. Accessed February 15 2022.

Linell, P. (2009) *Rethinking Language, Mind, and World Dialogically: Interactional and Contextual Theories of Human Sense-Making*. Charlotte, NC: Information Age Publishers. https://doi.org/10.1177/0959354310364279

Lowry, P.B., Romano, N.C., Jenkins, J.L. and Guthrie, R.W. (2009) The CMC interactivity model: How interactivity enhances communication quality and process satisfaction in lean-media groups. *Journal of Management Information Systems* 26 (1), 155–196. https://doi.org/10.2753/MIS0742-1222260107

Lyrigkou, C. (2018) Not to be overlooked: Agency in informal language contact. *Innovation in Language Learning and Teaching* 13 (3), 237–252. https://doi.org/10.1080/17501229.2018.1433182

Lyster, R., Saito, K. and Sato, M. (2013) Oral corrective feedback in second language classrooms. *Language Teaching* 46 (1), 1–40. https://doi.org/10.29344/0717621x.19.1587

MacIntyre, P.D. (1999) Language anxiety: A review of the research for language teachers. In D.J. Young (ed.) *Affect in Foreign Language and Second Language Learning* (pp. 24–45). Boston, MA: McGraw-Hill.

MacIntyre, P.D. and Gardner, R.C. (1994) The subtle effects of language anxiety on cognitive processing in the second language. *Language Learning* 44 (2), 283–305.

Marsick, V.J. and Watkins, K.E. (1990) *Informal and Incidental Learning in the Workplace*. London: Routledge.

Martin, J.R. and White, P.R. (2005) *The Language of Evaluation*. Basingstoke: Palgrave MacMillan.

McArthur, T. (1998) *The Concise Companion to the English Language*. New York: Oxford University Press.

McCafferty, S.G., Roebuck, R.F. and Wayland, R.P. (2001) Activity theory and the incidental learning of second-language vocabulary. *Language Awareness* 10 (4), 289–294. https://doi.org/10.1080/09658410108667040

McCroskey, J.C. (1984) The communication apprehension perspective. In J.A. Daly, J.C. McCroskey, J. Ayres, T. Hopf, D. Sonandre and T.A. Wongprasert (eds) *Avoiding Communication: Shyness, Reticence, and Communication Apprehension* (pp. 13–38). New York: Hampton Press.

Mercado, L.A. (2015) Integrating classroom learning and autonomous learning. In D. Nunan and J.C. Richards (eds) *Language Learning Beyond the Classroom* (pp. 189–201). New York: Routledge.

Mercer, S. (2016) Complexity and language teaching. In G. Hall (ed.) *The Routledge Handbook of English Language Teaching* (pp. 473–485). Abingdon: Routledge.

Miller, D. and Slater, D. (2000) *The Internet: An Ethnographic Approach*. Oxford: Berg.

Montoya-Weiss, M.M., Massey, A.P. and Clapper, D.L. (1998) On-line focus groups: Conceptual issues and a research tool. *European Journal of Marketing* 32 (7/8), 713–723. https://doi.org/10.1108/03090569810224100

Moors, G. (2008) Exploring the effect of a middle response category on response style in attitude measurement. *Quality and Quantity* 42 (6), 779–794. https://doi.org/10.1007/s11135-006-9067-x

Muir, C., Dörnyei, Z. and Adolphs, S. (2019) Role models in language learning: Results of a large-scale international survey. *Applied Linguistics* 1–24. https://doi.org/10.1093/applin/amz056

Nardi, B.A., Whittaker, S. and Bradner, E. (2000) Interaction and outeraction: Instant messaging in action. In *Proceedings of the 2000 ACM conference on computer-supported cooperative work* (pp. 79–88).

Nayar, P.B. (1997) ESL/EFL dichotomy today: Language politics or pragmatics? *TESOL Quarterly* 31 (1), 9–37. https://doi.org/10.2307/3587973

Norton, B. (2013) *Identity and Language Learning: Extending the Conversation* (2nd edn). Bristol: Multilingual Matters.

Norton Peirce, B. (1995) Social identity, investment, and language learning. *TESOL Quarterly* 29 (1), 9–31.

OECD (2015) *The OECD Model Survey on ICT Access and Usage by Households and Individuals (2nd revision)*. See https://www.oecd.org/sti/ieconomy/ICT-Model-Survey-Access-Usage-Households-Individuals.pdf. Accessed February 15 2022.

Orsatti, J. and Riemer, K. (2012) Identity and self-presentation: From a representational to a performative lens in studying social media engagement in organisations. *ACIS 2012: Location, Location, Location: Proceedings of the 23rd Australasian Conference on Information Systems 2012*, 1–12. See http://dro.deakin.edu.au/view/DU:30049060

Ozok, A.A. (2007) Survey design and implementation in HCI. In A. Sears and J. Jacko (eds) *Human-Computer Interaction: Development Process* (pp. 253–271). New York: Lawrence Erlbaum.

Pasfield-Neofitou, S.E. (2012) *Online Communication in a Second Language: Social Interaction, Language Use, and Learning Japanese*. Bristol: Multilingual Matters.

Prensky, M. (2001) Digital natives, digital immigrants part 1. *On the Horizon* 9 (5), 1–6. https://doi.org/10.1108/10748120110424816

Rice, R.E. (1992) Task analyzability, use of new media, and effectiveness: A multi-site exploration of media richness. *Organization Science* 3 (4), 475–500.

Rieder, A. (2003) Implicit and explicit learning in incidental vocabulary acquisition. *VIEWS* 12 (2), 24–39. See https://typo3.univie.ac.at/fileadmin/user_upload/dep_anglist/weitere_Uploads/Views/VIEWS122.PDF. Accessed February 15 2022.

Rühlemann, C. (2006) Coming to terms with conversational grammar. *International Journal of Corpus Linguistics* 11 (4), 385–409.

Rühlemann, C. and Donnell, M.B.O. (2014) Deixis. In K. Aijmer and C. Rühlemann (eds) *Corpus Pragmatics: A Handbook* (pp. 331–359). Cambridge: Cambridge University Press.

Russell, D.R. and Yañez, A. (2003) 'Big picture people rarely become historians': Genre systems and the contradictions of general education. In C. Bazerman and D.R. Russell (eds) *Writing Selves/Writing Societies: Research from Activity Perspectives* (pp.

331–362). Fort Collins, CO: The WAC Clearinghouse. See https://wac.colostate.edu/books/perspectives/selves-societies/. Accessed February 15 2022.

Sacks, H., Schegloff, E.A. and Jefferson, G. (1974) A simplest systematics for the organization of turn taking for conversation. *Language* 50, 696–735. https://doi.org/10.2307/412243

Satar, H.M. and Özdener, N. (2008) The effects of synchronous CMC on speaking proficiency and anxiety: Text versus voice chat. *Modern Language Journal* 92 (4), 595–613. https://doi.org/10.1111/j.1540-4781.2008.00789.x

Sauro, S. and Zourou, K. (2019) What are the digital wilds? *Language Learning & Technology* 23 (1), 1–7.

Schegloff, E.A. (2000) Overlapping talk and the organization of turn-taking for conversation. *Language in Society* 29 (1), 1–63. https://doi.org/10.1017/s0047404500001019

Schmidt, R.W. (1990) The role of consciousness in second language acquisition. *Applied Linguistics* 11 (2), 129–158.

Siegel, J. (2003) Social Context. In C. J. Doughty and M.H. Long (eds) *The Handbook of Second Language Acquisition* (pp. 178–223). Malden, MA: Blackwell.

Sockett, G. (2013) Understanding the online informal learning of English as a complex dynamic system: An emic approach. *ReCALL* 25 (1), 48–62. https://doi.org/10.1017/S095834401200033X

Sockett, G. (2014) *The Online Informal Learning of English*. Basingstoke: Palgrave Macmillan.

Spolsky, B. (1989) *Conditions for Second Language Learning*. Oxford: Oxford University Press.

Squires, L. (2016) *English in Computer-Mediated Communication*. Berlin: De Gruyter.

Sullivan, G.M. and Artino, A.R. (2013) Analyzing and interpreting data From Likert-type scales. *Journal of Graduate Medical Education* 5 (4), 541–542. https://doi.org/10.4300/jgme-5-4-18

Sundqvist, P. (2009) *Extramural English Matters: Out-of-School English and its Impact on Swedish Ninth Graders' Oral Proficiency and Vocabulary*. Karlstad: Karlstad University. See http://www.diva-portal.org/smash/get/diva2:275141/FULLTEXT03. Accessed February 15 2022.

Sundqvist, P. and Sylvén, L.K. (2014) Language-related computer use: Focus on young L2 English learners in Sweden. *ReCALL* 26 (01), 3–20. https://doi.org/10.1017/S0958344013000232

Sundqvist, P. and Sylvén, L.K. (2016) *Extramural English in Teaching and Learning: From Theory and Research to Practice*. London: Palgrave MacMillan.

Svalberg, A.M.L. (2007) Language awareness and language learning. *Language Teaching* 40 (4), 287–308. https://doi.org/10.1017/s0261444807004491

Swain, M. (2006) Languaging, agency and collaboration in advanced second language proficiency. In H. Byrnes (ed.) *Advanced Language Learning: The Contribution of Halliday and Vygotsky* (pp. 95–108). London: Continuum.

Sylvén, L.K. and Sundqvist, P. (2012) Gaming as extramural English L2 learning and L2 proficiency among young learners. *ReCALL* 24 (3), 302–321.

Taipale, S. (2016) Synchronicity matters: Defining the characteristics of digital generations. *Information, Communication & Society* 19 (1), 80–94. https://doi.org/10.1080/1369118X.2015.1093528

Tanis, M. and Postmes, T. (2003) Social cues and impression formation in CMC. *Journal of Communication* 53 (4), 676–693. https://doi.org/10.1093/joc/53.4.676

Thorne, S.L. and Reinhardt, J. (2008) 'Bridging activities', new media literacies, and advanced foreign language proficiency. *CALICO Journal* 25 (3), 558–572. https://doi.org/10.1017/S0958344012000274

Thorne, S.L., Sauro, S. and Smith, B. (2015) Technologies, identities, and expressive activity. *Annual Review of Applied Linguistics* 35 (2015), 215–233. https://doi.org/10.1017/S0267190514000257

Toffoli, D. (2020) *Informal Learning and Institution-wide Language Provision: University Language Learners in the 21st Century*. London: Palgrave Macmillan. See https://books.google.co.uk/books?id=T3vQDwAAQBAJ
Toffoli, D. and Sockett, G. (2015) University teachers' perceptions of Online Informal Learning of English (OILE). *Computer Assisted Language Learning* 28 (1), 7–21. https://doi.org/10.1080/09588221.2013.776970
Trinder, R. (2017) Informal and deliberate learning with new technologies. *ELT Journal* 71 (4), 401–412. https://doi.org/10.1093/elt/ccw117
Turkle, S. (1995) *Life on the Screen*. New York: Simon & Schuster.
Ushioda, E. (2011) Language learning motivation, self and identity: Current theoretical perspectives. *Computer Assisted Language Learning* 24 (3), 199–210. https://doi.org/10.1080/09588221.2010.538701
Ushioda, E. and Dörnyei, Z. (2009) Motivation, language identities and the L2 self: A theoretical overview. In Z. Dörnyei and E. Ushioda (eds) *Motivation, Language Identity and the L2 Self* (pp. 1–8). Bristol: Multilingual Matters.
Van Lier, L. (2004) *The Ecology and Semiotics of Language Learning*. Dordrecht: Kluwer Academic.
Vorderer, P., Krömer, N. and Schneider, F.M. (2016) Permanently online – permanently connected: Explorations into university students' use of social media and mobile smart devices. *Computers in Human Behavior* 63, 694–703. https://doi.org/10.1016/j.chb.2016.05.085
Wagner, J. (2018) Multilingual and multimodal interactions. *Applied Linguistics*, January, 99–107. https://doi.org/10.1093/applin/amx058
Walther, J.B. (1996) Computer-mediated communication: Impersonal, interpersonal, and hyperpersonal interaction. *Communication Research* 23 (1), 3–43. https://doi.org/10.1177/009365096023001001
Walther, J.B. (2007) Selective self-presentation in computer-mediated communication: Hyperpersonal dimensions of technology, language, and cognition. *Computers in Human Behavior* 23 (5), 2538–2557. https://doi.org/10.1016/j.chb.2006.05.002
Wang, V. and Tucker, J.V. (2016) Phatic systems in digital society. *Technology in Society* 46, 140–148. https://doi.org/10.1016/j.techsoc.2016.06.002
White, L. (1987) Against comprehensible input: The input hypothesis and the development of second language competence. *Applied Linguistics* 8 (2), 95–110. https://doi.org/10.1093/applin/8.2.95
White, R.V. (1988) *The ELT Curriculum*. Oxford: Blackwell.
Widdowson, H. (1998) Context, community and authentic language. *TESOL Quarterly* 32 (4), 705–716. https://doi.org/10.2307/3585679
Wilkins, D.A. (1976) *Notional Syllabuses*. Oxford: Oxford University Press.
Yamagata-Lynch, L.C. (2010) *Activity Systems Analysis Methods*. New York: Springer.
Yamashita, J. and Jiang, N. (2010) L1 influence on the acquisition of L2 collocations: Japanese ESL users and EFL learners acquiring English collocations. *TESOL Quarterly* 44 (4), 647–668. https://doi.org/10.5054/tq.2010.235998
Yashima, T. (2002) Willingness to communicate in a second language: The Japanese EFL context. *The Modern Language Journal* 86 (1), 54–66. https://doi.org/10.1111/1540-4781.00136
Yashima, T. (2009) International posture and the ideal L2 self in the Japanese EFL context. In Z. Dörnyei and E. Ushioda (eds) *Motivation, Language Identity and the L2 Self* (pp. 144–163). Bristol: Multilingual Matters.
Yates, S.J. (1996) Oral and written linguistic aspects of computer conferencing: A corpus based study. In S.C. Herring (ed.) *Computer-Mediated Communication: Linguistic, Social, and Cross-Cultural Perspectives* (pp. 29–46). Amsterdam: John Benjamins.
Young, E., Kim, A. and Brown, L. (2014) Negotiating pragmatic competence in computer mediated communication: The case of Korean address terms. *CALICO Journal* 31 (3), 264–284. https://doi.org/10.11139/cj.31.3.264-284

Yus, F. (2011) *Cyberpragmatics: Internet-Mediated Communication in Context*. Amsterdam: John Benjamins.

Yus, F. (2017) Contextual constraints and non-propositional effects in WhatsApp communication. *Journal of Pragmatics* 114, 1–42. https://doi.org/10.1016/j.pragma.2017.04.003

Zappavigna, M. (2011) Ambient affiliation: A linguistic perspective on Twitter. *New Media & Society* 13 (5), 788–806. https://doi.org/10.1177/1461444810385097

Zourou, K. (2019) A critical review of social networks for language learning beyond the classroom. In M. Dressman and R.W. Sadler (eds) *The Handbook of Informal Language Learning* (pp. 369–382). Hoboken, NJ: John Wiley & Sons Ltd. https://doi.org/https://doi.org/10.1002/9781119472384.ch24

Appendix A: Questionnaire

Introduction

Complete this survey for the chance to win a £50 Amazon voucher!

Tell us about how you use English as a second language online.

Please answer the question below to get started.

Please answer all questions in English.

(1) Please choose one of the following options:
  a. I am under 18 years old
  b. I am 18 years old or over

Before we begin.
Please read this <Information Sheet>. If you understand it and are happy to continue, please confirm below.

(2) I have read the information sheet and I understand it.

Please tell us a little about yourself.

(3) What is your primary nationality? ____________________
(4) What is your current country of residence? ____________________
(5) What is your first language? ________________
(6) What other languages do you speak? ____________________
(7) How old are you?

18–21	22–29	30–39	40–49	50–59	60–69	70+

(8) [Omitted]
(9) How would you describe your level of English?

Post-beginner level (I can hold simple conversations such as greetings and introducing someone, read simple materials and write a simple passage in elementary English).
Lower-intermediate level (I can talk about familiar daily topics, read materials about familiar everyday topics and write simple letters).
Intermediate level (I am able to talk about general matters of daily life, read general materials related to daily life and write simple passages)

Upper-intermediate level and over (I am able to talk about general matters of daily life and topics of my specialty, grasp the gist of lectures and broadcasts, read high-level materials such as newspapers and write about personal ideas).

Using English Online

For each item in the following questions please choose one of the six options.

(10) How often do you do these things **using English**?

	Several times a day	**Once a day**	**Several times a week**	**Once a week**	**Occasionally**	**Never**
Writing/reading personal (not work related) emails.						
Writing public comments on social network sites like Facebook, Twitter, Instagram.						
Exchanging messages with an individual person on instant messaging apps like WhatsApp, Facebook Messenger, QQ, WeChat.						
Exchanging messages in a group of people on instant messaging apps like WhatsApp, Facebook Messenger, QQ, WeChat.						

(11) How often do you do these things **using English**?

	Several times a day	Once a day	Several times a week	Once a week	Occasionally	Never
Writing/reading emails for work purposes.						

	Several times a day	Once a day	Several times a week	Once a week	Occasionally	Never
Using social network sites like Facebook for work purposes.						
Using instant messaging apps like WhatsApp for work purposes.						
Using professional networking sites like LinkedIn, Xing or Viadeo to communicate with professional acquaintances.						

(12) How often do you use **English** to talk about games, hobbies or interests?

	Several times a day	Once a day	Several times a week	Once a week	Occasionally	Never
In online forums or communities like Reddit.						
In real-time chatrooms.						
While playing online games.						

(13) How often do you use **English** for

	Several times a day	Once a day	Several times a week	Once a week	Occasionally	Never
Writing blogs?						
Reading and/or commenting on blogs?						

	Several times a day	Once a day	Several times a week	Once a week	Occasionally	Never
Writing comments on video or photo sites like YouTube, Flickr, Tumblr?						

(14) How often do you use **English** online to

	Several times a day	**Once a day**	**Several times a week**	**Once a week**	**Occasionally**	**Never**
Write reviews on websites like Tripadvisor, Amazon or Yelp?						
Read/write emails to customer service representatives of companies such as banks, mobile phone companies, energy suppliers?						
Chat online with customer service representatives of companies such as banks, mobile phone companies, energy suppliers?						
Arrange to exchange services with people offline, on community websites such as Airbnb, Couchsurfing or Freecycle?						

(15) How often do you meet new people online?

Often	Sometimes	Rarely	Never

Using Online Communication Technologies

For each technology in the following questions, please indicate how easy or difficult you find using **English**.

(16) Email. How easy do you find using **English** in email?

Very easy	Easy	Quite easy, but with some difficulties	Difficult	Very difficult

(If 'Quite easy', 'Difficult' or 'Very difficult'):

(17) Can you describe what you find difficult about using email in English? ___________

(18) Instant messaging (WhatsApp, Facebook Messenger, WeChat, Viber, etc.). How easy do you find using **English** in instant messaging?

Very easy	Easy	Quite easy, but with some difficulties	Difficult	Very difficult

(If 'Quite easy', 'Difficult' or 'Very difficult'):

(19) Can you describe what you find difficult about using email in English? ___________

(20) Discussing or commenting on posts, using **English** on discussion forums or social media sites.

Very easy	Easy	Quite easy, but with some difficulties	Difficult	Very difficult

(If 'Quite easy', 'Difficult' or 'Very difficult'):

(21) Can you describe what you find difficult about using English for discussing posts? ___________

(22) Chatting – Real-time chat, in chat rooms or during multiplayer games.

Very easy	Easy	Quite easy, but with some difficulties	Difficult	Very difficult

(If 'Quite easy', 'Difficult' or 'Very difficult'):

(23) Can you describe what you find difficult about using English in real-time chat? ___________

Social Activities Online

(24) How comfortable do you feel when taking part in the following activities **online** using **English**?

	Very comfortable	Quite comfortable	Quite uncomfortable	Very uncomfortable	I don't do this
Making new friends.					
Keeping in touch with existing friends.					

	Very comfortable	Quite comfortable	Quite uncomfortable	Very uncomfortable	I don't do this
Communicating with existing clients/ customers.					
Finding new clients/ customers.					
Working together with others in a project or game.					
Arranging to meet others face to face (including for non-personal reasons like accommodation, transportation or buying/ selling).					
Communicating with buyers/ sellers for shopping purposes.					
Managing personal matters such as banking, energy suppliers, phone/ internet suppliers, government administration.					
Stating your opinion in a discussion.					
Defending your opinion in a discussion.					
Disagreeing with someone.					
Offering advice to others (including writing reviews).					

Social Activities Offline

(25) And how comfortable do you feel when taking part in the same activities **offline** using **English**?

	Very comfortable	**Quite comfortable**	**Quite uncomfortable**	**Very uncomfortable**	**I don't do this**
Making new friends.					
Keeping in touch with existing friends.					
Communicating with existing clients/customers.					
Finding new clients/customers.					
Working together with others in a project or game.					
Arranging to meet others face to face (including for non-personal reasons like accommodation, transportation or buying/selling).					
Communicating with buyers/ sellers for shopping purposes.					
Managing personal matters such as banking, energy suppliers, phone/ internet suppliers, government administration.					
Stating your opinion in a discussion.					
Defending your opinion in a discussion.					
Disagreeing with someone.					
Offering advice to others (including writing reviews).					

Learning 'Online English'

(26) How much do you agree with the following statements?

	Strongly disagree	Disagree	More disagree than agree	More agree than disagree	Agree	Strongly agree
Using English to communicate online has improved my English skills.						
I have more opportunities to use English online than offline.						
I would be interested in learning more about the kind of English I use online.						
I would like more content related to online English use in the English textbooks I use.						

End of Questionnaire

Appendix B: Codebook from Qualitative Analysis

Nodes

Name	Description	Files	References
Attributes		4	717
Accuracy		4	145
Brevity		4	63
Clarity		4	98
Coherence		4	66
Complexity		4	83
Fluency	Interesting: ch1631 'It's needed to be fluent speaker to write quickly'. Includes comments regarding 'naturalness'. Also 'proper'/'appropriate' usage of words	4	262
Cognitive load		4	263
Multitasking		3	27
Time to prepare		4	151
Time to think	Search for 'think' to find missed cases of this. This is starting to incorporate a lot of 'thinking quickly' examples. Perhaps it could be 'cognitive load'? Would probably need to be redrawn a little. Formerly 'mental preparation'	4	85
Communicative competence		4	121
Comprehension		4	1059
Being understood		4	169
Causing offence		4	41
Cultural reference		4	21
Humor		3	18
Intercultural understanding	im245 example of how this could actually be 'intercultural communication' – 'unconfident to chat with foreign people' and the im252 is more like the difficulties of shared understanding in a global context. This should probably be combined with something that discusses the difficulties of very local meanings (e.g. im243)	4	73

(*Continued*)

Name	Description	Files	References
Misunderstanding		1	19
Situated meaning	This really refers to situated (contextual) meaning, possibly including pragmatic meanings or subjective meanings. Not completely sure 'implicit' is the right word. Also 'prosody' (ch386 says 'direction of phrase')	4	94
Understanding others	I have been coding all instances of 'I don't understand some words' as vocabulary and comprehension, but the comprehension aspect is possibly redundant	4	624
Other's L1		1	5
Others' level		4	65
Conveying meaning		4	1062
Describing things or situations	Look at this again to include comments regarding explaining specific/technical concepts. Also maybe combine with 'self-expression', 'expressing emotions', all of these things are communicating specific concepts with accuracy	4	81
Desired meaning		4	368
Details		3	23
Emotions	This is linked to affect - could be organized in terms of expressing affect in interaction vs affect regarding the interaction itself. But then affect (negative) also being quickly swallowed up by 'Communication Anxiety'	4	84
Ideas		4	218
Opinions	Combine with/subsume into 'Stance'	4	87
Stance		4	49
Thoughts		4	152
Discourse dynamics		4	888
Difficult to respond		2	22
Flow		3	45
Multi-party interaction		1	11
Participant behaviors		3	37
Antisocial behavior	Checked in all files	2	11
Behavior norms	Checked for all files	1	2
Unsupportive others		3	24
Pressure to respond		3	218
Speed		4	490
Stakes	So renamed this as 'stakes' in order to broaden it slightly to show the kinds of things that are at stake – jobs, credibility, face… In this way it also links to 'Others' perception of self', as that is also at stake (so therefore also, I suppose, the stuff I coded as 'manner')	3	10

(Continued)

Name	Description	Files	References
Time-consuming		3	55
Don't do it	Could use this as the starting point for a tree of nodes covering all the 'actually I don't do this' responses	4	543
Impression management		4	143
Awareness of audience		2	27
Projection		4	86
Reception		3	30
Intrapersonal issues		4	388
Communication apprehension		4	361
Choose not to participate		4	28
Communication skills		2	4
Dislike of discussion		1	2
Dislike of social networking		1	2
Introversion		2	8
Modal preference		2	6
Unknown interlocutors		3	5
Lack of exposure	Thinking about changing/incorporating 'lack of practice' or 'lack of opportunity'. This includes some examples like 'I have experience' when it suggests that this is problematic; there are other examples of this that simply suggest that the respondent doesn't do this, and therefore has no experience on which to comment (these are coded as 'don't do this'). Also think about a sub-group of 'L1 networks' to incorporate comments like em498: 'my friends don't use English so…'	4	249
L1 networks	Start em1921	4	22
Lack of practice	Difference with lack of exposure: exposure is lack of opportunities, lack of practice can be so despite opportunities present	2	23
Language learning		4	62
Disjunct with formal learning		4	38
Learning strategies		4	24
Native		4	185
Perception of NS ideal	Just coded im377 as this, but it's really about a perception of 'proper' language more generally, and doesn't mention native	4	129

(Continued)

Name	Description	Files	References
Non-standard language	Often referred to as 'daily' language. Might be worth differentiating mentions of 'colloquial' language. Difficult to know when to class things as this or as tenor, particularly mentions of 'informal' language. Where is the line between 'standard' and 'informal'? Surely there are plenty of standard informal phrases. 'Informal' language often coded as this, rather than as Tenor	4	1130
'Local' variation		2	17
Abbreviation		4	268
Age		1	1
Bad		2	3
Broken sentences		1	2
Casual		3	7
Colloquial		4	25
Common		3	6
Daily		3	28
English varieties		4	17
Informal		4	89
Nativist		4	49
Netspeak		2	11
New words	Includes new to the language and new to the respondent - differentiate the two	4	124
Proper		3	5
Slang		4	351
Spoken		3	12
Standard		3	7
Urban		3	5
Not difficult		4	73
Not difficult – affordance of English		2	3
Not difficult – others accommodate		2	3
Not difficult because informal		2	14
Oral production		4	83
Pronunciation		4	79
Speech mechanics		1	4

(Continued)

Name	Description	Files	References
Orthography		4	382
Emoji		3	9
Punctuation		2	26
Spelling		4	301
Typing skill		4	46
Production		4	1195
Compensatory strategies		4	23
Describing unknown word		4	20
Don't know what to say		3	13
Form		2	172
Message composition		2	15
Mistakes		4	241
Proof-reading		4	89
Recall	Maybe put this in vocabulary?	4	178
Word selection	Relate to 'finding the right word'?	4	464
Register	This should be concerns that cut across the three sub-fields of register. Good example is em130: 'Sometimes I have a problem when I se suitable word in mail'. Suitable could be by formality or by field	4	1203
Field		4	353
Background knowledge		1	21
Tenor	Mostly concerned with formality. Should probably recode this more specifically (whether it's a problem with formal or informal language)	4	520
Resources		4	236
Assistive language technologies		3	16
Dictionary		4	81
Dictionary inadequate		3	8
Internet search	Great example po1178	4	27
Machine translation		4	39
Online dictionary		4	15
Other		1	2
Unspecified		4	48
Technical issues		4	98
Auto-correct		4	28
Lean medium		3	5
Permanence of text		2	2
Traditional language categories		4	4114

(*Continued*)

Name	Description	Files	References
Four skills		4	509
Aural comprehension		4	96
Accents	Maybe rename this 'pronunciation – others' and combine with pronunciation renamed 'pronunciation – own'	3	59
Reading proficiency		4	46
Spoken proficiency		4	117
Writing proficiency	Think about combining writing and typing (but perhaps preserving the difference somehow)	4	250
Grammar		4	1204
Level	Bearing in mind this is self-reported level – look through and look for the kind of 'self-deprecation' noted by Barton and Lee	4	178
Syntax	This should really be something like 'sentence construction' – or maybe 'syntax'. Check back for examples of things like 'putting words/sentences together'. Then will need to check lit for relationship btw grammar and syntax	4	375
Vocabulary	The definition of this has been evolving slightly in my mind, and I'm now starting to include instances of 'how to use words' as vocab	4	1848
Formulaic language		4	637
Collocation		4	49
Expressions		4	356
Idioms		4	150
Phrasal verbs	These often mentioned alongside slang/idioms/expressions, etc. seems like learners perceive them in a similar way (possibly due to an overemphasis in learning?)	4	82
High frequency		4	23
Low frequency		4	20
Natural usage of words		2	13
Unfamiliar words		2	37
Translanguaging		4	331
Code-switching		3	8
Domain specific		1	4
L1 transfer		4	12
Language mapping		4	102
Thinking in a language		4	52
Translation		4	135
Word-for-word translation		4	18

Index

www.ingramcontent.com/pod-product-compliance
Ingram Content Group UK Ltd.
Pitfield, Milton Keynes, MK11 3LW, UK
UKHW021836150926
8656IPUK00003B/11

9781800413627